INSTITUTE OF ECONOMICS

WITH

KU-535-385

QA75.5
COM

WITHDRAWN

*Computer Science
and Scientific Computing*

ACADEMIC PRESS RAPID MANUSCRIPT REPRODUCTION

Computer Science and Scientific Computing

EDITED BY

James M. Ortega

Institute for Computer Applications in Science and Engineering
NASA Langley Research Center
Hampton, Virginia

*8 MAR 1977

WITHDRAWN

Proceedings of the
Third ICASE Conference on Scientific Computing
Williamsburg, Virginia
April 1 and 2, 1976

ACADEMIC PRESS   New York   San Francisco   London   1976
A Subsidiary of Harcourt Brace Jovanovich, Publishers

COPYRIGHT © 1976, BY ACADEMIC PRESS, INC.
ALL RIGHTS RESERVED.
NO PART OF THIS PUBLICATION MAY BE REPRODUCED OR
TRANSMITTED IN ANY FORM OR BY ANY MEANS, ELECTRONIC
OR MECHANICAL, INCLUDING PHOTOCOPY, RECORDING, OR ANY
INFORMATION STORAGE AND RETRIEVAL SYSTEM, WITHOUT
PERMISSION IN WRITING FROM THE PUBLISHER.

ACADEMIC PRESS, INC.
111 Fifth Avenue, New York, New York 10003

United Kingdom Edition published by
ACADEMIC PRESS, INC. (LONDON) LTD.
24/28 Oval Road, London NW1

Library of Congress Cataloging in Publication Data

Icase Conference on Scientific Computing, 3d, Wil-
    liamsburg, Va., 1976.
    Computer science and scientific computing.

    1.   Electronic data processing–Congresses.
2.   Science–Data processing–Congresses.   I.   Institute for Computer Applications in Science and Engineering.   II.   Ortega, James M., Date   III.   Ti-
tle.
QA75.5.I25   1976   001.6'4   76-25457
ISBN 0–12–528540–X

PRINTED IN THE UNITED STATES OF AMERICA

Contents

Contributors   vii

Preface   ix

Language as a Tool for Scientific Programming   1
Victor R. Basili

Data Definition, Structures, and Management in Scientific Computing   25
J. C. Browne

Computer-aided Design and Computer Science Technology   57
Robert E. Fulton and Susan J. Voigt

Scientific Applications of Symbolic Computation   83
Anthony C. Hearn

The Astrophysicist and the Computer   109
Icko Iben, Jr.

Turbulence and Numerical Wind Tunnels   127
Harvard Lomax

General Purpose Program for Finite Element Analysis: Some Computational Considerations   155
Pedro V. Marcal

Case Studies in Reliable Computing   163
W. M. McKeeman

Design of Large Hydrodynamics Codes   191
Steven A. Orszag

Software Tools for Computer Graphics   205
R. L. Phillips

Computers and Quantum Chemistry   227
Isaiah Shavitt

Computer Architecture in the 1980s   255
Harold S. Stone

Minicomputer Complexes: Progress and Prospects   283
Wm. A. Wulf

Contributors

Victor R. Basili
Department of Computer Science, University of Maryland, College Park, Maryland 20742

J. C. Browne
Department of Computer Science, University of Texas, Austin, Texas 78712

Robert E. Fulton
IPAD Development Section, NASA Langley Research Center, Hampton, Virginia 23665

Anthony C. Hearn
Department of Computer Science, University of Utah, Salt Lake City, Utah 84112

Icko Iben, Jr.
Department of Astronomy, University of Illinois, Urbana, Illinois 61801

Harvard Lomax
Computational Fluid Dynamics Branch, NASA Ames Research Center, Moffett Field, California 94035

Pedro V. Marcal
Marc Analysis Research Corporation, Palo Alto, California 94306

W. M. McKeeman
Department of Information Sciences, University of California, Santa Cruz, California 95060

Steven A. Orszag
Department of Mathematics, Massachusetts Institute of Technology, Cambridge, Massachusetts 02139

R. L. Phillips
Department of Aerospace Engineering, University of Michigan, Ann Arbor, Michigan 48105

Isaiah Shavitt
Chemical Physics Section, Battelle Memorial Institute, Columbus, Ohio 43201 and Department of Chemistry, Ohio State University, Columbus, Ohio 43210

Harold S. Stone
Department of Electrical and Computing Engineering, University of Massachusetts, Amherst, Massachusetts 01002

Wm. A. Wulf
Department of Computer Science, Carnegie-Mellon University, Pittsburgh, Pennsylvania 15213

Preface

Scientific computing is a highly diverse activity spanning a multitude of disciplines. It draws on mathematics for answers to such classical questions as the existence, uniqueness, and qualitative behavior of solutions of certain classes of mathematical problems. Numerical analysis, considered by some to be a subset of mathematics, provides rigorous analysis of algorithms, contributes to the development of new algorithms, and attempts to finalize this work in the form of modules (subroutines) for numerical solution of basic mathematical problems.

Scientific computing also draws on a number of areas in computer science and computer engineering: computer architecture, computer systems, programming languages, data management, symbolic computation, computer graphics, program correctness, etc. The intelligent use of computers has always required, of course, a detailed knowledge of the characteristics of the equipment being used. In the early days of scientific computing on electronic computers, the interaction of the user with the computer was direct and intimate. As operating systems, programming languages, and other systems software became ubiquitous and more sophisticated, the user needed to be aware of the details of the whole computer system, both hardware and software. Moreover, with each new advent in computer architecture, this cycle renews itself on an accelerating basis. For example, for the past few years certain people in scientific computing have grappled directly with new hardware at both ends of the computing scale: large vector or array processors, and mini- and microcomputers.

As problems have become larger, the need to organize and manage the data of the problem has become more acute and data management techniques probably will become increasingly important in scientific computing. For much the same reasons − large volumes of data, both input and output − the role of computer graphics also is growing; it is assumed, and certainly hoped, that the era of large piles of output listings is drawing to a close. Finally, several other areas of computer science, such as symbolic manipulation and techniques for writing correct and reliable programs, promise to have increasing impact on scientific computing.

The driving forces in scientific computing are, of course, the problems from science and engineering that are to be solved. Unfortunately, however, the lines of communication between mathematicians and computer scientists, on the one hand, and practitioners in the various application areas, on the other, have not always been as open and active as might be desired. Too many in the mathematical sciences are still motivated by a conception of problems as they existed in the application areas years or even decades ago. Conversely, many, if not most, of the applications areas have developed over the years a substantial computing technology in relative isolation from parallel developments in other applications areas as well as in computer science and numerical analysis.

A conference devoted to all the aspects of scientific computing would be so large as to be unwieldly. Hence, a more modest goal was set: to bring together some of the leading researchers in those computer science areas that have a direct bearing on scientific computing, and practitioners of a few representative application areas. The hope is that the exchange brought about by this conference – by the lectures as well as by personal interactions – will help in a small way to increase the communication between the various disciplines represented.

Whatever success the conference may have been is due to the efforts of a number of people. I am indebted to the Program Committee, consisting of C. William Gear, Peter Lykos, Harlan Mills, Martin Schultz, and John Shoosmith, for their efforts in the early stages of planning, and to the representatives of the cosponsoring societies: the Association for Computing Machinery, The American Chemical Society – Division of Computers in Chemistry, the American Institute of Aeronautics and Astronautics, the American Society of Civil Engineers – Structural Division, the Institute of Electrical and Electronics Engineers Computer Society, and the Society for Industrial and Applied Mathematics. Finally, the contributed papers and the local arrangements were expertly handled by Robert Voigt, ably assisted by Mmes. Linda Johnson and Barbara Porter of the ICASE staff.

J. M. Ortega

LANGUAGE AS A TOOL FOR SCIENTIFIC PROGRAMMING

Victor R. Basili
Computer Science Department
University of Maryland

ABSTRACT

Programming languages act as software development tools for
problems from a specific application area. The needs of the
various scientific programming applications vary greatly with the
size and style of the problems which include everything from
small numerical algorithms to large-scale systems. This latter
requires language primitives for a multitude of subproblems that
include the management of data, the interfaces with the system
at various levels, etc. One way of making available all the
necessary primitives is to develop one very large language to
cover all the needs. An alternative is to use a hierarchical
family of languages, each covering a different aspect of the
larger problem, e.g., a mathematical language, a data base management language, a graphics language, etc. The concept of a
family of languages built from a small common base offers a
modular, well-interfaced set of small specialized languages that
can support such software development characteristics as modularity, reliability, efficiency, and transportability. This
paper discusses the use of the hierarchical family concept in
the development of scientific programming systems.

I. INTRODUCTION

Tools are designed to aid in the construction of a product.
They help produce a better product and make the actual building
process easier. They help in the automation of the various
stages of development making the more tedious, difficult, and
error-prone aspects easier and more reliable.

Scientific programming leads to the development of products.
What do these products look like? They vary in size and complexity from library routines for basic mathematical functions
to self-contained programs encompassing basic algorithms to large

1

whole systems involving structural analysis (NASTRAN [NAS72], NONSAP [BAT74], . . .) or control center operations (MSOCC [NAS75], ATSOCC [DES75], . . .).

Tools have been developed to aid the scientific programmer in product development. Consider the problem from an historical perspective. In the beginning there was the bare machine. The solution to the scientific programming problem was expressed as a set of machine language instructions. The programmer developed everything from scratch every time, working only with the basic hardware. Almost immediately tools were developed to help specify programs in more human-related forms improving the machine environment in which the programmer worked.

The major emphasis in tools for expressing the problem solution has been in the development of higher-level programming languages. Such languages create an idealized, virtual computer that corresponds to the thinking habits and capabilities of the programmer, rather than to the limitations of the current technology.

One of the first tools developed was the library concept permitting the reuse of existing subprograms. In this way common tasks, such as mathematical functions, could be programmed once and used over and over again. These subprograms were a first step in defining a higher level set of the programming primitives suited to the user's needs and the application area.

A second tool was the development of symbolic codes. Assembly languages permitted the user to write in a symbolic notation to specify the instructions and locations of the machine. The use of mnemonics for instruction primitives made it easier for the programmer to relate to the data of the program. This higher level of specification was made possible by the assembler which translates the symbolic codes into the real machine codes.

Higher-level scientifically-oriented languages, such as FORTRAN and ALGOL, were developed to automate more powerful

2

forms of specification. They incorporated specifications for arithmetic expressions, data such as complex variables, control structures such as conditionals and iteration, and data structures such as arrays. These higher-level languages are translated using compilers or macroprocessors or executed via interpreters.

A set of high-level, more general-purpose languages, such as PL/1 and HALS/S [NEW73], offered facilities to the programmer not available in languages such as FORTRAN. These facilities included string processing and some control over the system environment in the form of overflow and underflow control.

In order to more closely associate the terminology for expressing the problem solution with the problem area, special purpose application oriented languages have been developed. Languages such as SNOBOL and LISP were developed early to handle string and list processing problems, respectively. There has been an ever-increasing number of very high-level languages that involve the solutions of set-theoretic problems (e.g., SETL [SCH73]), combinatorial problems (e.g., MADCAP [WEL70]), artificial intelligence based problems (e.g., SAIL [FEL72], PLANNER [SUS70]), graph algorithmic problems (e.g., GRAAL [RHE72], GEA [CRE70]), etc. Some of these languages have been called very high-level languages as they raise the level of specification far above that defined by the high-level languages, e.g., a primitive like the union operator in SETL would require a subroutine in FORTRAN.

Besides being used to raise the level of the machine to help the programmer express his program in the language of the problem area, tools have been developed to improve the environment in which the programs and programmer live. On top of the bare machine, monitors were developed to run the computer without stopping, automatically sequencing batches of jobs. This helped make more effective use of machine time and removed the programmer from pushing buttons on the bare machine. Under such a

3

system, however, interactive development was lost. In time, sequential batch processing gave way to demand systems. Using a multiple programming system with a virtual memory, each user was effectively given his own machine, in spite of the fact that he was one of many users. These systems gave the user a greater opportunity to share high-level resources such as text editors and file systems. They returned to the programmer the ability to interact with the machine, but this new software-extended machine was more powerful and several levels closer to man's problem areas.

Support tools have been developed which try to provide the programmer with an environment for developing and analyzing his programs at the level at which they are written. These support tools include debugging aids, testing and evaluation aids, and a variety of support programs including editors and data base analyzers.

Given this large assortment of tools, the programmer needs a mechanism for harnessing all these capabilities. Consider the definition of a programming language in this context. *A programming language is a standardized notation used to express a problem solution and communicate that solution to humans and computers.* (Note that the idea of expressing that solution to humans has gained considerable importance in light of the problems of correctness and maintainability.) The programming language must provide the user with control over whatever primitives are needed to express the problem solution and implement that solution as a correctly executing program. All of the tools mentioned earlier can be harnassed using programming language notation.

The definition given here emphasizes several important points which should characterize a programming language. These include ease of expression, the ability to write correct, readable, implementable and efficient programs. The ability to communicate with various computers implies portability. Another

4

important characteristic of a programming language is the ability
to reuse products developed in the language.

The next section discusses some of the capabilities and
characteristics a scientific programming language should have.
Section 3 recommends a method for defining a programming language
notation that achieves this set of capabilities and characteristics using the concept of a family of languages.

II. SCIENTIFIC PROGRAMMING LANGUAGE NEEDS

The scientific programming notation must provide the programmer with a set of capabilities for solving his problem and
this notation should have characteristics that support the ease
of expression, correctness, etc., of the solution algorithm.
First, consider some of the actual capabilities a scientific program via notation might encompass.

The most basic facility that is common across product size
and complexity is the ability to perform numerical calculations.
The notation should provide a basic set of arithmetic data types
including integer, real, complex. For operation on these basic
data types there should be a complete set of built-in operators
for each data type, along with complete libraries of special
functions. There should be clearly defined hierarchies of con-
versions, e.g., integer is a subset of real and real is a subset
of complex and mixed types are automatically converted to the
higher level type. The user should also have control over overflow and underflow with respect to the various operations.

There should be a variety of precisions for data types;
for example, there should be short and long reals, short integers,
etc. The user should have some control over precision in that it
should be easy to change precision across an entire program. One
way the need for a specific precision can be satisfied is by a
variable precision arithmetic package. This can be very inefficient however because the specified precision may not corres-
pond to the machine word size boundaries. Specific precision requirements could be satisfied more efficiently by permitting the

user to specify a minimum precision requirement and permitting
the compiler to impose a precision greater than the specified
precision that corresponds to some multiple of the machine word
size [INT75]. Precision hierarchies should be clearly defined
just as data type hierarchies. All functions should appear to the
user to be generic with respect to precision and data type.
There should be no need for the user to remember different function names for different data types and precisions.

The notation should provide a convenient format for arithmetic expressions. Since random reordering of expression evaluation can cause problems with precision critical computations, the
evaluation order of specific expressions must be preserved.
However, the user is also interested in optimization of non-
precision-critical expressions, so there should be some control
conventions or special formats to forbid reordering. For
example, the compiler might assume that normal parenthesized
expressions, or some special form of parenthesized expressions,
cannot be reordered.

What about the framework in which one imbeds arithmetic expressions? This includes the control structures, data structures,
and the runtime environment. There has been a great deal in the
literature about good sets of control structures for writing
algorithms [DAH72,MIL75]. These include the standard sequencing,
the ifthenelse, whiledo, etc. These structured control structures
aid in the development of readable, correct algorithms. Of special interest in scientific computations are an assignment
mechanism and the indexed loop statement, i.e., the for or do
loop. There are two formats for assignment. One is to consider
assignment as an operator, as in APL [PAK72]; the second is to
consider it as a statement as in FORTRAN. Studies [GAN75] have
shown that the assignment statement as opposed to the assignment
operator appears to be a less error prone construct. The main
benefits of the indexed loop statement are as an aid to correctness (automatic indexing built in) and for efficiency (the loop

6

variable can be specially treated in an optimal way if the use of
the index variable is limited to indexing, i.e., it is not available outside the loop and it cannot be assigned a value inside
the loop.)

With respect to data structures the standard workhorse has
been the array. However for many situations what is needed are
different methods of access. For example, one may want to access
an array of data both as a one-dimensional array and as a two-
dimensional array depending upon whether speed or ease of access
is of interest. Interestingly enough, FORTRAN allows the user
this kind of control over its array data structure. It permits
the programmer to use the array as a storage map over which different templates may be defined. Whether this facility was an
accident of design or purposeful, it is a widely used feature of
the language and gives the user a great deal of power with respect to data structuring. It is this kind of mechanism that
language designers are trying to improve upon and build into
languages in a less error prone way [LIS74,WUL76].

The runtime environment involves the language framework in
which the control and data structures are imbedded. For example,
the procedure organization (internal procedures, external procedures, nested procedures), the data scoping (block structure,
common blocks, equivalencing,...) and the existence of special
facilities (recursion, pointer variables, dynamically allocated
storage,...) all contribute to the complexity of the runtime environment. From the points of view of efficiency and ease of
understanding it is important to keep the runtime environment as
simple as possible. It is worth noting that FORTRAN has a relatively simple and efficient runtime environment compared to a
language like PL/1, which may account for part of its strong
support by the scientific programming community. A simple runtime environment framework can be a real asset in a programming
language.

The language facilities discussed so far have been a varia-
tion and extension of the facilities found in languages like
FORTRAN and ALGOL. However, many of the needs of scientific programming go beyond the facilities mentioned so far. For example,
string and character processing are needed for formatting outputs,
generating reports and processing data in nonnumeric form. Besides the string or character data types, basic operators are
needed along with conversion routines for changing between
numeric and nonnumeric data.

When the size of the problem and the amount of data become
large, the ability to interact with the system environment becomes necessary. The facility to read and write files is needed
for storing and retrieving large amounts of data. In order to
fit various segments of the program and data into memory at one
time, the user needs access to overlay capabilities. Larger
size implies more control over input and output routines and
devices. And, of course, as mentioned earlier, control over
interrupts plays an important role in handling overflow and underflow, etc.

As the problem gets more specialized, new features may become appropriate. Thus, the scientific programming notation
might provide some extensibility capabilities for creating new
features as necessary. For example, a matrix data type might be
a convenient primitive, along with a set of matrix operations.
It would be convenient for the programmer to be able to build
this into the notation easily to make expressing his problem
easier.

Thus far in the discussion we have tried to motivate a set
of capabilities building bottom up starting with existing capabilities in standard scientific programming languages, and
adding some of the facilities that are needed as the problem gets
larger or the application becomes more specialized. Let us
view the situation from the top down with respect to the needs of
large-scale scientific programming applications. These large-

scale applications involve the development of entire systems. Consider examples such as structural mechanics systems, e.g., NASTRAN, NONSAP, and control center systems, e.g., MSOCC, ATSOCC. Are these scientific or system applications? If they are examined from the user's point of view, they are definitely scientific applications.

What are these large scientific programming systems composed of? That varies with the particular application. However, there are some aspects that many of them have in common. At the very top is the user's interface to the system which is some form of system operation language (SOL). The power of the SOL is dependent upon the flexibility of the system and the sophistication of the user. SOLs vary from a set of push buttons to some limited form of a data input to some minimal form of sequential control to a full high-level language. Ideally there should be some flexibility in the level of the language. The unsophisticated user should be able to enter the system at a very high level using some standard prepared package routines. The more sophisticated user should be given more flexibility and be able to penetrate the system at the level of his expertise. Thus, the SOL should be both flexible and hierarchical.

To demonstrate the scope a programming notation must address for a large-scale scientific system, consider a particular application area, such as structural mechanics. What are the various aspects of such a system?

The user aspect involves an engineer who wants to check out some structure. At the top level he would like some simple form of data input for using a canned set of techniques. However, if the user is reasonably sophisticated and the canned techniques don't adapt well to the particular problem, he should be allowed to write a high-level algorithm to bring the power of the system to bear for his particular needs. The numerical analysis aspect involves many numerical algorithms for the solution of differential equations, non linear equations, eigenvalue extraction, etc.

9

There is a data base management aspect. This involves the definition of data structures for the structural elements, the definition of the grid point storage structure, the physical representation of these structures, and the access and storage techniques.
There is a graphics aspect. The user should be able to display the
input graphically for checking and the output for interpreting results easily. Finally, there is the systems aspect. One has to
build a system in which all of the above processing takes place.
This system should in fact include some interactive facility.

The above discussion is clearly superficial. It is merely
meant to demonstrate the wide variety of facilities required in
the notation for building large-scale scientific systems.

Having all of the above capabilities, the scientific programming notation should possess certain characteristics. Among
other things, it should support ease of problem expression,
the writing of correct, efficient, and portable code, and the
reuse of algorithms written in it. Let us consider these
characteristics one at a time.

One would like to express algorithms in a natural manner.
This implies the notation should be natural to the problem area.
For example, within the general problem area of mathematics there
is a specialized and different mathematical notation for the
algebraist and analyst. Each aid in expressing the problems of
the particular area explicitly and precisely and in an easy to
communicate form.

However, it is hard to define the right features for the
application area. Often knowing just the right notation is
part of the solution. We need to experiment with language
features. The notations of algebra and analysis have been refined over many years. To work on this problem of defining the
right notation for a particular application, one needs both a
language expert and an application area expert. Only the
application area expert can know the right abstractions for the
problem area. But the language expert is needed to model and

analyze these abstractions for ease and efficiency of implementation, error proneness, and interaction with other facilities in the language and the environment. We have learned a lot about language design in the last two decades and we should use this knowledge in the design of languages. For example, all new languages should be modeled using several modeling techniques [BAS75a,HOA73,HOA74,LUC68] to guarantee good design with respect to the criteria that each of the models demonstrates.

Correctness of a program is defined as the ability of the program to perform consistently with what we perceive to be its functional specifications. The programming language should support the writing of correct programs. The language should simplify rather than complicate the understanding of the problem solution. The complexity in understanding a program should be due to the complexity inherent in the algorithms, not due to the notation used. The notation should be clear and simple. A language natural to the problem area aids in correctness as it makes the statement of the solution easier to read and understand. The easier it is to read and understand a solution algorithm, the easier it is to certify its correctness. Aids in making a program readable are to structure it from top to bottom and to break it into small pieces. In order to achieve the goal of supporting correctness, a language should be simple, contain well-structured control and data structures, permit the breaking up of the algorithm into small pieces using procedures and macros, and contain high-level problem area oriented language primitives.

A program is considered efficient if it executes at as fast a speed and in as small a space as is necessary. The language should permit the efficient execution of programs written in it. The higher level the algorithm, the more information is exposed for optimization and the better job a compiler can do on improving the code generated. On the other hand, high level often implies general applicability in order to handle the majority of cases. This can often imply an inefficiency for a particular

11

application. For example, consider a language in which matrices
have been defined as a primitive data type with a full set of
operators including matrix multiplication. The multiplication
operation has been defined for the general case. Suppose the
particular subproblem calls for the multiplication of two triangular matrices. Using the standard built-in operator is inefficient. One would like to be able to substitute a more
efficient multiplication algorithm for the particular case involved. But this implies that the language permits the redef-
inition of language primitives at lower levels of abstraction.
That is, the programmer should be able to express the algorithm
at a high level and then alter the lower level design of the
algorithm primitives for a particular application when it is
necessary for reasons of efficiency.

A language supports portability when it permits the writing
of algorithms that can execute on different machines. Portability is a difficult, subtle problem that involves several
diverse subproblems. The numerical accuracy of arithmetic computations can vary even on machines with the same word size.
Techniques for dealing with this problem include variable length
arithmetic packages or a minimum precision (modulo word size)
specifications as mentioned earlier. Another problem area of
portability is text processing. One way of dealing with this
problem is to define a high-level string data type which is
word size independent. A third area of problems involves interfacing with a variety of host machine systems. One method of
handling this is to define programs to run on some level of
virtual machine that is acceptable across the various machine
architectures and systems and then to define that virtual machine
on top of the host system for each of those architectures.
This is commonly done using a runtime library. In general the
higher level the algorithms, the more portable they are. However,
more portability often means less efficiency. A language that
supports portability should contain one of the above mechanisms

12

for transporting numerical precision across machine architectures, high-level data types, the ability to keep nonportable aspects in one place, and a macro facility for parameterizing packets of information modulo word size.

Software is reusable if it can be used across several different projects with similar benefits. In order for software to be reusable, its function must be of a reasonably general nature, e.g., the square root and sine functions, it must be written in a general way and it must have a good, simple, straightforward set of specifications. The area of scientific programming has a better history of reusable software than most. Consider as examples some of the libraries of numerical analysis routines [INTE75,SMI75]. This is due largely to the easily recognizable, general nature of many scientific functions and the simplicity of their specifications. There are whole areas of scientific software development, however, that do not have a history of reuse. Consider telemetry software, for example.

Software written in a general way may perform less efficiently than hand-tailored software. However, if it is well written it should be possible to measure it and based on these measures modify it slightly in the appropraite places to perform to specification for the particular application.

A good, simple, straightforward set of specifications is not easy to accomplish, especially when the nature of the function is complex. A good high level algorithm can help in eliciting that specification. Specifications for software modules should also include an analysis of the algorithm, e.g., the efficiency of the algorithm with respect to the size of the input data. The language should support the development of a good library of well-specified software modules that are easy to modify if the time and space requirements are off. It should also be capable of interfacing efficiently with other languages and of expressing algorithms so that the essential function is clear and of a general nature.

This partial list of capabilities and characteristics for a scientific programming language contains a large number of seemingly contradictory requirements. It is quite possible we can't have a notation with all of the above characteristics. However, one would like to define a language tool in which we can maximize both the capabilities and the above characteristics.

III. A FAMILY OF PROGRAMMING LANGUAGES

To begin with, one language appears to be not enough. If we are to cover all the applications necessary, the language would be too large and contain too many contradictory features. The runtime environment needed to support such a language would be complex and inefficient. What we would like is a set of languages, each tailored to a particular subapplication. However, there are several drawbacks to building a large set of independent languages each tailored to a subapplication. For one thing, the design and development of new programming languages are fraught with many problems since each language would be an entirely new design experience. Secondly, if these languages were truly different in design, it would require the user to learn several totally different notations for solving the different aspects of the problem. Thirdly, there would be a proliferation of languages and compilers to maintain.

One possible approach that minimizes some of the above drawbacks is the development of a family of programming languages and compilers. The basic idea behind the family is that all the languages in the family contain a core design which consists of a minimal set of common language features and a simple common runtime environment. This core design defines the base language for which all other languages in the family are extensions. This also guarantees a basic common design for the compilers. The basic family concept can be viewed as a tree structure of languages in which each of the languages in a subtree is an extension of the language at the root of the subtree, i.e.,

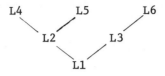

and

$$L4 = L2 \cup \{\text{new features of L4}\}.$$

Using the family approach permits the development of several application area languages, minimizing the difference between the languages and the compiler design effort. Since many of the constructs for various applications contain a similarity of design or interact with the environment in similar ways, experience derived from one design and development effort can be directly applicable to another. Since the notation for a particular application area may not be totally clear a priori, the family idea permits some experimentation without the cost of a totally new language and compiler development.

There are several approaches to minimizing the compiler development for a family of languages. One can develop an extensible language and build the family out of the extensible base language. The extension can be made either by a data definitional facility as in CLU [LIS74] or ALPHARD [WUL76] or by some form of full language extension as in ELF [CHE68] or IMP [IRO70]. The family of compilers can be built using a translator writing system [FEL68] or by extending some base core compiler [BAS75b]. A combination of two of the above techniques is recommended here, and they will be discussed a little more fully.

In the core extensible compiler approach, the base compiler for the base language is extended for each new language in the family, creating a family of compilers, each built out of the base core compiler. In order to achieve the resulting family of compilers, the core compiler must be easy to modify and easy to extend with new features. One experience with this technique, the SIMPL

family of languages and compilers [BAS76] has proved reasonably
successful with respect to extensibility by using specialized
software development techniques to develop the compiler [BAS75c].

Using the core extensible compiler approach, the compiler
C(L) for a new language in the family is built from the compiler
at its father node on the tree. This is done by making modifications (mod) to that compiler to adjust it to handle the new
features of the extension, i.e.,

$$C(L4) = C(L2)\underline{mod}\{L4\text{-fixes}\} \cup \{L4\text{-routines}\}$$

where the set of L4 routines represent the code for the L4
extensions to L2 and the set of L4 fixes represent the code
for modifying the L2 compiler to add those extensions. The
key to good extensible compiler design is to minimize the
number of modifications (fixes) and maximize the number of
independent routines.

Using a data extension facility, new data types and data
structures can be added to the language using a built-in data
definition facility. In order to achieve reasonable extensibility, the facility should be easy to use and permit efficient
implementation. Experience with forms of data abstraction
facilities in CLU, ALPHARD, and Concurrent PASCAL [HAN75] have
deomonstrated the benefits of this approach.

Here the effective compiler for the new language is again
built from the compiler at its father node on the tree. This is
done by adding a new set of library modules that represent the
new data types and structures and associated operators and access
mechanisms, respectively, of the new language, i.e.,

$$C(L4) = C(L2) \cup \{L4\text{-library}\}.$$

Each of the two techniques has different assets. The core
extensible compiler approach permits full language extension,
including new control structures and modifications to the runtime environment. It offers the most efficiency and permits a
full set of specialized error diagnostics to be built in. The
data definitional facility can be used only for data extensions,

16

but these are by far the most common in the range of subapplications. It is also a lot easier to do and can be performed by the average programmer, where the compiler extensions require more specialized training. Ideally, the first approach should be used for major application extensions and the second for smaller subapplication extensions.

Let us now apply this family concept to a large-scale system concept and analyze how the various application-oriented language features could be distributed across several languages in the family. Consider the structural mechanics system discussed earlier. There would be a language in the family for each application, i.e., an engineering application language, a numerical analysis language, a data base management language, a graphics language, etc. Each language would be built out of some base language (which may in fact be the system language). The application language may have several extensions, each of which adds on some higher level set of primitives, e.g., some set of standardized algorithms could be defined as a simple set of primitives. The family tree for the languages may take on a form such as

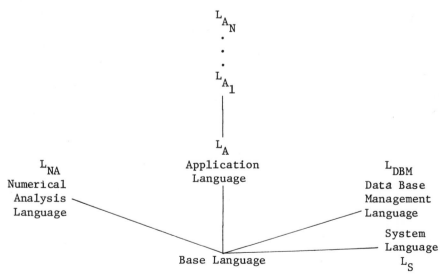

The system is then modularized so that each module is programmed in the appropriate language, i.e., the numerical analysis
module in the numerical analysis language L_{NA} , etc. The
application area module is programmed in the application area
language L_A . However, the SOL can be just as high an extension
of L_A as is appropriate for the sophistication of the user.

Each of these modules interfaces with one another through
an interfacing system. The interface system is part of the
basis for the family of languages and contains among other things
the compilers for the languages. The interface system is an
extension to the host operating system for whatever computer the
structured mechanics system is being developed. Together with
the host operating system, it makes up the virtual machine in
which the modules interact.

This kind of system offers a variety of SOLs. The unsophisticated user can interface into the system at the top level L_{A_N} .
The more sophisticated user can drop down any number of levels
to gain more power over the system by using lower level languages
in the hierarchy.

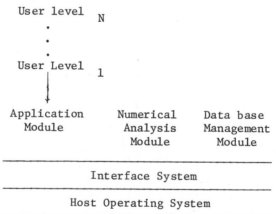

It is clear that the family of languages concept permits the
incorporation of the various capabilities required for a large-
scale scientific programming system. How does this concept rate
with regard to the criteria discussed earlier, i.e., ease of

expression, correctness, efficiency, portability and reusability?

With resepct to ease of expression, algorithms are written in a notation which is specialized to the application. In fact, since each language is reasonably independent of the application level, and primitives in one notation can be fine-tuned without affecting the primitives of another application, this permits a certain amount of experimentation, and primitives can be varied with experience.

High-level, application-oriented primitives make a solution algorithm easier to read and understand and therefore easier to prove correct. The specialized notation raises the level of the executing algorithm to the level at which the solution is developed. Individualized compilers tailor error diagnostics and recovery to the particular application.

Each language is small and relatively simple. Compilation of programs is very efficient, and recompilation of primitive definitions even at runtime is reasonably efficient. Each language is not complicated by a mix of features whose interaction may complicate the runtime environment. A more tailored runtime environment implies more efficient execution at runtime. Language features are specialized to meet the application and don't have to be generalized, inefficient versions of the feature. Because of the hierarchical structure of the languages, the programmer can use lower level languages to improve or fine-tune algorithms when necessary.

Higher level primitives mean more portable algorithms. The hierarchy with respect to the data abstractions permits the localization of the nonportable aspects of the program that can be recoded for a new machine architecture in a lower-level language in the hierarchy.

With regard to the development of reusable software, each application area has its own language. Thus, needed submodules are written in the target application notation rather than the host application notation. This makes it easier to recognize the essential function of the submodule and easier to write it in a more generally applicable way.

Several general comments should be made about the family approach. Since the languages are all members of a family, it is relatively easy to move from one language to another because of the common base. Whole new notations do not need to be learned. Interfacing with different languages is easier since there is a common base language/compiler system. However, good interfacing must be designed in from the start. The high-level primitives can remain fixed and be redefined at lower levels for purposes of portability or efficiency. There are several compilers to maintain although one approach might be to store one source in macro with expansions for each of the languages. It is harder to build an easily extendable/modifiable compiler and requires more care in development. But ease of modification should be an important property of any software. Some inefficencies exist with respect to the data abstractions passed between modules. However, these problems are being studied and the use of an interface system may help a great deal in effecting an efficient mechanism.

IV. SUMMARY

Scientific programming involves a multi-facted set of needs which vary from small programs to large systems among several subapplication areas. A scientific programming notation is needed for solving these problems in an effective way where effective means easy to express, correct, efficient, portable, and reusable. One way to conquer the complexity of the problem is to use as a notation a special application-oriented family of languages, one language for each subproblem area, and interface these languages into a portable system that can be built on top of a standard operating system.

REFERENCES

[BAS75a]   Basili, Victor R. A Structured Approach to Language
            Design. *Journal of Computer Languages, Vol 1,* pp.
            255-273 (1975).

[BAS75b]   Basili, V.R. and Turner, J. Computer Science Center,
            University of Maryland, Technical Report #269, 14
            pages. A transportable extendable compiler. *Soft-*
            ware Practice and Experience, Vol. 5, pp. 269-278
            (1975).

[BAS75c]   Basili, V. R. and Turner, A. J. Iterative Enhancement:
            A Practical Technique for Software Development. Pro-
            ceedings of the First National Conference on Software
            Engineering, Washington, D.C., September 11-12, 1975.

[BAS76]   Basili, Victor R. The SIMPL Family of Programming
            Languages and Compilers. Graphen-Sprachen und Al-
            gorithmen auf Graphen, Carl Hansen Verlag, Munich,
            Germany, 1976, pp. 49-85. Also Computer Science
            Technical Report #305, University of Maryland, June,
            1974.

[BAT74]   Bathe, Klaus-Jürgen, Wilson, Edwarld L. and Iding,
            Robert H. NONSAP A Structured Analysis Program for
            Static and Dynamic Response of Nonlinear Systems.
            Dept. of Civil Engineering, University of California,
            Berkeley, Report No. UCSESM74-3, February 1974.

[CHE68]   Cheatham, T. E., Jr., Fischer, A. and Jorrand, P.
            On the basis for ELF - an extensible language facility.
            Proc. AFIPS 1968 Fall Joint Comput. Conf., Vol. 33,
            Pt2, pp. 937-948. The Thompson Book Co., Washington,
            D.C.

[CRE70]   Crespi-Regluzzi, S. and Morpurgo,   A language for
            treating graphs. *COMM. ACM,* pp. 319-323, May, 1970.

[DAH72]   Dahl, O. -J., E. W. Dijkstra, and C. A. R. Hoare.
            Structured Programming. Academic Press, 1972.

[DES75]   desJardins, R. and Hahn, J.   ATS-6 Control Center
            Real-time Graphics Displays. Digest of Papers, IEEE
            COMPCON 75 Fall, Sept. 9-11, 1975, pp. 234-6.

[FEL68]   Feldman, J. and Gries, D.   Translator Writing Systems.
            COMM. ACM, 13, 2, (Feb. 1968) pp. 77-113.

[FEL72]   Feldman, J. A., et al.   Recent developments in SAIL-
            An ALGOL based language for artificial intelligence.
            Proceedings FJCC, AFIPS Press, Vol. 41 Part 2,
            Montvale, N.J. (1972) pp. 1193-1202.

[GAN75]   Gannon, John and Horning, James.   The Impact of Lan-
            guage Design on the Production of Reliable Software.
            Proceedings of the Interantional Conference on
            Reliable Software, April 1975, pp. 10-22.

[HAN75]   Hansen, Per Brinch.   The Purpose of Concurrent PASCAL.
            Proceedings of the International Conference on
            Reliable Software, April 1975, pp. 305-309.

[HOA73]   Hoare, C. A. R. and Wirth, N.   An Axiomatic Defini-
            tion of the Programming Language PASCAL. Acta
            Informatica 2, pp. 335-355, 1973.

[HOA74]   Hoare, C. A. R. and Lauer, P. E.   Consistent and
            Complementry Formal Theories of the Semantics of
            Programming Languages. Acta Informatica, Vol. 3,
            fasc: 2, 1974, pp. 135-153, Springer-Verlag-Berlin.

[INT75]   CS-4 Language Reference Manual and CS-4 Operating
            System Interface. Intermetrics, Inc., Cambridge,
            Mass. October, 1975.

[INTE75]   IMSL Library 2 Reference Manual, International
            Mathematical and Statistical Libraries, INC.,
            Houston, Texas, 1975.

[IRO70]   Irons, E. T. "Experience with an Extensible Language".
            COMM. ACM, 13, 1 (Jan. 1970), pp. 31-40.

[LIS74]   Liskov, B. and Zilles, S.   Programming with Abstract
            Data Types. Proceedings of a Symposium on Very High
            Level Languages, March, 1974, SIGPLAN Notices, Vol. 9,

No. 4 April 1974.

[LUC68]   Lucas, P. Lauer, P., and Stiglertner, H. Method and
            notation for formal definition of programming lan-
            guages. IBM Tech. Rep. 25-087, IBM Lab., Vienna,
            1968, 107 pages.

[MIL75]   Mills, H. D. How to Write Correct Programs and Know
            It. Proceedings of the International Conference on
            Reliable Software. Los Angeles, California, April,
            1975, pp. 363-370.

[NAS72]   NASTRAN User's Manual. NASA SP-222(01). NASA
            Scientific and Technical Information Office, Wash-
            ington, D. C., June 1972.

[NAS75]   Multi-Satellite Operations Control Center (MSOCC)
            Systems Manual. NASA/Goddard Space Flight Center,
            August 1975.

[NEW73]   Newbold, P. M. and Helmers, C. T., Jr. HAL/S Lan-
            guage Specification. Intermetics, Inc. Cambridge,
            Mass. April 1973.

[PAK72]   Pakin, Sandra. APL\360 Reference Manual. SRA, 1972.

[RHE72]   Rheinboldt, W. C., Basili, V. R. and Mesytenyi, C.
            On a Programming Language for graph algorithms. *BIT*
            12 (1972) pp. 220-241.

[SCH73]   Schwartz, J. On Programming: An Interim Report on
            the SETL Project, Installment I, II, 1973. Also
            Computer Science Department Courant Institute of
            Mathematical Science, New York University.

[SMI74]   Smith, B. T., Boyle, J. M., Garbow, B. S., Ikebe,
            Y., Klema, V. C., Moler, C. B. Lecture Notes in
            Computer Science V6: Matrix Eigensystem Routines -
            EISPACK Guide. New York: Springer 1974.

[SUS70]   Sussman, G. J. etal. MICRO-PLANNER Reference Manual
            MIT Artif. Intel. Lab., Memo No. 57.1 (April 1970).

[WEL70]   Wells, M. B.   Elements of Combinatorial Computing.
           Pergamon, Oxford, 1970.

[WUL76]   Wulf, Wm. A., London, Ralph, L., Shaw, Mary.
           Abstraction and Verification in ALPHARD.   February
           1976, (unpublished memorandum). Department of Computer
           Science, Carnegie Mellon University.

DATA DEFINITION, STRUCTURES, AND MANAGEMENT
IN SCIENTIFIC COMPUTING

J.C. Browne
Departments of Computer Science and Physics
and the Computation Center
The University of Texas
Austin, Texas   78712

ABSTRACT

This article deals primarily with the data structures of
scientific computing and their representation and management.
The coverage is at a fundamental although not elementary level.
Emphasis is placed on applicable concepts and techniques. The
goal is to put into the hands of engineers and scientists who
use computer systems some computer science technology which is
not yet widely available in contemporary software systems and/or
programming language systems. The topics covered include fundamentals of abstract data structure, data representation and
storage mapping functions for data structures, program control
of executable storage, and an illustration of a data management
system. Procedures for imbedding desired or needed data structuring and data management technology into the programming systems
generally used for scientific computing are suggested.

I. NEEDS, PURPOSES, GOALS AND COVERAGE

It is reasonable to assume that most of the difficulties
encountered in expressing scientific and engineering problems
in the programming language systems available for scientific
computing on current computers arises from inadequacies in the
data structuring, storage management and data management capabilities implemented in these language systems. The computer
system is being used more and more in scientific computing to
organize, store and manage data instead of serving only as a
computational instrument. This trend will exacerbate the need
for powerful data structuring and storage management capabilities.
Contemporary concepts of data structures and data management are

not, however, generally available in the programming languages and programming systems most used for scientific and engineering computing. The enormous inertia associated with the production, wide dissemination and development of a broad user base for a new programming language system means that most scientific and engineering computing problems will be expressed in past and current language systems for perhaps decades to come. The scientist or engineer who wishes to apply computers to his problems must expect to continue to supply for himself solutions to the problems of data structuring and representation, data management and storage management with little direct assistance from the programming language system. Thus the practicing scientist-engineer must extend his range of knowledge beyond his discipline area and the numerical algorithms which have become a standard part of modern scientific and engineering education and practice to include some fundamental knowledge in the areas of data structuring, data representation and data management. The purpose of this paper is to expound in fundamental but hopefully applicable terms the developing computer science technology for data structuring and representation, storage management and data management and to bring to the attention of the scientific and engineering community some of the applications of this technology which is being developed. This purpose is pursued with recognition of the barriers to its successful prosecution. Potential users of the developing computer science technology are not interested in computing per se, but in the problems of their professional and discipline competencies. There is a natural tendency in practicing professionals of all disciplines to use familiar techniques and algorithms which they have already used successfully. The goal, nonetheless, is that the scientist and engineer will be assisted by this article to use developing computer science knowledge and technology to more easily and effectively specify and implement programs for his discipline area problems.

The coverage of techniques and applications will necessarily be highly selective. The focus will be on the concepts and techniques judged most likely to be of service in numerical codes and in data storage and data management systems for scientific and engineering purposes. Topics of significance such as linked storage, sort/merge and searching will be regretfully left out or dealt with only by reference.

The literature citations are to the sources judged by this author as being most readable and most readily available.

II. CONTEMPORARY PROGRAMMING LANGUAGE SYSTEMS

A programming language system should provide the following capabilities if it is to be a convenient and effective vehicle for expression for solution processes for scientific and engineering computing:

o A set of primitive and system defined data structures

o A set of operations on these primitive and system defined data structures

o A set of composition rules for hierarchically composing primitive and system defined data structures into structures appropriate for the application

o A set of composition rules for hierarchically composing primitive or system defined operations into operations convenient for the solution process to be executed

o A set of capabilities for managing the resources committed to a program by the computer system, in particular the executable memory and file memory resources

o An interface to capabilities defined in the operating system or in the system libraries

Let us examine some of the familiar programming systems [1,2] for scientific and engineering use, ALGOL-60 [3], FORTRAN [4], and PL/1 [5]. The primitive data objects in all of these include the standard ones of numerical application: reals, integers, etc. The system defined data structures all include arrays of identical objects of up to several dimensions. PL/1 has a considerably richer variety of primitive data objects including strings and system defined data structures which include hierarchical records. The facilities for composition of extended user defined operations, i.e., functions, subroutines, procedures, are quite powerful in all three language systems.

There is however, only very limited capacity for hierarchical composition of system defined data structures into more complex user-oriented structures. These language systems thus lack a convenient capacity for extending system defined data types. Thus to utilize a data concept not directly available, i.e., a sparse matrix, it is necessary for the programmer to explicitly construct the structure, the representation and the addressing function for a sparse array. It may be difficult in the light of current day knowledge to comprehend why the designers of the language system felt that the data structures provided were an adequate basis for the expression of scientific and engineering problems when they provided such an elegant and powerful capability for extending the operational set into user defined operations. This state of affairs, however, reflects the status of maturity of computer science at the time of definition and implementation of each of these languages. The study of computational processes was a very early concern of computer science. The development of adequate concepts and mechanisms for data structures has been a much more recent concern. The concept of composition extensibility of data structures appears in newer languages such as PL/1, ALGOL 68 [6] and PASCAL [7] and is a central theme in the so-called extensible languages [8,9].

The convenience of interfacing operating systems and system library capabilities is also impacted by the limited set of data structures directly definable.

Program controlled storage management is another concept not well developed in early programming languages. FORTRAN supports directly only static storage assignments. ALGOL-60 has an implicit dynamic storage management in its block structure but does

not allow explicit program control of storage. PL/1 possesses
well thought out capabilities for program control of storage
management.

None of these programming language systems contain adequate
built-in capabilities for expressing data management or data
storage in the multilevel memory environments characteristic of
third generation computer systems.

III. DATA STRUCTURE AND DATA REPRESENTATION

The properties of data and the definition of theories of
data and data structures has been a dominant theme of computer
science research and development for the past six or eight years.
The driving force is to determine means of specifying and writing programs whose properties ("proof of correctness") can be
rigorously established [10,11]. A primary thrust has been to
establish the properties of data structures independently of
their representation in a particular environment [12, 13, 14].
This work has of necessity generated insight both into the
properties of data and the representation of data.

An abstract data structure consists of a conceptual object,
e.g., a sparse array, a name or name set for referring to the
object and a set of operations on the object. The set of operations defined for the structure constitute the only means of
learning the properties of the structure and accessing its values.

A realization of a data structure consists of a storage
mapping function which maps the name space of the data structure
onto a memory structure and the definition of the operations on
the structure in terms of primitive operations.

These definitions are completed by defining a storage or
memory. A cell is a physical realization which holds a value.
Memory consists of an ordered collection of cells. An address is
the location in memory for a given cell. A value is an instantiation of a data object or data structure. A mapping function
accepts a name as input and produces the address of a cell (or
cells) in memory as an output.

The definition and realization of a data structure thus consists of a sequence of actions:

o A structure declaration which defines the data type

o A name assignment which associates the name with a type or structure

o The definition of the operations on the structure. The only required operations are of course storage and retrieval.

o An allocation of memory to the named instantiation of the data structure

o The definition of the mapping function which maps the name space onto the allocated memory space

This sequence of steps is seldom clearly delineated in traditional programming languages. A FORTRAN DIMENSION or COMMON declaration of a rectangular array executes all of the above steps except the definition of operations upon the array. DIMENSION A(10,10) recognizes the square array as a data structure of the program, associates the name A with the array, assigns 100 contiguous cells of memory each of which will hold a floating point number and assigns the implicit familiar mapping function

$$\text{Address } [A(I,J)] = \text{Address } A(1,1)+$$
$$10(I-1) + (J-1).$$

The definition of operations on an array (except for I/O operations) must be defined by the programmer in terms of operations on the primitive data objects. The declaration DECLARE (A) CONTROLLED (*,*) appearing in a PL/1 procedure associates the name A with a square array of real numbers but makes no explicit storage allocation. [PL/1 allows for program control of storage management of CONTROLLED data structures by ALLOCATE AND FREE statements.] The same mapping as used by FORTRAN is implicitly supplied. PL/1, however, extends the meaning of arithmetic operations to include arrays so that B= A+A results in an array, B, each of whose elements is twice the value of the corresponding value of A. PL/1 has the most flexible data structuring capabilities of any language used for scientific or engineering computing.

It will be clear in the experience of most readers that none of the generally available scientific and engineering programming languages have the capability to directly define the range of data structures which commonly occur in even standard numerical analysis. Examples not directly definable which occur frequently are sparse matrices, matrices with varying numbers of rows and columns and general tetrahedral arrays. It appears that the scientist or engineer who wishes to program processes involving such structures must create both the definition and the implementation of the data structure as well as the operations upon the data structure from the whole cloth of the general programming language capability. The aspect of this problem not commonly familiar to the scientist and engineer is representation of data in the computer memory system structure and the definition and implementation of storage mapping functions. We now turn to the examination of the properties and characteristics of storage mapping functions.

IV. STORAGE MAPPING FUNCTIONS AND DATA REPRESENTATION

It is convenient to classify storage mapping functions according to some of the following definitions:

- o Direct access: A data representation or storage structure has the direct access property if there exists a storage mapping function which maps the name onto an address in a one to one fashion using only the index portion of the name, as in an array or record.

- o Key value computation: A storage mapping function which utilizes some or all of the name as a key value for direct computation of an address. The one to one property is not required. This differs from the direct access by the absence of the requirement for one to one mapping and by the possible use of the nonindex portion of the name.

o Indexing function: A data representation where the execution of the storage mapping function involves searching and extraction of tabulated information (key values) concerning the relative address of an instantiation of a data structure or data element within a data structure.

o Associative representation: A data representation where some or all of the name is stored with the value, usually for the need of determining the uniqueness of the address computed by the address mapping function.

o Linked representation: A data representation where the addresses of preceding and succeeding cells in the representation are stored along with the value and perhaps the name or a key value.

It is commonly the case that a given representation and storage mapping function may combine several techniques to obtain an efficient complete and one-to-one mapping.

There are a number of texts on data structures [15, 16, 18, 19] and programming languages [1, 2, 20] which discuss data representations, storage mapping functions and data storage. Knuth [15,16] is the most complete source for work prior to publication dates in the areas of his coverage.

V. ELEMENTARY EXAMPLES OF STORAGE REPRESENTATIONS AND STORAGE MAPPING FUNCTIONS

The most familiar non-trivial data representation and mapping is undoubtedly that for an array of identical objects. The FORTRAN declaration DIMENSION A(10,10) generates lexicographical or "row-major" storage. The elements of each row are stored. contiguiously in cells of advancing address. The storage mapping function is

$$\text{Address } [A(I,J)] = f_1(I,J) = \text{Address } [A(1,1)] + 10(I-1) + (J-1)$$

This mapping function is a direct access storage mapping function. The direct access property allows a fetch and retrieval

without storage of key value or name information in the memory
cell. It is thus appropriate for the circumstance that there is
a value of interest to be associated with each name $A(I,J)$.
This mapping function also has the useful property that a sequence
of cell addresses along a row or column can be generated by only
an addition for each member of the sequence. It is thus very
efficient for row/column sequential referencing as well as rather
efficient for random accessing.

$$\text{Address } [A(I,J)] = f_2 \, (I,J) = \text{Address } [A(1,1)] + (I \times J) \text{MOD } N$$

This mapping function (with $N = 101$) does generate an address in
the correct boundary for each ordered pair. The addresses
generated are not, however, unique for a given I or J. For
example, $I = 2$, $J = 2$ and $I = 4$, $J = 1$ and $I = 1$, $J = 4$ all
generate the same address and thus point to the same cell. Thus
f_2 is not suitable for use without some further specification.
Let it be stipulated that each cell contain the index part (key
value) of the name (I,J) as well as the value. Stipulate further
that if f_2 attempts to store in an already occupied cell, it seeks
an empty cell by circularly searching the total sequence of cells
towards smaller addresses and that if f_2 generates an address to
a cell which does not contain an entry desired it searches for
the desired value circularly toward lower addresses as previously.
This extended form of f_2 then generates a unique address for each
name $A(I,J)$.

f_1 is clearly much more efficient than f_2 both with respect
to computation and storage requirements for the case where $A(I,J)$
is small and dense. Consider the case where the dimension of
I and J are large, e.g., 10^4, but the matrix is sparse, e.g.,
approximately 10^5 non-zero different elements with random addressing pattern. Then f_1 cannot be practically applied in current
memory systems but f_2 with $N = $ approximately 1.2×10^5 and the cell
size capable of holding both the index part of the name and the

value will be reasonably efficient. f_2 is of course a very simple example representation of the so-called "hashing" functions [15]. Such functions are typically of interest when the dimensionality of the name space is much larger than the value set and its required cell address space.

A third type of mapping function is the indexing or directory function. It is defined through extraction of values from tables of key values or indices. These techniques are again very useful where the dimensionality of its name space is very much greater than the dimensionality of the number of required values. An example is a common procedure [17] for storing sparse matrices. Let us define a mapping function which stores and retrieves non-zero entries of a sparse matrix by its columns. The data is stored by scanning the columns of the matrix from top to bottom and then from left to right, storing the non-zero elements in a vector called VALUE-ROW. The value of each row element is stored together with its row index. The ordinal position in VALUE-ROW of the first non-zero element of each column is stored in a vector called COLUMN ORIGIN in order of the scan. The address of the VALUE-ROW cell for the I row and the J column entry is found by searching COLUMN-ORIGIN for the position of the row in VALUE-ROW and initiating a search for the desired cell at that position in the VALUE-ROW vector. This mapping function clearly allows a very efficient scan of the entire array by column (or rows if stored by rows). Note that this technique is easily extended to n dimensions by adding additional vectors of pointers. A third dimension can, for example, be added by regarding each plane or matrix as an element in a vector of square arrays. The required addition is a vector of pointers to the origin in the COLUMN-ORIGIN table for each square array.

The class of mapping functions which maps very large name spaces onto smaller address spaces has been prominently studied in the context of data management systems. The name space in this

application area is typically and characteristically enormous
compared even to very large auxiliary storage devices. It is
also always not elementary to formulate directly computable
mapping functions for physical devices whose cell addresses do not
define a linear space. We will discuss some of these techniques
rather sketchily in later sections.

VI. SOME MORE GENERAL DATA STRUCTURES AND THEIR REPRESENTATIONS
     AND MAPPING FUNCTIONS

A. GENERAL RECTANGULAR ARRAYS

It is usually desired to store rectangular arrays in a representation where the elements of a row or column occupy contiguously addressed cells. Let us assume lexicographical ordering
where the elements of a row are stored sequentially. It is
possible to obtain a direct access addressing function for regular
arrays of general dimensionality where a value occupies a single
memory cell. Let ℓ_i and u_i be respectively the lower and upper
bounds on the dimensionality of an array in the ith dimension
and the I_i be the current value of the index for dimension I. Then

$$\text{address}[A(I_1,I_2,\ldots I_k)] = \text{base address} - \sum_{1 \le n \le k} a_n \ell_n + \sum_{1 \le n \le k} a_n I_n$$

where $a_n = \prod_{n < j < k} (u_j - \ell_j + 1)$

B. DIAGONALLY BLOCKED ARRAYS

It is possible to obtain direct access functions for many
array shapes. Ehrich [21] displays an algorithm which will
generate direct access functions for n dimensional triangular
arrays which have s zero diagonals including the main diagonal.
If n is the number of dimensions and s is the number of zero
diagonals starting with the main diagonal, then n = 2, s = 0 is
a lower triangular array and n = 2, s = 1 is a lower triangular
array with the main diagonal missing. Let I_i be the current index
of the I dimension. Then the storage mapping function for these
arrays is given by

$$\text{address } [A(I_1,I_2 \ldots I_n)] = \sum_{k=1}^{n} \binom{I_k + (n-k)(s-1)}{n-k-1} + \text{base address}$$

C. RECORD ARRAYS WITH NON-IDENTICAL ELEMENTS

It is possible to generate direct access expressions for structures for which all elements are not primitive data objects. Let us look at data structures similar to PL/1 STRUCTURES or COBOL RECORDS [22]. Such structures are often used to define the content of the logical records of a data management system. Let us as an example define data for the design cycle of a wing section. This is shown in Figure 1.

1 Wing Section [40]	1 WS [40]
2 Surface Description [20]	2 SD [20]
2 Design History [10]	2 DH [10]
3 Design Data [6]	3 DD [6]
3 Plant Code [5]	3 PC [5]
2 Evaluation Data [10]	2 ED [10]
3 Test Data [6]	3 TD [6]
3 Performance Rating [2]	3 PR [2]

Figure 1: Record Definition for Wing Section Data

This structure defines the occurence of 40 data records on the design and evaluation of wing sections. The number on the left defines the level in the definition hierarchy. The indentation and the level numbers are of course redundant in this graphical representation. The structure is clearly a tree. The components at any level with no immediately succeeding components at a lower level are terminal nodes of the tree. The bracketed numbers on the right hand side of the terminating nodes are the number of primitive data objects in each instance of the defined object. The bracketed numbers on the right hand side of the non-terminal nodes in the tree are the number of instances of the structure for which storage is to be allocated. Figure 2 shows the tree representation of the structure.

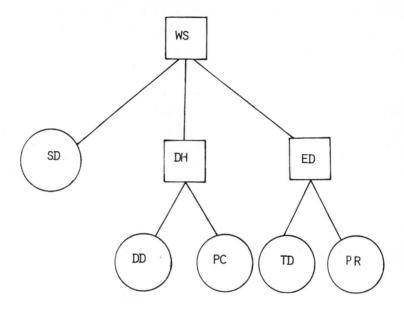

Figure 2. Tree Diagram of Wing Section Data Record

It is convenient to describe the structure in tabular form.

TABLE 1:   Tabular Representation of Record Structure

Level	1	1	2	2	3	3	2	3	3
Name	N	WS	SD	DH	DD	PC	ED	TD	PR
Count	C	40	20	10	6	5	10	6	2
	Q	0	0	20	0	6	130	0	6
	M	210	1	11	1	1	8	1	1

It is desired to allocate storage for each record in a contiguous block with each terminal node of the tree being stored contiguously for each instance of the structure or sub-structure.   Let us define a reference expression which orders the names of the structures from left to right by level.

$$A_1(I_1)A_2(I_2)A_3(I_3)$$
$$A_1(I_1)A_2(I_2)A_3$$

37

The reference expression $WS(I_1)SD(I_2)DH(I_3)$ refers to the I_3^{th} storage element within the I_2^{th} instance of SD within the I_1^{th} instance of WS. $WS(I_1)SD(I_2)$ refers to the I_2^{th} instance of SD within the I_1^{th} instance of WS while $WS(I_1)SD$ refers to all 10 instances of SD within the I_1^{th} instance of WS. A storage mapping function for these expressions of the following form can be derived [22].

$$\text{Address } [A_1(I_1)A_2(I_2)\ldots A_k(I_k)] = \sum_{i=i}^{k} [Q(A_i) +$$
$$M(A_i)(I_i-1)]$$

where $Q(A_i)$ and $M(A_i)$ are constants for each record element.

The constants Q and M can be defined recursively.

1. If A_i is a terminal node of the structure, then
$M(A_i) = 1$.

2. If A is a structure or sub-structure with a typical instance $B_1\ldots B_n$
$$M(A_i) = \sum_{i=i}^{n} C(B_i)M(B_i)$$

3. If $B_1\ldots B_n$ is a sub-structure definition,
then $Q(B_1) = 0$
$Q(B_j) = Q(B_{j-1}) + C(B_{j-1})$, $j>1$
$Q(A) = 0$, for root of tree

4. If B_n is the last item in a sub-structure $B_1\ldots B_n$ of A, then
$$M(A) = Q(B_n) + C(B_n)M(B_n)$$

Figure 3 is a flow chart for construction of Q and M from the level numbers and counts of the record definitions. The last two rows of Table 1 give an example of the calculation for the record defined in Figure 1. In the flow chart the level indices are used instead of the component name. This technique will of course generate the familiar formula for arrays of identical elements.

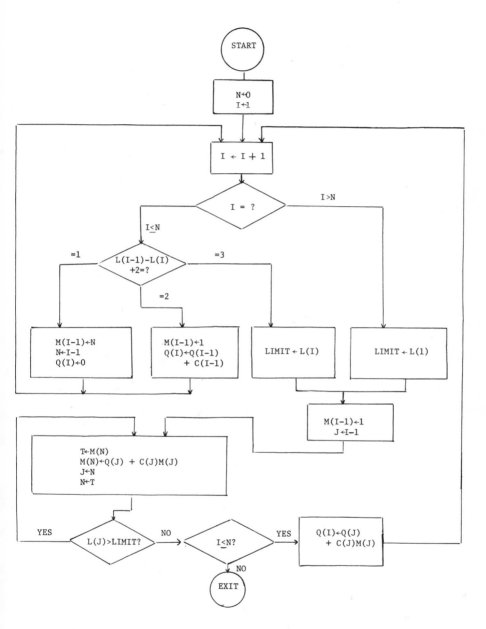

Figure 3: Flow Chart of Address Constant Computation

D. SPARSE ARRAYS

A sparse array is not actually sparse. The correct statement is that the value of many elements can be predicted without
examination. If an application generated a matrix whose elements were with only a few exceptions, unity, then it would not
be necessary to store the unit valued elements. That matrix
would be a "sparse matrix" in terms of its storage representation
even though there were no zero elements. We will, however,
adhere to the convention of calling arrays with a large fraction
of zero elements "sparse arrays." Sparse arrays in scattered,
blocked and banded forms have been the data structures which
have held the attention of numerical analysts, scientists and
engineers executing numerical calculations. There are three
standard addressing techniques: bit maps, row or column indexing
and linked storage allocation. There are many accounts of these
techniques and their application in the literature. A recent
survey article [23] gives a representative set of citations.
The notion of using a scatter storage and hash coding techniques
as a data representation and storage mapping function for sparse
arrays has received relatively little attention. That it potentially has advantages is seen even in the very simple example
given in the section on "ELEMENTARY EXAMPLES OF STORAGE
REPRESENTATION AND STORAGE MAPPING FUNCTIONS." The first
published account found by this author of a systematic exploration
of the use of hash coding for sparse arrays is de Villers and
Wilson [30]. It is surely the case that others have utilized
this technique without formal description. Part of the lack of
use may also arise in the difficulty of adapting hash coding
techniques to row-wise or column-wise scans of the matrices.
Hash coding techniques probably deserve much more attention as a
storage mapping function for sparse arrays.

E. DYNAMIC ARRAYS

The occurrence of arrays whose number of rows and columns
change dynamically is fairly common.

There has grown up a sizeable literature concerning the use of linked list data representations for this situation. It is not yet widely appreciated that direct access storage mapping functions can be obtained for dynamic arrays. Rosenberg [24, 25, 26], Stockmeyer [27], and Rosenberg and Stockmeyer [28,29] have developed data representations and storage mapping functions for extendable arrays which are computationally reasonable and allow row or column traversal. The use of the techniques is not without cost as they tend to utilize storage rather poorly in the present formulations. Dynamic arrays can be conveniently classified by two properties: Can the number of rows and columns be bounded? Is row or column traversal required? We have space only for a few examples of the possible storage mapping functions. The so-called "Square shells" mapping function for arrays in two dimensions is as follows:

$$\text{address } [(i,j)] = \text{base address} + (m-1)^2 + m + j - 1$$
$$m = \max(i,j)$$

This function is applicable to fully extensible arrays. It has the unpleasant property that in the worst case it may spread an array of s elements over a total address space of dimension s^2. An addressing function which applies to boundedly extensible arrays of maximum size s and has the property of additive row traversal is

$$\text{address } [A(i,j)] = i+j-1, \text{ if } s \leq 3$$
$$= (i-1)(N(s)-1) + (j-1)N(s) + 1, \text{ if } s > 3$$
$$N(s) = \left|\left| \frac{1}{2} + (s + \frac{1}{4})^{1/2} \right|\right| ; \qquad || \quad || = \text{integer part}$$

There is a sizeable potential impact for direct access storage mapping functions for extendable arrays in the area of management of sparse matrices on auxiliary storage.

VII. DATA MANAGEMENT

Data Management Systems are often thought of as being a separate subject from the data structuring and data access area

that we have previously been discussing. It is my contention
that the concepts are essentially similar. The difference lies
in the properties of the data structures, the name spaces and
the address spaces typically associated with data management
system applications as contrasted to those associated with
scientific computing. The data structures of data management
systems are typically less regular and have more complex
structures. The name spaces are typically many orders of
magnitude greater than for common scientific programs. Consider
as examples the space of all possible surnames in the English
language or the possible inventory numbers for all spare parts
of operational aircraft in the U.S. Air Force. The value sets
are usually very large but generally orders of magnitude
smaller than the name spaces. This implies that the data
instantiations will be very sparse with respect to the name
space (very sparse array!!). The total physical address spaces,
disks, drums and tapes are often non-linear in both logical and
physical characteristics. These factors have important influ-
ences on the choice of data representation and storage mapping
functions used in data management systems. A characteristic
which might be described as fundamental is persistence. The
value sets of data management systems tend to have lifetimes
very long with respect to program execution. The value sets of
scientific and engineering computing are typically transient
within a program execution. A characteristic associated with
longevity is updating or partial alteration of the value set.
A final characteristic is that the storage mapping functions
are often sequences of functions which map to/from a user defined
data structure to/from a representation in executable memory
and then to/from another representation in auxiliary memory.

The subject of data management systems is in its entirety
clearly a subject very far beyond the few pages we can allocate
here. The focus will be on illustrating some concepts and
techniques which may be useful in the design and implementation

of data storage and retrieval systems for numerical data or experimental data tabulations. Introductions to data management systems can be found in Martin [31] and Date [32].

The approach to be taken here will be to illustrate the structure of a typical data management system using as an example a system whose purpose is to store and retrieve design data on wing sections of an aircraft. The essential components are:

1. A data structure definition capability: This will include a set of primitive data objects and a set of composition rules which will enable a user to create a structure which represents the objects of interest. The set of primitive objects and composition rules comprise what is often called the data definition model or data model in the data management system literature. A structure defined by the composition rules will be said to constitute a logical record.

2. A storage mapping function which enables access to the components of a logical data structure or logical record.

3. A representation which packs logical records onto physical records in executable memory.

4. A storage mapping function which determines the address of a logical block and the address of the physical block which contains it.

5. A block transfer function which transmits physical records to and from auxiliary memory.

6. A query language which allows the user to express his storage/retrieval requests in an application-oriented format. Commercial data management systems often have very highly developed query languages. It is often the interface which sells the system more than its internal performance. It is generally the case in scientific/ engineering computing that simple or specialized query languages will be all that is required. The users of the system will often be familiar with programming and

programming systems.

Standard commercial data management systems are generally not designed to handle the high volume numeric data associated with scientific and engineering computing. We will therefore define for illustration a simple data management system which will handle storage and retrieval of a hypothetical data base consisting of wing section stress values. We will proceed by defining each of the components previously described.

1. Data definition model: The primitive objects which we will need will be character strings, real numbers, integer numbers and real vectors. We will allow the compositon of arbitrary tree structures utilizing these primitive data types. Figure 4 defines a logical record for a wing section.

   1 Wing Section [15]

      2 Aircraft Designation C[10]

      2 Design Parameters

         3 Thickness R[1]

         3 Flexibility R[1]

         3 Strut Spacing R[1]

      2 Stress Values R[25]

   Figure 4. Logical Record Definition for Wing Section Stress Data

The record consists of a character string for the aircraft designation, a set of design parameters including thickness, flexibility coefficient and strut spacing, each of which is a real number and a set of stress values which is a vector of length 25 of real numbers. Figure 5 is a tree structure for this data.

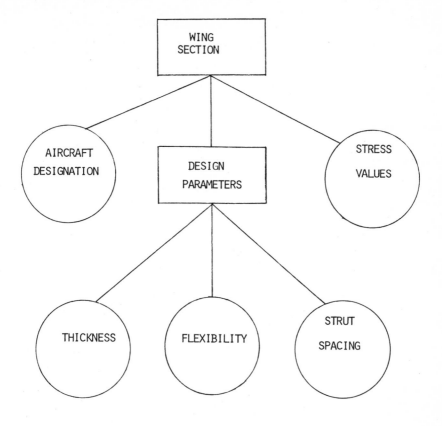

Figure 5. *Tree Structure of Wing Section Logical Record*

The [15] following the record declaration declares that a physical record will contain 15 logical records. The primary purpose of this system is to be able to examine the stress values as a function of design parameters. It is anticipated that entire records will be added or deleted from the file but that records will seldom be altered or modified.

2.   Storage mapping functions for logical records: We can use the storage mapping function defined earlier in the section on RECORDS for these logical records.

3. Data representation in physical memory: The logical record will be organized and stored on physical record blocks (PRB) of 512 words in length. Each logical record will require 30 words. Fifteen logical records will be stored on each physical record block. Forty-five of the remaining sixty-two words will be used for the numbers in the PRB of logical record instantiations which contain a given design parameter value.

4. A storage mapping function for accessing logical records from physical records: The storage mapping function will utilize an inverted file structure [31]. Each design parameter will be represented as an inverted file. An inverted file is a tabulation of record addresses associated with a given name or structure component whereas a normal file contains the values associated with each name or structure component. Each entry in the inverted files for design parameters will consist of a design parameter and the number (=address) of each physical block which contains a logical record with that design parameter value and a pointer to the address on that physical block of the set of position numbers for logical records containing that particular design parameter value. Each entry in the inverted file on a given design parameter is sorted in ascending order on the design paramenter values. The inverted files will also be stored on 512 word PRB's. It will be assumed for simplicity that the set of entries for a given design parameter will always fit on a single PRB.

There will be a directory to each inverted file which is kept in executable memory. The directory entries for a given inverted file will consist of the largest and smallest value for a design parameter which

is stored on a given inverted file PRB together with the
number (= address) of the PRB holding those inverted
file entries.

5. Physical record transmission: We will assume that the
operating system provides a convenient capability for
transmitting fixed length blocks to and from disk storage.

6. Query language: The query language will consist of a
knowledge of the table structures.

A summary of the relationships between the storage mapping
function and a given physical record is illustrated in Figure 6.

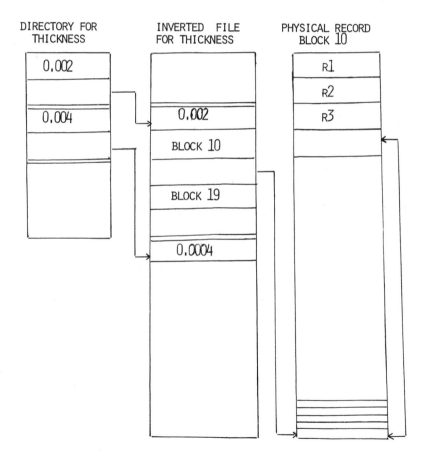

Figure 6. File Structures For Wing Section Data

This data management system structure will support queries
for logical records which specify one, two, or three design parameters. To find all records which have a particular design
parameter, say thickness = 0.002", the following process would
ensue:

o A search would be made on the directory for thickness
  to locate the inverted file page containing 0.002" for
  the thickness design parameter. This PRB would be loaded
  into executable memory.

o A search of this page of the inverted file for thickness
  would return the set of physical record blocks containing
  the logical records with that thickness parameter and the
  pointer to the physical record block section which holds
  the positions on the PRB of the logical records containing the given design parameter.

o These physical records could then be read in from the
  disk. The logical records would be extracted from the
  PRB's and examined one by one using the record addressing scheme.

To obtain all records which have two particular attributes,
say a thickness of 0.002" and a strut separation of 0.8', one
would carry out an indentical search on the inverted files for
both thickness and strut separation. The intersection of the
two lists of physical record blocks will contain all of the
logical records which have the specified value for both parameters.

A simple system such as just described can be implemented
with only a few weeks of work in FORTRAN under a reasonably
modern operating system. There are of course many optional data
representations and mapping functions which could be used.
Fairly readable descriptions of many of these can be found in
Martin [31], Date [32], and Bertiss [19].

VIII.   STORAGE MANAGEMENT FOR DATA AND PROGRAM DATA STORAGE MANAGEMENT

Storage may be allocated (bound) to the data structures declared and defined in a program at three different times [33]. The earliest is at compile time when the compiler determines the amount of storage that must be reserved and issues directives causing the loader to reserve the appropriate amount of storage on loading. The second time at which allocations may be made is at load time. Some loaders have a capability for interpreting parametric assignments issued by compilers and utilizing parameters supplied at load time to carry out space allocation. The third time at which storage can be allocated is at execution time. In this case, storage is assigned to data structures as they are used or as the program moves its execution to the scope of definition of a given data structure. The first two binding times are both fairly described as being static with respect to program execution. The latter is usually referred to as a dynamic allocation or dynamic binding. There are two subcases of dynamic binding. One is where the system allocates storage automatically whenever the program moves in and out of the scope of definition of a data structure and the other is allocation under program control. ALGOL 60 implementations characteristically utilize a dynamic storage management capability. PL/1 for example has both system controlled dynamic storage management and programmer controlled dynamic storage management.

FORTRAN in virtually all of its implementations statically allocates storage at compile time. Thus unless a program is to have its dimensionality of its data structures altered and be recompiled before each run, data declarations at the main program level must be dimensioned for the largest expected occurrence of the data sets. Thus much allocated storage may be unused during an average execution of the program. This flaw is not intrinsic to FORTRAN language definition. It can be alleviated by a slight extension to allow a compiler to emit parametric allocations at compile time and the construct of a linking, relocating loader which will accept as input assignments of these parameters and load accordingly. This does not represent a major extension of capability in either the compiler or the loader. A linking relocated loader capable of executing this function was designed and implemented for use on the ICL ATLAS [34]. The FORTRAN compiler for the ATLAS was never constructed to take advantage of this unique and desirable feature.

ALGOL-60, in most implementations, manages dynamic storage by allocation from a push-down stack. Data structures are allocated storage as the program moves its execution into the scope of definition of each data item. Storage is deallocated as the program leaves the scope of definition of a given data item. There are a number of awkwardnesses in this scheme. The programmer cannot directly express his knowledge of the useful scope of data but must try to represent the scope by block structuring of the program. Additionally, in order to have variables remain available from incarnation to incarnation of a block, it is necessary to declare variables as OWN variables. This causes them to remain static. It causes their storage allocation to be permanent throughout the execution life of the entire program.

PL/1 has a quite effective set of provisions for execution time storage management. All three types of storage allocation are available. Variables can be declared as STATIC or CONTROLLED. STATIC variables are assigned fixed storage for the duration of program execution, whereas variables which are declared as controlled will have storage assigned to them by the execution of ALLOCATE statements and storage deleted from them by execution of FREE statements. Variables declared to be neither STATIC nor CONTROLLED are managed dynamically by the system.

Since most scientific programs are still written in FORTRAN, it is desirable to consider mechanisms for imbedding dynamic storage management in FORTRAN. A number of such schemes have

been published in the literature [35, 36] and many installations
have available one or more such packages on their system library.
Bertiss [19] gives a tutorial description of such systems. The
general characteristic is to assign a large common block and
a set of mapping functions which map data on to this linear
space under the programmer's control. These packages have great
variance in their capability and the convenience of their
utilizations.

A. PROGRAM STORAGE MANAGEMENT

It is often the case that a very large and complex program
will consist of a set of processes whose action is essentially
serial. This implies that the loading of a complete program
set results in a great deal of program and data being loaded into
allocated memory and the memory then being unused for long periods
of time. It is a fairly general characteristic of such programs
that their execution cycles have tree or graph structures.

The paged memory concept [37, 38] whereby a programmer's
allocated memory space is divided into pages some of which are
kept on external storage when not needed, provides an answer to
this problem. However, the answer often involves a computational
cost which is non-trivial in its application [39, 40, 41].
Paging has the basic problem of not reflecting the programmer's
knowledge of the system but rather forcing the hardware to react
to changes as they occur. The concept of segmentation [37, 38]
associates a name with a given block of storage. The name is
usually related to the value sets stored in the storage block.
Hardware implementation of segmentation which stores segments
not in active use on external storage does not suffer the liability
of paging in that the logical association of names to storage
allows the programmer to utilize his knowledge of execution
structure. Program overlay is a software implementation of
segmentation.

It is commonly the case that a programmer's knowledge of the
processes of a program may be incomplete.

For example, a program has been 'obtained from another site, or the program may be the composition of the work of a number of individuals. In such cases advantage should be taken of the technology which is available for analysis of programs to produce optimal overlay structures [42, 43, 44, 45]. An overlay structure can be represented as a graph in which each node is a program and each arc is labeled by the probability that this arc will be traversed in a typical execution. It is thus possible to construct a program which will apply constraints and produce an "optimal" overlay structure. For example, it is possible to construct a program [46] which will analyze a given FORTRAN routine into a set of overlays under the constraints of a given maximum size. The definition of optimality depends upon the amount of information given on the program. If complete information on graph traversal can be provided then the decomposition can be described as having optimal running time within a given storage constraint.

IX. A PROPOSAL

It is clear that everyone writing FORTRAN programs which involve any extensive data structuring or data mangement requires the use of imbedded capabilities for data definition, dynamic storage management and data management facilities. The capabilities are now replicated by many workers on many computer installations. This is very wasteful of effort and makes transporting of programs difficult. I propose that ANSI, ACM, IEEE or someone undertake the definition of a standard set of capabilities in each of these areas for imbedding in FORTRAN.

REFERENCES

1. Sammet, J. [1969], "Programming Languages: History and Fundamentals," Prentice-Hall, Englewood Cliffs, N.J. This is a standard reference work for background on programming languages.

2. Pratt, T.W. [1973], "Programming Languages: Design and Implementation" Prentice-Hall, Englewood Cliffs, N.J. A readable summary of the properties and characteristics of common programming languages.

3. Naur, P. (ed.) [1963], "Revised Report on the Algorithmic language ALGOL 60," *Comm. ACM 6*, 1, 1-17.

4. ANSI [1966], American National Standard FORTRAN (ANS X 3.9-1966) American National Standards Institute, New York.

5. IBM Corporation, IBM System 360 Operating Manual: PL/1 Language Specifications, *IBM Reference Manual GC 28-6571*, White Plains, New York, 1965.

6. Van Wijngaarden, A. (ed.), B. Mailloux, J. Peck, C. Koster [1965], "Report on the Algorithmic Language ALGOL 68," *Numerishe Mathematik 16*, 2, 79-218.

7. Wirth, N., K. Jensen [1975], "PASCAL-USER Manual and Report," Springer-Verlag, New York.

8. Cheatham, T.E. [1966], "The Introduction of Definitional Facilities into Higher Level Languages" *Proc. AFIPS 1966 Fall Joint Computer Conference 29*, 623-637.

9. Wegbreit, B. [1971], "The ECL Programming System" *Proc. AFIPS Fall Joint Computer Conference 39*, 253-262.

10. Hoare, C.A.R [1972a], "Proof of Correctness of Data Representation," *Acta Informatica 1*, 271-281.

11. Good, D.I. [1975], "Provable Programming," *Proceedings International Conference on Reliable Software*, 411-419.

12. Hoare, C.A.R. [1972b], "Notes on Data Structuring" in *Structured Programming* by O.J. Dahl, E.W. Dijkstra and C.A.R Hoare, Academic Press, New York.

13. Liskov, B. and S. Zilles [1975], "Specification Techniques for Data Abstraction," *Proc. International Conference on Reliable Software,* 72-87.

14. Flon, L. [1975], "A Survey of Some Issues Concerning Abstract Data Types," *Computer Science Dept. Report, Carnegie-Mellan University,* Pittsburgh, Penn.

15. Knuth, D.E. [1973], *The Art of Computer Programming, Vol. 3,* "Sorting and Searching," Addison-Wesley, Reading Mass.

16. Knuth, D.E. [1968], *The Art of Computer Programming, Vol. 1,* "Fundamental Algorithms," Addison-Wesley, Reading Mass.

17. Brandon, D.M. [1976], "The Implementation and Use of Sparse Matrix Techniques in General Simulation Programs," *Computer J. 17,*4, 165-171.

18. Elson, M. [1974], "Data Structure," Science Research Associates, Palo Alto, Calif.

19. Bertiss, A.T. [1975], "Data Structure: Theory and Practice" Academic Press, New York, 2d Ed.

20. Elson, M. [1973], "Concepts of Programming Languages," Science Research Associates, Palo Alto, Calif.

21. Ehrich, H.D. [1974], "Theory of Direct Access Storage Functions," *Proc. IFIPS Congress,* North Holland Press, Amsterdam, 6,647.

22. Deud, P. [1966], "On a Storage Mapping Function for Data Structures," *Comm. ACM 9,* 5, 344-347.

23. Pooch, U.W. and Nieder, A. [1973], "A Survey of Indexing Techniques for Sparse Matrices," *Computing Surveys 5,* 2, 109-133.

24. Rosenberg, A.L. [1974], "Allocating Storage for Extendible Arrays," *Journal ACM 21,* 4, 652-670.

25. Rosenberg, A.L. [1975a], "Managing Storage for Extendible Arrays," *SIAM J. Comp 4,* 3, 287-306.

26. Rosenberg, A.L. [1975b] "Preserving Proximity in Arrays," *SIAM J. Comp. 4*, 4, 443–460.

27. Stockmeyer, L.J. [1973], Extendible Array Realizations with Additive Traversal," *IBM Research Report RC-4578*.

28. Rosenberg, A.L., and L.J. Stockmeyer, [1975a], "Hashing Schemes for Extendible Arrays," *IBM Research Report 5564*.

29. Rosenberg, A.L., and L.J. Stockmeyer [1975b], "Storage Schemes for Boundedly Extensible Arrays," *IBM Research Report 5586*.

30. deVilliers [1974], E.D.S. and L.B. Wilson, "Hash Coding Methods for Sparse Arrays," *BIT 14*, 347–358 (1974).

31. Martin, J. "Computer Data-Base Organization," Prentice-Hall, Englewood Cliffs, New Jersey.

32. Date, C.J. [1975], "An Introduction to Database Systems," Addison-Wesley Publ. Co., Reading, Mass.

33. Elson [1974], Ref. 20, Chapter 5, discusses binding times for storage allocation and data values.

34. Curtis, A.R. and Pyle, I.C. [1962], "A Proposed Target Language for Compilers on ATLAS," *Computer J. 5*, 100–106.

35. Sakoda,J.M.[1968], "DYSTAL: Dynamic Storage Allocation Language in FORTRAN," in *Symbol Manipulation Languages and Techniques*, (D.G. Bobrow, ed.) pp. 302–311, North Holland Publ. Co., Amsterdam.

36. Chung-Phillips, A. and R.W. Rosen [1975], "A Note on Dynamic Data Storage in FORTRAN IV," *Computer J. 18*, 342–343.

37. Shaw, A.C. [1974], "The Logical Design of Operating Systems," Chapter 5, Prentice-Hall, Inc., Englewood Cliffs, N.J.

38. Madnick, S. and Donavon, J.R. [1974], "Operating Systems," McGraw-Hill Publ. Co., New York.

39. McKellar, A.C. and Coffman, E.C. [1969], "Organizing Matrices and Matrix Operations for Paged Memory Systems," *Comm. ACM 12*, 153–165.

40. Moler, C.B. [1972], "Matrix Operations with FORTRAN and Paging," *Comm. ACM 15, 268-270.*

41. Elshoff, J.L. [1974], "Some Programming Techniques for Processing Multi-Dimensional Matrices in a Paging Environment," *Proc. AFIPS 43,* 185-193.

42. Baer, J.L. and Caughey, R. [1972], "Segmentation and Optimization of Programs from Cyclic Structure Analysis," *Proc. AFIPS (SJCC) 40,* 23-25.

43. Van Hoep, E.W. [1971], "Automatic Segmentation Based on Baerlean Connectivity," *Proc. AFIPS (SJCC) 38,* 491-495.

44. Lowe, T.C., "Automatic Segmentation of Cycle Program Structure Based on Connectivity and Program Timing," *Comm. ACM 13,* 3-6 (1970).

45. Kernighan, B.W. [1971], "Optimal Sequential Partitioning of Graphs," *J. ACM 18,* 36-40.

46. Weiss, L., Greenawalt, E.M., and Browne, J.C., unpublished memorandum, Computer Sciences Department, University of Texas, 1972.

COMPUTER-AIDED DESIGN AND COMPUTER SCIENCE TECHNOLOGY

Robert E. Fulton and Susan J. Voigt
NASA Langley Research Center

ABSTRACT

Digital computers are important to the design of complex aerospace vehicles. Developments in computer-aided design (CAD) technology continue but, generally, such developments are dis-jointed improvements in specific areas. Research on and defini-tion of comprehensive integrated CAD systems, together with the continued evolution of computer hardware, has highlighted areas where advances in computer science could have substantial impact on CAD. This paper discusses some important CAD capabilities required to support aerospace design in the areas of interactive support, information management, and computer hardware advances and discusses some computer science developments which may con-tribute significantly to making such capabilities possible.

INTRODUCTION

Digital computers are used in many ways to support engineers in design work. The broad class of technology associated with such use is denoted herein as Computer-Aided Design (CAD). While early CAD was primarily directed toward improved analysis proce-dures, recent developments have extended CAD to include such functions as interactive computations, automation of design decisions, tutorial assistance to designers, graphical display of results, and management of information (Ref. 1). While these developments have been principally disjointed, efforts are being initiated to integrate such functions into comprehensive CAD sys-tems such as the planned NASA IPAD[*] system (Refs. 2-7). The definition and development of integrated CAD systems, together with the continued evolution of computer hardware, has indicated areas for improvement in computer science technology which need to be addressed to maximize the benefits of integrated CAD

---

[*] Integrated Programs for Aerospace-Vehicle Design.

systems and to facilitate their long-term viability. The purpose
of this paper is to describe some of the CAD requirements and the
resulting computer science advances needed to support aerospace
design. Topics considered include interactive support, information management, and computer hardware advances. A brief description of the aerospace design environment is given first to help
in understanding computer support requirements. The results of
the paper are based on studies of existing CAD systems (see, for
example, Refs. 8-21), numerous discussions with their developers,
and the definition of the planned NASA IPAD system (Fig. 1),
(Refs. 5-7). IPAD is to be a prototype computer-aided design
software system to provide company-wide access to design information and will be incrementally developed on two different computers with extensive user involvement throughout definition,
design, and software checkout.

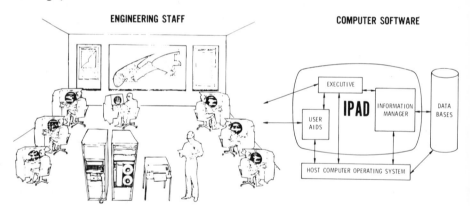

- $10M, 5 YEAR DEVELOPMENT PLAN
- INCREMENTALLY RELEASED ON 2 DIFFERENT COMPUTERS
- HEAVY INDUSTRY INVOLVEMENT

*Fig. 1   IPAD - A NASA-sponsored computer-aided design system for
the aerospace industry*

THE AEROSPACE DESIGN ENVIRONMENT

The aerospace design process is composed of numerous tasks
which grow in number and complexity as a vehicle design is
refined. Many engineering disciplines are involved, each with

its own specific interests and requirements (Fig. 2). Staff sizes may range from a few at the beginning to hundreds or thousands in the later stages of design. Design begins with gross treatments of widely varying vehicle options and evolves to careful and detailed consideration of one specific option. A typical vehicle development cycle (for example, the 747 aircraft), can take as long as five years from beginning of preliminary design to first vehicle delivery.

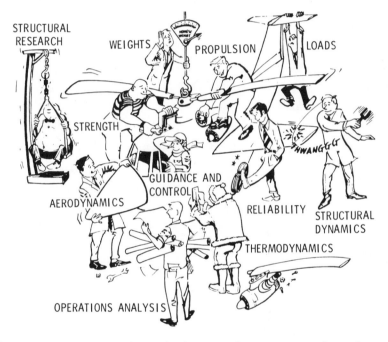

Fig. 2 Aerospace-vehicle design requires cooperation of many disciplines (courtesy McDonnell Aircraft Co.)

While the total design activity is often characterized by three levels denoted conceptual, preliminary, and detail, the dividing lines and precise definitions for each level, as well as any intermediate stages, are not clearly established and can be different for different design organizations. Typical goals for each design level are:

Conceptual Design: Assess relative merits of a broad range of vehicle parameters to determine promising alternative configurations;

Preliminary Design: Conduct in-depth studies of selected alternative configurations to refine their shape, structure, and systems and to improve prediction of performance, weights, and costs;

Detailed Design: Verify and refine design of one vehicle configuration and define all technical details preparatory to fabrication.

Furthermore, because of the effort, time, and interrelationship of design activities on a complex vehicle, design levels are not carried out in series, but include substantial parallel work. Such parallel work is necessary to perform numerous iterations on a design within a tight development schedule. These iterations and the design activities conducted in parallel cause design data to continually change. Hence, the staff from one discipline of necessity often uses input data which are not current from another discipline. Control of this process requires configuration management of design data with certified updates at specific intervals.

In the early stages of conceptual design, the quantity of data is small and only a few key disciplines are considered, together with gross configuration or mission parameters. In the preliminary design stage, additional disciplines and effects are included and technical depth grows. In the detailed design stage, the in-depth studies require detailed consideration of all disciplines necessary for full vehicle design. The amount of data generated increases with subsequent design levels. Furthermore, problems of data handling and organization are compounded by the broad spectrum of projects simultaneously underway at one company. Thus, through the iterative process of definition and evaluation, aerospace product design is largely communication

among managers, designers, technical disciplinarians, and computer programs (Fig. 3).

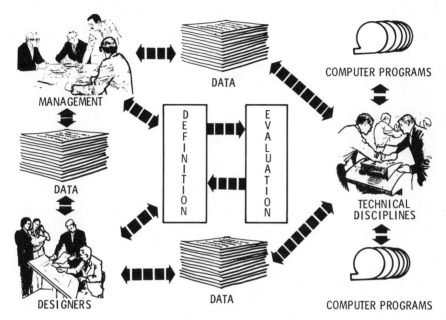

MANAGEMENT

DATA

COMPUTER PROGRAMS

DATA

DEFINITION

EVALUATION

DESIGNERS

DATA

TECHNICAL DISCIPLINES

COMPUTER PROGRAMS

Fig. 3 Aerospace product design is largely communication

An aerospace corporation may have several thousand engineers
working on a mix of engineering design activities with many of
these activities supported by a complex of computer hardware and
software which can be denoted the computer environment. This
environment usually includes several computers, possibly of
different manufacture or vintage, and may include several different minicomputers. Some or all of this capability may be time-
shared and/or networked together locally or in some cases nation-
ally. Peripheral devices likely include numerous tape and disc
devices, alphanumeric and graphic display terminals, digitizers,
etc. The variety of makes and types of computers and peripherals
is often the result of fragmented evolution of the computer complex driven by increasing corporation needs, computer science
advances, and specialized requirements. A measure of daily
company computer hardware requirements for a typical mix of

projects at various design levels is shown in Figure 4. This indicates the need for more computer capacity than can be provided by a single computer with the power of a CDC 6600, support for about 100 interactive terminals, and massive amounts of on-line or readily accessible data storage.

DESIGN LEVELS	CPU hr CDC 6600	I/O RATE (WORDS/6600 CP sec)	DATA STORAGE ($\approx$ 60 BIT WORDS)	SIMULTANEOUS INTERACTIVE PORTS
I - RESEARCH	~ 1.0	~ 40000	~ 1 M	~3
II - CRITERIA SELECT.	.3	30000	1 M	1
III - SIZING	5.1	30000	110 M	3
IV - REFINEMENT	16.4	30000	600 M	20
V - VERIFICATION	8.3	45000	2750 M	20
VI-IX - PRODUCTION	2.0	70000	1000 M	50
OTHER	~ 9.0	~100000	~ 40 M	~3
TOTAL	42.1	50000 (WEIGHTED MEAN)	4510 M	100

Fig. 4   Company daily computer hardware requirements can be large (eight concurrent design projects at varying levels)

Each corporation also has a wide variety of software available, some developed in-house and some obtained from outside sources. In the engineering applications area, there exist thousands of computer programs, together with a few computer-aided design systems which aim toward multidisciplinary tasks and contain individualized data management systems appropriate for their use. Most companies also have some level of Computer-Aided Manufacturing (CAM) installed and this capability is continually expanding. The engineering programs and data management software can have major interfaces and interactions with computer-aided manufacturing activities (Refs. 22-23). Often both engineering and manufacturing need access to the same information and manufacturing constraints can have a significant effect on design.

This total computer software/hardware complex to support design and manufacturing represents a multimillion dollar investment which has evolved over many years of continuous development. Corporations have placed their financial security on the reliability of that complex to perform certain critical functions in the vehicle development process. This reliance is based on extensive quantified experience with the performance and reliability of the complex, and abrupt changes which might jeopardize this complex usually are not allowed to take place. Yet, because of the changing nature of computer technology, a corporation's computer environment undergoes significant alterations over each three-to-five-year period.

In the midst of this environment of computer programs, computer hardware, and data, is the typical designer (Fig. 5). He is surrounded by a maze of computer science tools. Computer programs abound, each with its own peculiar engineering capabilities,

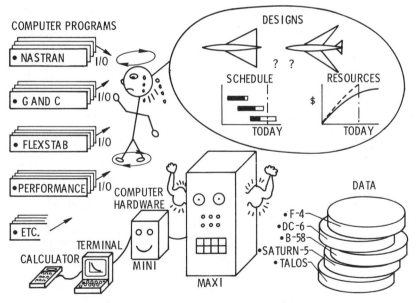

Fig. 5 The designer's problem

software characteristics, and input formats. Data exist on numerous past designs and are being created on his own project at an astounding rate. A variety of computer hardware is available with various costs, response times, and capabilities. Too often,

however, the designer feels he is drowning in data and starved
for information. His goal is to decide on a design, yet he is
often behind schedule and overspent on resources. The challenge
to computer science and computer-aided design technology is to
help him, not to bury him. Many potential computer science
advances are possible, but some appear to be particularly important to advancements in computer-aided design. Some areas helpful to the designer are discussed in the following sections on
interactive support, information management, hardware advancements, and computer science developments. While some features
are partly or fully available on certain computer systems, an
integrated capability, widely available, is needed to provide the
comprehensive CAD system of the future.

INTERACTIVE SUPPORT

The interactive terminal is normally the primary interface
between the computer system and the engineering designer. Thus,
substantial capability to support interactive activity is needed.
This includes assorted user aids, facilities for interactive
design, and capabilities for interactive computation.

User Aids

Extensive user aids are needed by the designer to take full
advantage of the combined capabilities of the interactive terminal
and computer complex (Fig. 6). These include standard languages
for communication with the computers, as well as standard data
formats. The computer system should provide support to engineering standards which can be installed to aid in design communications. For example, standard engineering procedures, notations,
dimensions, etc., should be available and/or be readily created
to provide a consistent language for communication among specific
groups of designers. Options should permit the use of system-
provided standards or for the insertion of a company's own standards. Other user aids should include a good interactive language
which is both easy to use and to understand and a wide assortment

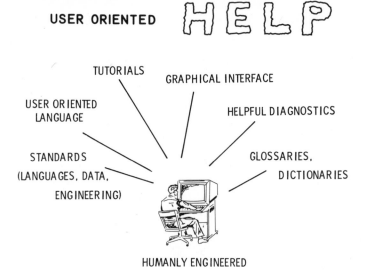

Fig. 6 Important user aids

of tutorial aids and helpful messages to guide both experienced and inexperienced users. (Speakeasy, Ref. 24, is a good example of such a capability.) Also required are capabilities for graphics, error diagnostics with explicit descriptions of the cause of failures, and a feature permitting a wide assortment of glossaries and dictionaries to help the user search through the myriad of available capabilities. Particularly important to all the user aids is that they be humanly engineered not only to meet prescribed requirements, but also to allow for important human characteristics such as rate of comprehension, response times, and fatigue levels.

Interactive Design

A particularly important ingredient in CAD is the capability for interactive design (Fig. 7). Interactive design features important to the user include facilities to create and modify sketches or drawings at an interactive terminal, define and refine dimensions, and create and modify configurations. Especially important is the capability to display results of related analytical calculations, data searches, etc. All such capabilities

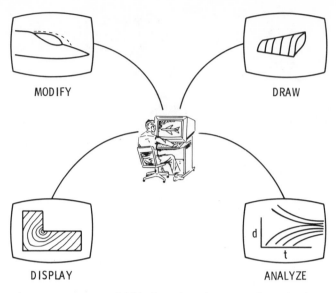

Fig. 7 Key capabilities for interactive design

should be geared to enhancing the designer's ability to visualize
the physical configuration and dimensions of vehicles and components and to make design changes. He should be able to selec-
tively view data in various ways such as a geometric cross
section of a component or specific items cutting across a data
hierarchy, displaying these data in numerical or graphical form
at his terminal. The graphical support required to permit interactive design includes (Fig. 8) the facility for drawing three-
dimensional figures encompassing such features as lines, conics,
surfaces, translation, rotation, scaling, and perspectives. Also
required is graphical capability for preparing charts with such
support features as labeling, grid preparation, curve fitting,
and a wide assortment of data plotting capabilities.

Interactive Computations

   Many design analyses are done most effectively when the
designer can interact with the computations. Computer response
times to interactive users are functions of many factors including computer hardware and software, transmission rates, and
demand. Nevertheless, it is essential that response times be

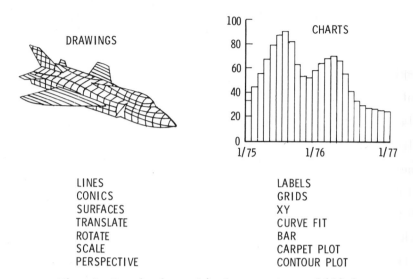

DRAWINGS

CHARTS

LINES	LABELS
CONICS	GRIDS
SURFACES	XY
TRANSLATE	CURVE FIT
ROTATE	BAR
SCALE	CARPET PLOT
PERSPECTIVE	CONTOUR PLOT

Fig. 8   Required graphical support capabilities

adequate to maintain the user's thought continuity. Figure 9
illustrates a hypothetical sequence of commands to set up and run
stress and flutter analyses of structural configurations of the
tail of a space shuttle vehicle. The commands shown on the

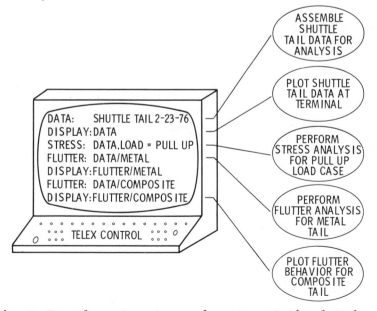

DATA: SHUTTLE TAIL 2-23-76
DISPLAY:DATA
STRESS: DATA,LOAD = PULL UP
FLUTTER: DATA/METAL
DISPLAY:FLUTTER/METAL
FLUTTER: DATA/COMPOSITE
DISPLAY:FLUTTER/COMPOSITE

TELEX CONTROL

ASSEMBLE
SHUTTLE
TAIL DATA FOR
ANALYSIS

PLOT SHUTTLE
TAIL DATA AT
TERMINAL

PERFORM
STRESS ANALYSIS
FOR PULL UP
LOAD CASE

PERFORM
FLUTTER ANALYSIS
FOR METAL
TAIL

PLOT FLUTTER
BEHAVIOR FOR
COMPOSITE
TAIL

Fig. 9   Procedures to set up and run computational tasks

display include both analysis and display events. It is important that commands such as these, many of which are possible with existing operating systems (see Ref. 15), be simple and user-oriented and each command result in the automatic collection, assembly, and/or organization of procedures, computer programs, and data stored in a data base. Utilities are also needed to aid the user in the installation of computer programs to carry out such analysis and design tasks. For example, assistance is needed to resolve differences in programing language dialects, input/output formats, overall program designs, etc., to facilitate program installation. Also important are capabilities to change previously stored computer programs by altering, adding or deleting statements, and, where appropriate, to maintain a chronological record of such changes. (Many of these features are available in current systems.)

The computer systems capabilities required for interactive computations include (1) the simultaneous support of many interactive users on a variety of terminals, (2) the ability for communication between users at their own individual terminals, (3) the capability to build and save procedures consisting of sequences of commands with sufficient control structures and parameter substitution features so that a sequence of parametric studies might be run with very simple procedure calls, and (4) communication capability between an interactive user and an executing batch job so that progress of a complex engineering analysis can be monitored from the interactive terminal. For the latter case, for example, the user needs the ability to view output files while a job is in progress. This may involve interruption and suspension of the job while the user assesses intermediate results. Also, the facility is needed to arbitrarily interrupt a program (1) to a pause state for short-term interruption (e.g., lunch break), (2) to a hold state for a longer term interruption (hours, days, or weeks) with the ability to view partial output prior to resumption, and (3) quite importantly, to a suspended state, to interactively insert and perform alternate tasks and resume the original job based upon results of the intervening task. Both the interactive user control over the batch job, and the suspend to perform alternate tasks with resumption at a later time, are important advances necessary for adequate systems support for the engineering designer.

INFORMATION MANAGEMENT

Information involved in the design process includes both computer programs and technical and management data. The computer can be a major resource for managing such design information and a full spectrum of information management capabilities is needed. The following sections give some insight into the special characteristics of design information and the associated data management requirements.

Characteristics of Design Information

Design information has some interesting and somewhat unique characteristics which make its management challenging. For example, engineering data may be accompanied by long descriptors to identify the source, theoretical basis, and other background information necessary to establish credentials and applicability. Also, it is common for the work in large aerospace projects to be distributed among major subcontractors. Figure 10, for example, identifies the prime contractor and selected subcontractors for various components of the space shuttle orbiter. The shuttle subcontractors are geographically dispersed, represent independent corporate entities, and some not shown are even from foreign countries. Communication among individual subcontractors is difficult at best, and each subcontractor likely has a unique computer system as its corporation's main computational facility. Because design is an evolutionary process, data describing each respective component represent only gross characteristics in the early stages of design and this information is refined and expanded as design progresses. At the same time, the design of

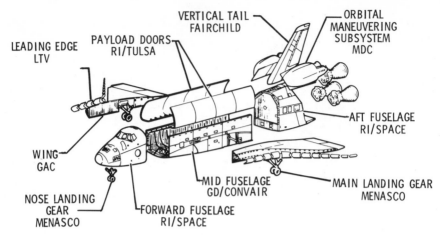

*Fig. 10   The space shuttle orbitor, a multicompany project
(Prime contractor: Rockwell International)*

one component by a subcontractor usually requires information on
components assigned to other subcontractors. The timely and
reliable exchange of critical design information to meet tight
development schedules can be a major difficulty.

Within each aerospace company, design data bases are also
large and complex (Fig. 11). Some data are intended for general
company access such as the actual code for a "company standard"
computer program, directories and dictionaries describing available programs, menus of procedures, tutorial aids, standard data
such as material properties or airfoil designs, and archival
information on previous vehicles. Other data may have limited
accessibility. Such data may be associated with a particular
design project and might include both geometry and analysis data
for various candidate configurations, test data, and classified
data on weapons systems. Other limited access data might include
project management information on resources, schedules, and
progress on various tasks and private or working data files for
individual designers.

The design data base content is dynamic and changes in size
and characteristics as the design matures. Thus, the data structure should be flexible. A simple tree structure, as shown in

70

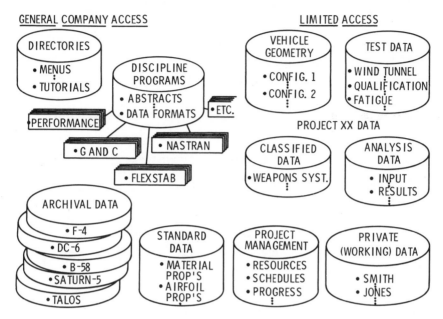

Fig. 11 Data bases are large, varied, and complex
(size range 10^6-10^{10} named items)

Figure 12 for geometric data, is unlikely to be adequate for all
needs. Here, structural components data have been organized into
a tree; yet, subsystems such as avionics and hydraulics require
specific information from several components, indicating the need
for data cross sections. The CODASYL concepts of schema and sub-
schema (Ref. 25), permitting different logical views of the data,
provide a means to accommodate this engineering requirement.
However, extensions to the CODASYL approach are necessary to
accommodate other characteristics of engineering data (Ref. 26).

As illustrated in Figure 10, the data on different components may be developed and stored at geographically dispersed
locations, in different data formats, and on computers of different manufacture. The only common data base among these dispersed
activities at the beginning may be the set of master dimensions
characterizing overall vehicle geometry and key interfaces.
Internal details are developed and generated by these

71

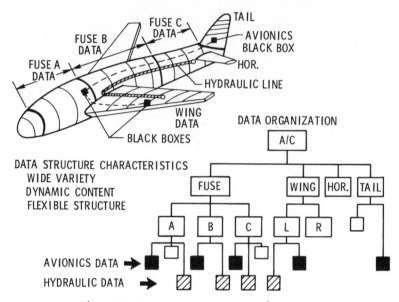

Fig. 12   Data structure requirements

geographically dispersed organizations as the design evolves.
Since many of the design activities depend on detailed information about other components, there is a need for periodic coordi-
nation to insure compatibility of the data being generated. A
common, centrally located data base with suitable controls may
be one approach to solving this problem. At present, the design
interface problems of subsystems such as avionics and hydraulics
can only be resolved through use of full-scale vehicle mockups,
a costly, time-consuming, and often inflexible process with which
to make design decisions. Computer-aided design and particularly
interactive graphics could be more effectively utilized to support such design problems if the required information could be
suitably managed.

Data Management Requirements

The effective management of large design data bases imposes
several requirements. First of all, it is important that the
data can be made independent from the machine. Then data can be
shared among companies having different computing facilities, as

well as distributed among various processors with ready access by all who need the data. As illustrated in Figure 12, flexible data structures are important, and data content should be separated from the storage structure so that restructuring can be readily carried out if and when new requirements occur. Engineering designers may formulate complex and unpredictable queries of the data management system, but the data still should be rapidly retrieved to be responsive to the designer's creative thought processes. As a minimum, statistical studies are needed of typical engineering designer queries to determine the most frequent types, so that a data management system can be designed to respond to the most common needs of the engineering community.

Some data of interest to a designer will be archival in nature and, hence, the data management system should be capable of handling data in a hierarchy of storage media to allow ready access to such archival data. Some specialized computer systems currently provide access to archival permanent files, for example, by advising the user and informing the operator to mount a particular tape, causing the user only a slight delay in data access. As an adjunct to the archival data requirement, it is important that existing data collections generated external to a large integrated data management system be used with the integrated data without totally reformatting or regenerating the existing data. Since system failures will always occur, the data base system should provide adequate backup and recovery so that a user's data are transparent to any failures (i.e., restored to the form prior to the failure).

Data integrity is critically important to aerospace design and the user must have confidence in data reliability. A computer-aided design system must provide safeguards against both accidental and intentional modification, destruction, or disclosure of the data. Data entry techniques must permit only authorized entry, and all activities and transactions in the data base should be audited with audit trail records maintained. Data also should be checked frequently for validity to insure integrity has been preserved, and backup procedures regularly followed to allow for quick recovery in case of any loss. Insuring data security is vitally important in CAD, particularly when an integrated data base is used and some data can be accessed by competitive companies. Information management practices, physical protection, and systems security techniques can all be combined to provide the necessary data security. Management procedures, personnel practices, maintaining logs, providing protection against natural threats, using physical locks, and limiting access to the computing facilities and data storage areas are some of the ways to protect data. The computer system also can help insure security through access controls, operating system features, encryption, and correct software (to prevent accidental penetration).

HARDWARE ADVANCEMENTS

Trends suggest future computer hardware developments will provide faster, cheaper processing and large capacity mass storage facilities (e.g., Refs. 27-28). In this future computing environment, a wider variety of hardware will be available to the designer on which he can conduct computing and data management activities (Fig. 13). It may be cost-effective to use different hardware for different portions of the task. For example, he might prepare the input geometry on a small minicomputer, conduct initial preprocessing calculations on a larger minicomputer, carry out selected calculations on a large computer, and use a supercomputer for the bulk of the number crunching. To provide for such a scenario, a multimachine operating system is needed to support distributed computing, permitting computation to be split among several processors, as well as to carry out management of distributed data and data transfer. Special-purpose dedicated processors may be an effective way to facilitate the data management and control in a distributed computing environment.

Computer hardware advances that will have significant impact on computer-aided design include inexpensive, high-speed graphics

74

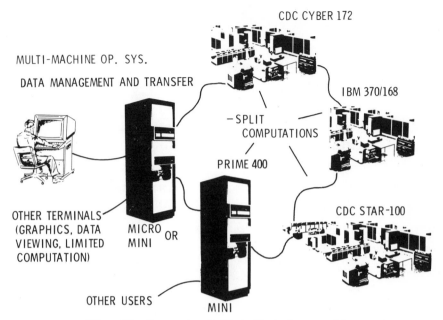

Fig. 13 Support of distributed computing

on interchangeable devices; faster communication rates for better response times; distributed computation and data exchange; improved memories and large mass storage devices to support the large data requirements of the design process; and reliable and inexpensive off-line storage capabilities. In addition, the reductions in cost of computer components imply that individual design groups will be able to afford their own computers, and with advances in networking technology, these design groups will be able to tie their computers into the integrated system.

COMPUTER SCIENCE DEVELOPMENTS

Several recent developments in computer science probably will have great impact on future computer-aided design systems. Such CAD systems represent a large investment by the engineering community and, in addition, require retraining and reorientation of the designers to adapt to the new, more automated techniques. Hence, these systems must be long-lived and highly reliable,

placing great requirements on the integrity of the computing
hardware and software.

Software engineering practices are becoming more accepted in
the design and development of computer software (Refs. 29-32).
The resulting software designs are better documented, more modular, and easier to maintain. Code generated following structured
programing rules has clearer logic, is more readable, and is
separated into manageable pieces. The resulting software product
is better tested, more reliable, and its performance predicted
for a variety of circumstances. Certainly all of these goals
have not been met to date in large computer systems developments,
but the techniques are now available and, in time, these practices
should become widely accepted.

More development is needed in the area of high-level languages for implementation of reliable, maintainable, portable
software. Pioneering work such as that by Basili (Ref. 33) in
families of languages where each member is specially tailored for
specific applications may lead to greater advances in software
through improved isolation of machine dependence allowing for
easy migration to new systems, and longer-lived, maintainable
programs. Computerized modeling and simulation of software
designs prior to implementation should identify bottlenecks and
problem areas before coding even begins (Ref. 34). Moreover,
such modeling may identify unacceptable designs prior to expend-
ing any development effort.

Substantial emphasis has been placed recently on several
approaches to reliable software development including management
techniques, verification, and testing (Refs. 35-36). Such procedures are still developing, but hold promise for development of
future systems to meet high reliability requirements.

With rapid advances in hardware developments and increasing
emphasis on distributed computing, the communication protocol
between systems and the ability to transform data from one processor environment to another are of increasing importance. In the

projected network environment needed to support future CAD, these developments will have vital impact. As computer devices change more rapidly, the transformation of existing code and data from one device to another will become more common and techniques to provide for automated transformations and device independence will be needed. Standardization of data and file formats would be a major aid in this area.

CONCLUDING REMARKS

Computers are widely used in design of aerospace vehicles and their role will continue to expand. Future developments in computer science and computer-aided design systems should make analysis of vehicle designs more efficient, provide improved capability to integrate design team activities, and greatly aid the management and analysis of massive amounts of design information.

As computer technology advances, aerospace design procedures and associated computer programs will continually evolve in a multiuser, multidisciplinary and multicompany environment. To protect investments in existing software and related user expertise, however, the CAD environment cannot change abruptly, but the software should migrate gracefully to new plateaus of capability with minimum impact to production and users. Computer science techniques to facilitate migration of software to alternate host computers and new computing systems is a prime need for CAD systems of the future.

Many user requirements discussed in the paper are operational on specific computer installations, yet are not widely available. Ways are needed to improve the computing capabilities available to the aerospace industry in several computer science areas including interactive computing, management of engineering information, distributed computing, multimachine operating systems, program reliability, and continued software enhancement. Specific areas where gains would be particularly helpful include increased standardization, facilities to aid in transfer of code and data among computer systems, the ability to control batch jobs from an interactive terminal, and the capability to suspend tasks in order to perform other tasks and subsequently resume suspended tasks. As such computer science advances occur, the designer can be relieved of many tedious design tasks and provided a more creative and stimulating work environment in which to design the complex aerospace vehicles of the future.

REFERENCES

1. Sobieszczanski, J. E., Susan J. Voigt, and Robert E. Fulton [1974]. "On Computer-Aided Design of Aerospace Vehicles," *Structural Optimization Symposium*, L. Schmit (Ed.), ASME Special Publication AMD, Vol. 7, pp. 135-160, presented at *Symposium on Structural Optimization, 1974 ASME Winter Annual Meeting*, Nov. 17-21, 1974, New York, N.Y.

2. Garrocq, C. A., and M. J. Hurley [1974]. "The IPAD System: A Future Management/Engineering/Design Environment," presented at the *ACM/IEEE 11th Design Automation Workshop*, June 17-19, 1974, Denver, Colorado.

3. Miller, R. E., Jr., S. D. Hanson, A. S. Kawaguchi, D. D. Redhed, and J. W. Southall [1974]. "An Executive Summary of the Feasibility Study of an Integrated Program for Aerospace-Vehicle Design (IPAD)," presented at the *ACM/IEEE 11th Design Automation Workshop*, June 17-19, 1974, Denver, Colorado.

4. Miller, R. E., Jr., S. D. Hanson, A. S. Kawaguchi, D. D. Redhed, and J. W. Southall [1974]. "Cost-Effectiveness of Integrated Analysis/Design Systems (IPAD)," presented at the *AIAA 6th Aircraft Design, Flight Test and Operations Meeting*, Los Angeles, California, August 12-14, 1974, AIAA Paper No. 74-960.

5. "Feasibility Study of an Integrated Program for Aerospace-Vehicle Design (IPAD)," The Boeing Company, Contract NAS1-11441, 1973, NASA CR 132390-97.

6. "Feasibility Study of an Integrated Program for Aerospace-Vehicle Design (IPAD)," General Dynamics/Convair, Contract NAS1-11431, 1973, NASA CR 132401-06.

7. Santa, J. E., and T. R. Whiting [1974]. "Application of IPAD to Missile Design," Report under Contract NAS1-12346 to McDonnell Douglas Astronautics Company, April 1974, NASA CR-132671.

8. Heldenfels, R. R. [1973]. "Automating the Design Process: Progress, Problems, Prospects, Potential," presented at *14th AIAA/ASME/SAE Structures, Structural Dynamics, and Materials Conference*, Williamsburg, Virginia, March 20-22, 1973, AIAA Paper No. 73-410.

9. Heldenfels, R. R. [1973]. "Integrated, Computer Aided Design of Aircraft," presented at *AGARD/NATO Flight Mechanics Panel Symposium*, Florence, Italy, October 1-4, 1973.

10. Heldenfels, R. R. [1974]. "Automation of the Aircraft Design Process," presented at *IXth Congress of the International Council of the Aeronautical Sciences*, Haifa, Israel, August 25-30, 1974.

11. Rau, T. R., and J. P. Decker [1974]. "ODIN-Optimal Design Integration System for Synthesis of Aerospace Vehicles," *AIAA 12th Aerospace Sciences Meeting*, Washington, D.C., January 30-February 1, 1974, AIAA Paper No. 74-72.

12. Fulton, R. E., J. Sobieszczanski, and E. J. Landrum [1972]. "An Integrated Computer System for Preliminary Design of Advanced Aircraft," *4th AIAA Aircraft Design Conference*, Los Angeles, California, August 1972, AIAA Paper No. 72-796.

13. Fulton, R. E., J. Sobieszczanski, O. O. Storaasli, E. J. Landrum, and D. D. Loendorf [1973]. "Application of Computer-Aided Aircraft Design in a Multidisciplinary Environment," presented at *14th AIAA/ASME/SAE Structures, Structural Dynamics, and Materials Conference*, Williamsburg, Virginia, March 20-22, 1973, AIAA Paper No. 73-353.

14. Giles, Gary L., Charles L. Blackburn, and Sidney C. Dixon [1972]. "Automated Procedures for Sizing Aerospace Vehicle Structures (SAVES)," *AIAA Journal of Aircraft, Vol. 9, No. 12,* December 1972, pp. 812-819.

15. Sobieszczanski, J. [1975]. "Building a Computer-Aided Design Capability Using a Standard Time Share Operating System," in Integrated Design and Analysis of Aerospace Structures, R. Hartung (Ed.), ASME Special Publication, 1975, pp. 93-112, presented at *ASME Winter Annual Meeting,* Houston, Texas, November 30-December 5, 1975.

16. English, C. H. [1973]. "Computer Aided Design-Drafting (CADD) - Engineering/Manufacturing Tool," *Journal of Aircraft, Vol. 10, No. 12,* December 1973, pp. 747-752.

17. Lafavor, S. A., and A. E. Doelling [1975]. "Some Implications of Interactive Computer Applications to Aircraft Development," in Integrated Design and Analysis of Aerospace Structures, R. Hartung (Ed.), ASME Special Publication, 1975, pp. 1-22, presented at *ASME Winter Annual Meeting,* Houston, Texas, November 30-December 5, 1975.

18. Wennagel, G. J., P. W. Mason, and J. D. Rosenbaum [1968]. "Ideas, Integrated Design and Analysis System," Paper No. 687028, Society of Automotive Engineers, Atlanta, Georgia, October 1968.

19. Loshigian, H. H., J. D. Rosenbaum, and G. J. Wennagel [1975]. "RAVES - Rapid Aerospace Vehicle Evaluation System," in Integrated Design and Analysis of Aerospace Structures, R. Hartung (Ed.), ASME Special Publication, 1975, pp. 23-55, presented at *ASME Winter Annual Meeting,* Houston, Texas, November 30-December 5, 1975.

20. Ascani, L. [1975]. "The Role of Integrated Computer Systems in Preliminary Design," in Integrated Design and Analysis of Aerospace Structures, R. Hartung (Ed.), ASME Special Publication, 1975, pp. 71-91, presented at *ASME Winter Annual Meeting,* Houston, Texas, November 30-December 5, 1975.

21. Rhodes, Thomas R. [1973]. "The Computer-Aided Design Environment Project (COMRADE)," *National Computer Conference, AFIPS Conference Proceedings, Vol. 42,* 1973, pp. 319-324.

22. "Design/Manufacturing Interface," AIA Project MC 74.4, Report to the Manufacturing Committee, Aerospace Industries Association of America, Inc., Washington, D.C., October 1974.

23. Buffum, H. E. [1974]. "Air Force Computer-Aided Manufacturing (AFCAM) Master Plan," Report AFML-TR-74-104, Vols. I-V, Boeing Commercial Airplane Company under contract to Air Force Materials Lab., WPAFB, July 1974.

24. Cohen, S. [1974]. "Speakeasy, An Evolutionary System," Proceedings of *Symposium on Very High Level Languages, ACM SIGPLAN NOTICES, Vol. 9, No. 4,* April 1974, pp. 118-126.

25. CODASYL Data Base Task Group Report, April 1971, available from ACM, 267 pages.

26. Bandurski, A. E., and D. Jefferson [1975]. "Enhancements to the DBTG Model for Computer-Aided Ship Design," Proceedings of *Workshop on Data Bases for Interactive Design,* University of Waterloo, September 15-17, 1975, ACM.

27. Turn, Rein [1974]. Computers in the 1980's, Columbia University Press, New York, 1974.

28. Withington, F. G. [1975]. "Beyond 1984: A Technology Forecast," *Datamation,* January 1975, pp. 54-73.

29. Liskov, B. H. [1972]. "A Design Methodology for Reliable Software Systems," *Fall Joint Computer Conference,* 1972, pp. 191-199.

30. Mills, H. D. [1973]. "On the Development of Large Reliable Programs," *IEEE Symposium on Computer Software Reliability,* 1973, pp. 155-159.

31. Henderson, P., and R. A. Snowdon [1974]. "A Tool for Structured Program Development," Information Processing 74, N. Holland Pub. Co., 1974, pp. 204-207.

32. Stucki, L. G. [1975]. "Automated Tools and Techniques Assisting in Software Development," in Practical Strategies for Developing Large Software Systems, E. Horowitz, Ed., Addison-Wesley Pub. Co., 1975, pp. 171-189.

33. Basili, V. R. [1974]. "The SIMPL Family of Programing Languages and Compilers," University of Maryland, Comp. Sci. Ctr., TR-305, June 1974.

34. Browne, J. C., K. M. Chandy, R. M. Brown, T. W. Keller, D. F. Towsley, and C. W. Dissly [1975]. "Hierarchical Techniques for the Development of Realistic Models of Complex Computer Systems," *Proc. IEEE, Vol. 63, No. 6,* June 1975, pp. 966-975.

35. Williams, R. D. [1975]. "Managing the Development of Reliable Software," *Proc. 1975 International Conference on Reliable Software, ACM SIGPLAN NOTICES, Vol. 10, No. 6,* June 1975, pp. 3-8.

36. Ramamoorthy, C. V., and S. F. Ho [1975]. "Testing Large Software With Automated Software Evaluation Systems," *Proc. 1975 International Conference on Reliable Software, ACM SIGPLAN NOTICES, Vol. 10, No. 6,* June 1975, pp. 382-394.

SCIENTIFIC APPLICATIONS OF SYMBOLIC COMPUTATION

Anthony C. Hearn

C.N.R.S., Marseilles, France
and the University of Utah

ABSTRACT

This paper reviews the use of symbolic computation systems for problem solving in scientific research. The nature of the field is described, and particular examples are considered from celestial mechanics, quantum electrodynamics and general relativity. Symbolic integration and some more recent applications of algebra systems are also discussed.

1. INTRODUCTION

The ability of the computer to perform algebraic and more general symbolic computations has been exploited by researchers in several fields for over a decade now. As a result, previously intractable problems are now solved routinely often by fairly elementary algebraic systems. This paper is intended as a review of some of these successful applications in order to acquaint the general reader with the potential of today's available systems as tools for scientific problem solving. However, as there are now over 500 papers which consider some aspect or application of symbolic computation, this particular paper cannot itself hope to a complete review of the field. So examples will be chosen which illustrate some important aspects of the subject, and references will be made to published reviews in particular areas so that the reader can fill in the gaps. As a starting point in this direction, a review which comes closest to covering the whole applications area is that of Barton and Fitch (1) to which we shall often refer.

The plan of this paper is as follows. In Section 2 we shall discuss the nature of symbolic computation so that the reader unfamiliar with this area can understand the scope of the subject. Particular applications are considered in some detail in Section 3, and we conclude in Section 4 with a discussion of future trends as predicted from today's research in the area.

2. THE NATURE OF SYMBOLIC COMPUTATION

In order to introduce the nature and scope of symbolic computation, let us begin by comparing a simple FORTRAN calculation with a similar algebraic one. The example to be used is the computation of Legendre polynomials by the usual recurrence relation, for which the following FORTRAN program segment could be used:

```
          DIMENSION P(11)
          P(1)=1
          P(2)=X
          DO 10 N=3,11
          P(N)=((2*N-3)*X*P(N-1)-(N-2)*P(N-2))/(N-1)
          N1=N-1
       10 WRITE (6,20)N1,P(N)
       20 FORMAT (3HOP(,I1,4H)=,F5.1)
```

Given that X is assigned a value in the program, and apart from a possible change in the WRITE statement, this program segment will run correctly under most FORTRAN systems, and produce output for, say, X = 2.0 of the form:

```
          P(2)=  5.5
          P(3)= 17.0
             ...
```

On the other hand, if we forgot to give X a value, then our program would terminate with an error. However, suppose our programming system was sufficiently general that it could represent the variable X as an undetermined symbol and carry out polynomial operations in the unknown X as it iterates through the loop. Then with an appropriate change in the format statement our results might come out like this:

84

$$P(2) = 3/2*X**2-1/2$$

$$P(3) = 5/2*X**3-3/2*X$$

...

This example shows one of the basic differences between a numerical calculation using FORTRAN, for example, and an algebraic calculation in which indeterminates such as X with no pre-assigned numerical value can appear, and expressions themselves have algebraic rather than numerical values. Furthermore, by the use of integer and rational number arithmetic, the results are exact rather than approximate. Systems exist which can do such polynomial manipulation using either a FORTRAN or ALGOL-like syntax, with of course additional declarations and syntatical constructs to handle the more complicated data-types. For example in ALTRAN (2), a FORTRAN based system, the above program segment might take the form:

```
ALGEBRAIC (X:10) ARRAY (0:10) P
INTEGER N
P(0)=1
P(1)=X
DO N=2,10
    P(N)=((2*N-1)*X*P(N-1)-(N-1)*P(N-2))/N
    WRITE P(N)
DOEND
```

What else can these systems do? At the other end of the spectrum, we have the following possible expression (%E being e)

$$INTEGRATE (X*\%E**X/(X+1)**2, X),$$

which if given to the algebraic system MACSYMA (3) will produce the printed result

$$\frac{\%E^X}{X+1}.$$

Between these two extremes of simple polynomial manipulation on the one hand and the sophisticated analytic integration of complicated expressions on the other there exists a wide range of facilities now offered by algebraic systems. Many of these facilities will be described as we consider various application examples of the available systems.

One might ask whether symbolic computation is limited to algebraic simplification. After all, parsing and compilation of a FORTRAN program are symbolic operations, so are they included? The consensus on this point is that they are not and that one limits symbolic computation to techniques which solve problems outside of computer science rather than say program compilation which is a problem of computer science itself. However, even this definition includes subjects other than algebraic manipulation such as analysis of graphs, which we shall touch on briefly later. However, our main concerns will be with algebraic manipulation.

Our discussion has mentioned the existence of algebraic systems, and it is true that if you want to do such calculations at present, you must use a special program for this purpose. One might therefore ask why symbolic computation systems cannot be made available as subroutines to be loaded into a standard FORTRAN job, so that they can be used as needed as part of a combined numerical and algebraic calculation. There are several reasons why this hasn't happened. First, although important systems such as ALTRAN are based on FORTRAN, a user cannot write an efficient numerical program which includes a symbolic computation step in it because FORTRAN is normally a compile, load and go system. Therefore, since one generates algebraic expressions during the go step, one has no way of compiling them into efficient code in the same job step. The only way to do this is to pass such expressions on to another job or job step, at which point the whole purpose of doing the algebraic calculation in a numerical system is lost. In fact, the main reason such systems are implemented in FORTRAN is to provide for portability and standardization or to utilize its numerical subroutine library and system support capabilities (such as I/O). However, there is a growing feeling among algebraic system designers that such

86

systems should provide more efficient numerical computations
then they now allow, thus possibly bypassing the use of numerical
programming systems entirely. To alleviate this problem for the
time being, most available systems have the ability to produce
output in a FORTRAN compatible format which can then be used in a
later job or job step for numerical calculations.

Another deterrent to using a purely numerical programming
system for symbolic calculations is that the data structures used
in these calculations, such as polynomials and power series, are
quite different from those of numerical computation where integers and floating point numbers are the principal concern.
Algebraic data structures clearly vary in size considerably
during expression evaluation and therefore the storage management
can be quite complicated, although the techniques for doing this
are well understood (4). Unfortunately, FORTRAN does not provide
the necessary tools for doing this in an efficient manner, and so
they must usually be provided in assembly language. Many systems
have therefore bypassed the use of numerical systems for embed-
ding and utilized languages with storage management facilities
already built in, such as LISP (5), or the majority of the
system has been written in assembly language.

So we are dealing with systems or programs essentially
independent from numerical systems but with languages similar in
form to their numerical counterparts. One notable exception to
the latter statement is SCRATCHPAD (6), which has incorporated a
completely new language design whose purpose is to provide a
more natural mathematical notation for problems. For example,
in SCRATCHPAD, we could compute and print the first eleven
Legendre polynomials by the statements:

```
p<0>=1
p<1>=x
n in (2,3,...,10)
p<n>=((2*n-1)*x*p<n-1>-(n-1)*p<n-2>)/n
n in (0,1,...,10)
p<n>
```

Other examples of programming styles in algebraic systems are given in Ref. (1).

The computational characteristics of symbolic calculations are also quite different from numerical calculations. Roundoff is not a problem since, as was mentioned earlier, exact results may be obtained. The stability and convergence problems of numerical approximations are also not relevant. On the other hand, symbolic computation has its set of own difficulties. A common one in practice is that even though most calculations start from short expressions, the expressions formed during intermediate stages of the calculations are often quite large even if the answer isn't, and may in fact exceed the available storage, aborting the computation. This problem of intermediate expression swell as it has been called remains of constant concern in symbolic calculations, and often requires much inno-vation to overcome. Another difficulty is the fact that many of the necessary algorithms, such as those for polynomial factor-ization, have potentially exponential growth rates associated with them. Much of the theoretical work in the field during the past five years has been devoted to overcoming such problems. Considerable progress has in fact occurred, the benefits of which should be passed on to users in the near future.

A third problem relates to the fact that it is only possible theoretically to put upper bounds on the computation times associated with symbolic computations, unlike numerical calcula-tions where it is often possible to determine average computing times. To put this problem in the right perspective, consider the evaluation of a symbolic determinant of order 10. If every element of the matrix is distinct, the determinant will have in general 10!, or over 3,000,000 terms in the answer. Apart from being incomprehensible, such a result would take a nontrivial time to derive. However, most scientific problems have various symmetries in their specification which put constraints on the form of the matrices with which one works. For example, the matrix may in fact be singular, and the recognition of this may take an algebra program negligible time. To get the value 0 for such a determinant may have very important consequences in a calculation, and so a researcher may attempt to evaluate the determinant for this reason. However, he must be prepared to get an answer as large as 3,000,000 terms if his guess isn't right, and so the estimate of the time required to discover whether the determinant is really zero may be prohibitive in the worst case, although in practice such an upper bound may rarely be reached.

With these thoughts in mind, we can now look at some of the typical calculations which have been completed in this area, and use these to gain further insight into the nature of symbolic computation.

3. SPECIFIC APPLICATIONS

A perusal of essentially all successful applications of symbolic computation so far reveals that they involve problems solved by means of perturbation theories. Hand calculations which can be tractably taken to a given order are then extended one or two more orders by computer. Because of the exponential nature of such techniques, at this point expressions grow so large using current systems that the computational time and sheer incomprehensibility of the output limit any further extension. In addition, with a few notable exceptions, most of the calculations have been an adjunct to a numerical calculation. In other words, part of the calculation was done algebraically and these results then used to determine a final numerical solution for the problem.

Consider for example the field of celestial mechanics where researchers have made much use of algebraic systems in the past decade. Here the most tedious task to be faced is in the construction of an analytic perturbation theory; in other words a formula for calculating the position or rotational properties of a body at any instant in time. The body might be the Moon, a planet or more topically an artificial satellite or space station. To construct such theories requires solving the differential equations which describe the motion of the body. Since solutions rarely exist in closed form, one solves them by a technique of repeated approximation and expresses the solution as a power series in terms of the small parameters of the theory, such as the body eccentricities.

The most famous such calculation is surely Delaunay's work in the Lunar Theory (7), in which the coordinates of the Moon are computed to the seventh order in the small quantities. Like most hand calculations of this type, this investigation involved working with thousands of terms. In Delaunay's case the computations took 20 years. When Deprit, Henrard and Rom (8) repeated this calculation by computer in 1970, they found only one error in Delaunay's computation of the secularized Hamiltonian up to the ninth order, a major part of the work; certainly a great tribute to Delaunay's skill and dedication.

What types of manipulation are involved in these calculations? The most frequently considered series in celestial mechanics turn out not to be power series, but Poisson series, which have the form:

$$Q(\underset{\sim}{x}, \underset{\sim}{y}) = \underset{\underset{\sim}{j}}{\Sigma} \; P_{\underset{\sim}{j}} \cos(\underset{\sim}{j} \cdot \underset{\sim}{y}) + Q_{\underset{\sim}{j}} \sin(\underset{\sim}{j} \cdot \underset{\sim}{y}), \quad (1)$$

where $\underset{\sim}{x}$ is a vector of polynomial variables, $\underset{\sim}{y}$ a vector of trigonometrical variables and $\underset{\sim}{j}$ is a vector of integers. $P_{\underset{\sim}{j}}$ and $Q_{\underset{\sim}{j}}$ are polynomials, indexed by $\underset{\sim}{j}$, in the polynomial variables $\underset{\sim}{x}$ whose coefficients may be rational or floating point numbers. It is clear that by the use of the trigonometrical identities

$$\sin x \; \sin y = \frac{1}{2} \cos(x - y) - \frac{1}{2} \cos(x + y)$$

$$\sin x \; \cos y = \frac{1}{2} \sin(x + y) + \frac{1}{2} \sin(x - y) \quad (2)$$

$$\cos x \; \cos y = \frac{1}{2} \cos(x + y) + \frac{1}{2} \cos(x - y)$$

such series are closed under the operations of addition, sub-
traction, multiplication and differentiation. By making suitable
assumptions about the size of the parameters in the series, we
can also define operations of division, integration and substitution which do not lead outside this class. Finally, an
important theoretical consideration is that Poisson series can be
written in a unique canonical form, in other words a form to
which all equivalent expressions can be uniquely reduced. This
form can then be used to define the simplification of Poisson
series expressions. This means we can avoid many of the problems
associated with general expression manipulation which we shall
return to later. Such problems arise for example in recognizing
that

$$\log \tan(x + \tfrac{1}{4}\pi) - \sinh^{-1} \tan 2x = 0 \qquad (3)$$

The importance and mathematical simplicity of Poisson series
has led to the construction of many systems for their manipulation, including that of Rom (9) used in repeating the Delaunay
calculations, Jeffreys' system TRIGMAN (10) which is written in
FORTRAN and fairly portable, and CAMAL (11) which has also been
used extensively for calculations in general relativity, is well
documented and easily obtainable. Further examples are given in
the reviews by Jeffreys (12) and Barton and Fitch (1).

To see how Poisson series arise in a natural way in celestial mechanics calculations, let me repeat Barton and Fitch's
discussion of the computation of the series solution to Kepler's
equation by repeated approximation, which is the starting point
for many of these calculations. We are interested in obtaining
the solution for E, as a function of u and e, of the implicit
equation

$$E = u + e \sin E \qquad (4)$$

where e is to be regarded as a small quantity, typically the
eccentricity of an elliptic orbit. Although the problem is

capable of a formal solution in terms of Bessel functions, since
we normally require the solution correct to a given order in e
(say tenth) it is computationally easier if we adopt a repeated
approximation procedure. From the Kepler equation, it is obvious
that $E = u$ to zero order in e. Then, supposing that $E = u + A_k$
is the solution correct to order k in e, we can easily see that
A_k satisfies the equation

$$A_{k+1} = e \, \sin(u + A_k), \tag{5}$$

where the right hand member of Eq. (5) is to be taken to order
$k + 1$ in e. Thus an approximation algorithm may be stated as
follows:

$$E = u + \lim_{n \to \infty} A_n \tag{6}$$

where

$$A_0 = 0$$

$$A_{k+1} = \left[e\sin u \left\{ 1 - \frac{A_k^2}{2!} + \frac{A_k^4}{4!} \dots \right\} + e\cos u \left\{ A_k - \frac{A_k^3}{3!} + \dots \right\} \right]_{k+1}$$

The outer brackets in the above expression indicate that terms of
degree greater than $k + 1$ are to be ignored in the calculation.
By using the trigonometrical relations given in Eq. (2), we can
express the result of this computation as a linear expression in
the trigonometrical functions; that is in the form of a Poisson
series.

This computation is clearly only a small part of say the
complete Delaunay result, but does illustrate the types of
expressions to be manipulated. Barton and Fitch (1) go on to
consider the steps involved in the remainder of the Delaunay
calculation, as well as looking at other examples of the application of Poisson series processors. The reader is encouraged to
study these calculations in order to gain some idea of the sheer
enormity of the computations involved.

The second application I would like to consider is in the field of quantum electrodynamics (or QED), an area where one tries to understand the detailed interactions of electrons and photons by means of relativistic quantum mechanics. The most commonly used calculational method is due to Feynman (13) who showed that one could develop a perturbation theory of such interactions with an expansion parameter of about 1/137 (the so-called fine structure constant). The starting point for this method is a diagrammatic representation of the particular process under study.

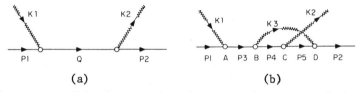

(a)   (b)

Fig. 1 Possible interactions between electrons and photons.

For example, in Figure 1 we have two such diagrams which occur in the representation of the process which occurs when a quantum of radiation (that is, a photon) interacts with an electron. From these diagrams, Feynman developed a method of calculating the contribution of any given diagram to the determination of a physical quantity. The order of perturbation is related very simply to the number of vertices in a diagram. Therefore since the most important contributions come from the simplest diagrams one can quickly get a rough approximation to the answer. However, as the accuracy of experiments has increased, the need for more and more precise calculations has required more and more complicated diagrams to be studied. To understand the complexity of such calculations it is necessary to look in some detail at the way they are done.

Feynman's method gives you a one-to-one mapping between diagrams like those in Figure 1 and expressions like

$$\sum_{\mu,\nu} \text{Trace } \{(\gamma \cdot p2 + M) \ \gamma_\mu \ (\gamma \cdot p2 + \gamma \cdot k2 + M) \ \gamma_\nu$$

$$\times (\gamma \cdot p1 + M) \ \gamma_\nu \ (\gamma \cdot p2 + \gamma \cdot k2 + M) \ \gamma_\mu \}, \qquad (7)$$

which, apart from some simple multiplicative factors, is the contribution of Figure 1(a) to the experimentally measurable cross-section. The rules for this mapping are quite straightforward and may be found in any suitable textbook on relativistic quantum mechanics, e.g. (14).

In the above expression, γ_μ represents a set of four 4×4 noncommuting matrices known as Dirac matrices which satisfy the relation

$$\gamma_{\mu\nu} + \gamma_{\nu\mu} = 2 \ \delta_{\mu\nu} \ I. \qquad (8)$$

The Greek indices range from 1 to 4, I is the unit 4×4 matrix and $\delta_{\mu\nu}$ is the Kronecker delta function defined by

$$\delta_{\mu\nu} = \begin{cases} 1 \text{ if } \mu = \nu \\ 0 \text{ if } \mu \neq \nu. \end{cases} \qquad (9)$$

M is the electron mass multiplied by a unit 4×4 matrix, and $p1$, $p2$, $k1$ and $k2$ are four-component vectors representing the electron and photon momenta as in Figure 1. Thus $\gamma \cdot p1$ represents the sum

$$\gamma_1 \ p1_1 + \gamma_2 \ p1_2 + \gamma_3 \ p1_3 + \gamma_4 \ p1_4. \qquad (10)$$

However, because of the relativistic invariance of the result, one rarely has to study the individual components of the vectors, but only their scalar products, so calculations are less complicated than they might be.

Thus the result of taking the trace of the 4×4 matrix expression in the curly brackets in Eq. (7) and summing over the tensor indices is a scalar. In principle, this computation is straightforward. Equation (8) implies that the trace of the product of an odd number of gamma matrices is zero, and the trace of the product of 2n such matrices may be expressed in

94

terms of the trace of 2n-2 products by a simple recurrence relation, given for example in Ref. (14). However, a naive calculation can be disastrous. For example, the trace of a single
product of 12 gamma matrices generates over 10,000 terms, many of
which prove to be equal when contraction over the tensor indices
is taken. This problem has motivated the development of more
sophisticated algorithms, most of which involve summation over
the repeated tensor indices before taking the trace. A description of one such algorithm, due to Kahane (15), may be found in
Ref. (1). Fairly complete reviews of the symbolic calculations
which have been done in QED may be found by studying Refs. (16),
(17), (18) and (19).

From a computational point of view, such calculations involve quite straightforward though lengthy symbol manipulation.
Like Poisson series, the rules for simplification are well defined
although a little more exotic than those for polynomial manipulation. In addition, one needs a mechanism for substitution for
variables and simple expressions. Although denominators occur in
some expressions, rational algebra is not necessary, because the
denominators have a simple structure and can therefore be re-
placed by variables in the numerator. The most widely used
systems for such calculations have been REDUCE (20) and
SCHOONSCHIP (21). The former is a LISP-based system which is
also well suited to more general calculations than just QED and
has a large number of published applications in many fields to
its credit. The latter system is written in COMPASS for the CDC
6000 and 7000 series computers and also has a long application
list, though all essentially in QED. A third system of some
interest is a FORTRAN based program ASHMEDAI (22), which also has
been used in some important calculations.

To give one a feel for the scope of current calculations in
this area, it is worth looking at the most important such calculation undertaken during the past few years. This is undoubtedly
the computation of the sixth order corrections to the anomalous

magnetic moment of the electron. The analytic form for the
fourth order contribution was completed by hand in 1957 (23).
Because of the sheer magnitude of the calculation, the sixth
order result, which involves looking at 72 diagrams, has been
completed by a group effort involving many different independent
researchers. To be sure that the result is correct, each diagram has by now been computed independently by two different
groups, usually with different algebra programs. The complete
answer is still not known analytically because some of the integrations involved were performed numerically.

The need for integration in these calculations is apparent
if we look again at Figure 1(b). An electrical analogy is often
used to explain the problem; just as current flows through an
electrical circuit, momentum flows through these diagrams. If we
assume that the initial momenta are known, then we know the
momentum in line AB by momentum conservation at vertex A, by
analogy to current conservation in the electrical case. However,
at vertex B the momentum splits into two paths, so we no longer
know the values of the individual momenta in lines BC and the
wavy line BD but only their sum. So an integration over this
unknown momentum is necessary to get the required result.

The integrals which arise in these calculations are messy
and tedious, rather than being sophisticated, as one usually
starts with rational functions. However, as integration over
several variables is required, the results come out in terms of
generalized Spence functions in most cases. Examples of such
integrations are given in Ref. (24) and (25), which describe
programs in SCHOONSCHIP and REDUCE for evaluating integrals of
the form

$$I(k,m,n,r,s) = \int_0^1 dy \int_0^1 dx \int_0^1 dw \int_0^1 dz \ z^r w^s x^{2k-3+n-m}$$
$$\times \ y^{k-2+n} \ \Delta^m / \beta^n \Gamma^k$$

where

$$\beta = 1 - xy(1-wz + w^2z^2)$$
$$\Delta = 1 - x(1-wz\ (1-w)) \tag{11}$$
$$\Gamma = w^2\ x\ \beta + y\ \Delta^2,$$

which arise in some fourth order computations in QED. For example

$$I(1,0,2,2,3) = \frac{1}{6}\pi^2 - \frac{1}{3}\pi^2\ \log\ 2 + \frac{1}{2}\zeta(3) + \frac{1}{3},$$

$$\tag{12}$$

where $\zeta(3)$ is the Riemann zeta function. Currently, two groups (26, 27) are trying to find the whole sixth order result analytically by computer and considerable progress has been made. Although their methods are different, the procedure involves expanding expressions in partial fractions and integrating term by term. To give you an idea of the relative times involved in this work, Levine, Perisho and Roskies (26) give statistics for the analytic evaluation of one of the more difficult of the 72 graphs in the sixth order calculation. Their method involved trace evaluation, two straightforward integrations, a partial fraction expansion of the result followed by two further integrations. Using the ASHMEDAI program, the times on a Univac 1108 were 2 minutes for the traces and first two integrals, 18 minutes for the partial fraction expansion and 15 minutes for the two final integrations. It is interesting to note that the trace taking, the original stumbling block for the hand calculations which motivated the development of such computer programs in the first place, is now only a small part of the whole computer calculation.

In fact, it is interesting to see that once the basic trace problem was solved, researchers in this area started looking at other ways of using symbolic computation in their work. Analytic integration is one such example. Another application involved looking at ways to actually generate and manipulate the diagrams which occur in a given problem. Once such a diagram is written

down, it is a fairly simple procedure to generate the matrix
elements which were the starting point of the previous discussion
(28). The most difficult problem here is to recognize topolog-
ically equivalent diagrams, but a recently developed program (29)
seems to have solved this problem in an efficient manner. Some
earlier programs are described in Ref. (19). If one is ever
interested in looking at eighth order calculations, where over
1000 diagrams contribute to the magnetic moment correction, such
graphical programs should be essential even if only used as a
bookkeeping device.

These two very successful applications of symbolic computation, celestial mechanics and quantum electrodynamics, are
prototypical of a large number of the successes in this field.
Both are problems with well-defined rules of simplification, even
if the non-standard algebra was responsible for the early development of special purpose systems to handle this. Major application successes were already in evidence five years ago, and the
work during the past five years has been concerned with extending
the earlier successes to harder and harder problems, or tackling
new problems, such as the integration example in QED. At the
same time, problems in other areas such as fluid mechanics,
plasma physics, electrical network theory and queuing theory,
which were amenable to solution by polynomial or power series
manipulation were being solved by systems such as ALTRAN (and its
predecessor ALPAK), FORMAC (30) and REDUCE which possessed the
necessary facilities for performing these tasks. A considerable
number of applications of these programs have been described in
the literature. Another convenient system for such calculations
is Engeli's SYMBAL (31).

There was, however, another group of important calculations
being carried out at the same time which involved the manipulation
of more general expressions than the examples so far. Since
there is no canonical form for a sufficiently large class of
expressions (32) the designers of algebra systems for such appli-

cations must either try to solve a very complicated simplification problem for which no clear cut solution exists, or provide sufficiently general substitution facilities so that users can input their own set of rules for simplification. A particularly good example of such calculations, and one for which good reviews exist (1, 33) is general relativity, where the calculations considered are concerned with a very large set of elementary functions for which many complicated simplification rules exist.

Applications in this area have been mainly concerned with the field equations which express the relationship between the geometrical structure of the four dimensional space and the distribution of mass and energy within it. These field equations are very complicated even for physically simple cases and involve exponential and circular functions in their description. An account of the systems which have been used to solve such problems is given in the cited references. Among the most widespread in use are FORMAC, CAMAL and LAM and its predecessors (34). Each of these systems, as is true for the other systems mentioned earlier in this paper, take a different approach to the problem of simplification, and an amusing review of this subject may be found in Ref. (35).

Another application of algebraic manipulation involving general expressions which deserves consideration in its own right is the problem of analytic integration. This is different from our previous applications in that it is in mathematics rather than physics or related areas, and it is certainly not a perturbation problem. However its importance to the latter fields is obvious. Considerable progress has been made in solving this problem during the past decade and it is now possible to integrate a wide variety of expressions automatically. Most of the effort has been directed toward the problem of indefinite integration which we shall consider here, although some work on definite integration has also been reported (36, 37). Of course, given the result of an indefinite integral we can always find the

equivalent definite integral by substitution. However, as is well
known, closed form solutions exist for many definite integrals
where the indefinite form does not, and special methods such as
contour integration are applicable in these cases.

Although earlier programs existed, the first truly effective
program in this area was Moses' SIN program, which in an improved
form provides the basis for the MACSYMA integration facility, an
example of whose use was shown earlier. The structure of this
program is described in some detail in Moses' review of the field
(38). SIN works very much like a scientist when confronted with
an expression to be integrated. It first of all tries a cheap
general method which, if it succeeds, gives the result very
quickly. This general method involves the so-called "derivative
divides" test which determines by pattern matching whether the
integral can be written in the form

$$\int c \, f(u(x)) \, u'(x) \, dx$$

If this test succeeds, then the integral can be immediately
written down if the integral of f is known. This part of the program also expands the integral to its fullest extent, and then
expresses the integral of a sum as the sum of integrals in order
to reduce the complexity of the integrands. For example,

$$\int (\sin x + \cos x)^3 \, dx$$

would be written in the form

$$\int 3 \sin^2 x \cos x \, dx + \int 3 \cos^2 x \sin x \, dx +$$
$$\int \sin^3 x \, dx + \int \cos^3 x \, dx,$$

the first two terms of which satisfy the derivative divides test.
If this general method fails, as for the last two terms in the
above, special methods which are specific to a certain class of
integrals are tried. For example, if the integrand contains trigonometrical functions, the substitution $t = \tan \theta/2$ would be
attempted, if it is a rational function than the well known

100

Hermite's method (39) would be used. Again, even though these methods are narrow in scope, they provide efficient solutions when they are applicable. In addition, the integration examples we mentioned in QED are of this type because they are amenable to special case algorithms and Hermite's method.

Clearly a large class of interesting integrals will not be evaluated by the above techniques and, at this point, an entirely different approach to the problem is taken based on an algorithmic approach to integration developed by Risch (40). This particular method requires a radical transformation of the integrand; for example, sines and cosines are converted to complex exponentials. Since, as pointed out by Moses (38), a user prefers to see his answer in terms of the same sort of functions as the problem was presented, such transformations should only be used when there is no other more straightforward way to evaluate the integral.

The complete Risch algorithm is of extreme importance because it provides a procedure for deciding if an integral exists within a given class of functions. If the integral does exist, the algorithm finds it. If it does not exist, the algorithm states this. It is very important to understand the difference between such a decision procedure and the usual methods for integration which either find the integral or leave us not knowing if the integral exists or not. In other words the search for a "closed form" solution to an integration problem is a search for the form of the integral if it exists in the class of functions we are considering. The Risch algorithm can tell us this and in the affirmative case provide the result. This is, after all, all we can reasonably hope for in integration; if the integral does not exist in the current class of functions under consideration a new function must be introduced anyway. Risch's algorithm is quite complicated, and beyond the scope of this paper to describe, but a readable account of it may be found in Refs. (1) and (38). In broad terms, it is based on a generalization of Liouville's theorem, well known to every student of mathematical analysis, and uses a method similar to the Hermite algorithm to determine the parts of the integral if they exist in closed form. In principle, a computer program could now be written which provides for the indefinite integration of any expression in a class of functions sufficiently large to satisfy all physicists and engineers. However, there remain several theoretical and practical difficulties in the implementation of this algorithm and at present programs only exist for functions which are so-called monomial transcendental extensions of the rational functions (that is, exponentials or logarithms of the rational functions). However, there is considerable current research in progress aimed at enlarging this class, and some results should be forthcoming shortly.

4. FUTURE TRENDS

It should be clear from the examples shown in this paper that symbolic computation can play a useful role in a wide range of scientific applications, and there is no doubt that this range will increase as more and more researchers discover the possibilities inherent in this approach. However, I see three main problems which limit the applicability of today's available systems, but fortunately current research is seeking solutions to these, so that no doubt they will be overcome in the next few years.

The first problem is concerned with the production of large expressions. As was mentioned earlier, most symbolic calculations can only carry a hand perturbation calculation further by one or two orders at most. At that point, expressions become so large and unwieldly that not only does the computing time increase dramatically, but the results are thoroughly intractable. However, one of the reasons for the explosive growth of expressions is that many algorithms used internally by existing systems require expressions in an expanded form. So any structure in the

input expressions, especially factor structure, is immediately
destroyed by this expansion. However, as had been pointed out
most succinctly by Brown (41) there are ways of consistently
handling expressions in a factored form, and the use of these and
similar ideas should shortly have an impact on the field as they
are incorporated into available systems. The recognition of
common sub-expressions in an expression and their renaming by a
single parameter, or the deferred expansion of a function or
variable in an expression can also be very important. Systematic
ways of handling this problem are being studied by several groups,
and some practical experience with such techniques in a plasma
physics calculation has recently been published (42).

A second problem from the average user's point of view is
that as programming systems, algebra programs are not always
designed in the most transparent manner, and so the user is often
frustrated in trying to understand what is going on in a calculation. Finally, the range of facilities offered by available
systems is limited, and it is not easy for the average user to
extend them in a straightforward manner.

There are now trends in computing methodology which can help
solve these latter two problems and which will, I believe, cause
symbolic computation systems to have an even greater impact in
the years ahead. The consistent introduction of types at a very
basic level, software portability, modularity and structured
programming are all examples of such developments. The result in
the near future will be algebraic systems which have well designed modular construction, easily understandable programming
language syntax and semantics and robustness and portability far
in excess of today's systems. Efforts towards machine-indepen-
dent implementations of such systems will find immediate use on
the new inexpensive hardware which is being predicted.

Another point to consider is that symbolic computation and
algebraic manipulation are now recognized as having much wider
application than previously considered. For example, algebraic

manipulation methods find an obvious place in such tasks as program verification (43), optimization (44) and error analysis (45).
Although these applications are only just beginning, we should
see more such activity in the next few years.

Another approach in the use of algebraic manipulation
systems detectable during the past few years has been the increasing use of such systems for making a quick check of the
validity of some physical idea which would otherwise be difficult
or impossible to resolve in a reasonable time by hand. An
example of such use was given in a paper by Gibbons and Russell-
Clark (46), which showed, using CAMAL, that a solution of
Einstein's vacuum field equations put forward as a possible
description of a black hole lacked several of the necessary
properties. Another example was reported recently by Cohen (47)
who used REDUCE to look for valid perturbation expansion techniques for solving a problem in fluid mechanics. In this case,
he could learn in an evening at an interactive console whether a
particular method was applicable by seeing if the secular terms
were eliminated in second order. Such calculations would have
taken many months by hand and would therefore probably have never
been taken to that order. Calculations of this type are often
not reported in the literature unless the results are dramatic;
the researcher accepts such techniques as another problem solving
tool and uses them when appropriate. This is especially true for
users with access to interactive systems like MACSYMA and REDUCE
which encourage casual use because of the ease of access to the
program. In batch oriented environments, this access is less
easy, especially if a user has to see the results of one step
before going on the next as was the case in the fluid mechanics
calculation discussed above.

In the long-term, I believe that we shall see the emergence
of computing systems which can provide algebraic manipulation at
very low cost for a wide spectrum of users, including even high
school and college students in addition to scientists. We should

have programming systems sufficiently well designed and understood to support tasks far beyond our present capabilities. For example, the problems of simplification of general expressions should also be better understood in a few years. I believe that we shall then have in time a complete programmed solution of the classical indefinite and definite integration problems. Once such tasks are successfully accomplished, we shall begin to see systems developed which can provide formal solutions for more complicated problem representations such as integral and differential equations.

Even more interesting is the possibility that since many scientific problems are formulated in terms of fundamental conservation laws, we may be able to attempt solutions directly in terms of these laws rather than to follow the traditional practice of producing approximate solutions by linearization and perturbation methods. This is but one example of the possible impact of such work on scientific problem solving, and there are no doubt countless others which will emerge in the years ahead.

ACKNOWLEDGMENTS

The author's work is supported in part by the National Science Foundation under Grant No. GJ-32181. The figure was taken from Ref. (17), copyright 1971, Association for Computing Machinery, and reprinted by permission.

REFERENCES

(1)   BARTON, D. and FITCH, J.P., *Rep. Prog. Phys.* *35* (1972) 235-314.

(2)   BROWN, W.S., *ALTRAN User's Manual*, Third Edition, Bell Laboratories, 1973.

(3)   BOGEN, R. et al., *MACSYMA Reference Manual*, Project MAC M.I.T., Cambridge, Mass., 1974.

(4)   KNUTH, D.E., *The Art of Computer Programming, Vol 1. Fundamental Algorithms* and *Vol. 2, Seminumerical Algorithms*, Addison Wesley, Reading, Mass. (1968).

(5) McCARTHY, J. et al., *LISP 1.5 Programmer's Manual*, M.I.T. Press, Cambridge, Mass. (1965).

(6) JENKS, R.D., *The SCRATCHPAD Language, SIGPLAN Notices*, ACM, New York, *9* (1974) 101-111.

(7) DELAUNAY, C., *Théorie du Mouvement de la Lune* (Extraits des Mém. Acad. Sci.), Mallet-Bachelier, Paris, 1860.

(8) DEPRIT, A., HENRARD, J. and ROM, A., *Science 168* (1970) 1569-1570.

(9) ROM, A., *Celest. Mech. 3* (1971) 331-345.

(10) JEFFREYS, W.H., *Celest. Mech.* 2 (1970) 474-480.

(11) FITCH J.P., *CAMAL User's Manual*, Computer Lab., Cambridge, U.K. (1975).

(12) JEFFREYS, W.H., *Comm. ACM 14* (1971) 538-541.

(13) FEYNMAN, R.P., *Phys. Rev. 76* (1949) 769-789.

(14) BJORKEN, J.D. and DRELL, S.D., *Relativistic Quantum Mechanics*, McGraw-Hill, New York, 1964.

(15) KAHANE, J., *J. Math. Phys. 9* (1968) 1732-1738.

(16) CAMPBELL, J.A., *Comp. Phys. Comm. 1* (1970) 251-264.

(17) HEARN, A.C., *Comm. ACM 14* (1971) 511-516.

(18) HEARN, A.C., *Computer Solution of Symbolic Problems in Theoretical Physics, Computing as a Language of Physics*, IAEA, Vienna (1972) 567-596.

(19) CAMPBELL, J.A., *Acta Phys. Austriaca Suppl. XIII* (1974) 595-647.

(20) HEARN, A.C., *REDUCE User's Manual*, Second Edition, University of Utah, 1973.

(21) STRUBBE, H., *Comp. Phys. Comm. 8* (1974) 1-30.

(22) PERISHO, R.C., *ASHMEDAI User's Guide*, U.S.A.E.C. Rep. No. COO-3066-44 (1975).

(23) PETERMANN, A., *Helv. Phys. Acta 30* (1957) 407-408.

(24) MAISON, D. and PETERMANN, A., *Comp. Phys. Comm. 7* (1974) 121-134.

(25) FOX, J.A. and HEARN, A.C., *J. Comp. Phys.* *14* (1974) 301-317.

(26) LEVINE, M.J., PERISHO, R.C. and ROSKIES, R., *Would You Believe More Graphs for g-2?*, Univ. Pittsburgh Preprint PITT-153 (1975).

(27) BARBIERI, R., CAFFO, M. and REMIDDI, E., *Phys. Lett. 57B* (1975) 460-462.

(28) CAMPBELL, J.A. and HEARN, A.C., *J. Comp. Phys*, 5 (1970) 280-327.

(29) SASAKI, T., *Automatic Generation of Feynman Graphs in QED*, Rikagaku Kenkyusho, Wako-Shi, Saitama, Japan, Preprint 1975.

(30) TOBEY, R.G. et al., *PL/I-FORMAC Symbolic Mathematics Interpreter*, SHARE Contributed Program Library, No 360 D-0.3.3.004 (1969).

(31) ENGELI, M., *An Enhanced SYMBAL System*, SIGSAM Bulletin, ACM, New York No. *36* (1975) 21-29.

(32) RICHARDSON, D., Ph.D. Thesis, Univ. of Bristol (1966).

(33) BARTON, D. and FITCH, J.P., *Comm. ACM 14* (1971) 542-547.

(34) D'INVERNO, R.A., *Comp. J. 12* (1969) 124-127.

(35) MOSES, J., *Comm. ACM 14* (1971) 527-537.

(36) WANG, P., *Symbolic Evaluation of Definite Integrals by Residue Theory in MACSYMA*, *Proc. IFIP Congress 74* (1974) 823-827.

(37) CAMPBELL, J.A., *Applications of Symbolic Programs to Complex Analysis*, *Proc. ACM Annual Conf. 72* (1972) 836-839.

(38) MOSES, J., *Comm. ACM* (1971) 548-560.

(39) HARDY, G.H., *The Integration of Functions of a Single Variable*, Second Edition, CUP, Cambridge, England (1916).

(40) RISCH, R., *Trans. AMS 139* (1969) 167-189.

(41) BROWN W.S., *On Computing with Factored Rational Expressions*, *SIGSAM Bulletin*, ACM, New York, No. *31* (1974) 27-34.

(42) KERNER, W. and STEUERWALD, J., *Comp. Phys. Comm. 9* (1975) 337-349.

(43)　LONDON, R. and MUSSER, D.R., *The Application of a Symbolic Mathematical System to Program Verification*, Proc. ACM Annual Conf. *74* (1974) 265-273.

(44)　STOUTEMYER, D., *Trans. Math. Software 1* (1975) 147-164.

(45)　STOUTEMYER, D., *Trans. Math. Software* (to be published).

(46)　GIBBONS, G.W. and RUSSELL-CLARK, R.A., *Phys. Rev. Lett. 30* (1973) 398-399.

(47)　COHEN, I., *Perturbation Calculations in Fluid Mechanics Using REDUCE, SIGSAM Bulletin,* ACM, New York, No. *36* (1975) 8 (abstract only).

THE ASTROPHYSICIST AND THE COMPUTER

Icko Iben, Jr.

University of Illinois at Urbana-Champaign

ABSTRACT

Revolutionary advances in our understanding of stellar structure and evolution, stellar pulsations and explosions, the synthesis of elements in stars and in the Big Bang, and the dynamics
of many-body systems have closely paralleled the development of
computer technology. Each order-of-magnitude increment in computing power has led to the solution of long standing problems and
ushered in a new era of exploration.

Currently, however, the access of the astronomer to the machines which he is now capable of exploiting efficiently and
effectively is exceedingly limited. The problem is threefold:
(1) astronomy is a small profession and is unable to muster the
necessary numerical and financial support for its own large scale
computing facility; (2) many of the most interesting astrophysical problems are CPU bound and solution has a very noticeable
impact on local machine utilization - the astronomer usually
loses in the battle for time since the policy of most service
installations is to satisfy the largest number of customers possible, regardless of merit; (3) usage of remote facilities is
hampered by the need in most instances for physical relocation of
the astronomer, the second class citizenship of the astronomer at
the host installation, and the hassle of conversion from one system to another.

Most of the problems just cited are political in nature and
can never be satisfactorily resolved. However, several steps
toward alleviating the current impasse are to be recommended.
First, those in the business of designing machines and providing

basic software could, in conjunction with systems programmers at
university installations, expend some effort in providing a universal job control language (in the spirit of Fortran) and a standardized editing language that would considerably ease the pain
and frustration of moving programs from one installation to the
next and getting them to work. Second, the transfer of data
bases from one installation to the next could be immeasurably
improved if all manufacturers would provide all installations
with standard conversion packages that allowed tapes written at
one installation to be read at another with a minimum of programmer intervention. Finally, purveyors of service could alter
their standard philosophy that good service means primarily a
large job throughput rate. Most of our current understanding of
the inner workings of stars could not have been achieved without
the existence of large scale computers. Many of the existing
problems facing the astronomer now simply cannot be solved except
on the most powerful computers available. It is a tragic fact
of life that really important problems about the nature of our
universe wait for solution while powerful computers waste time
on infinite numbers of trivial problems that could be solved on
a wooden slide rule. In scheduling algorithms some provision
should be made to assure that problems for which the computer is
really essential, and not just a convenience, receive adequate
attention.

I. INTRODUCTION

The astrophysics-oriented astronomer needs huge amounts of
time on the fastest computers available and rapid, interactive
access to these computers. In return, he can provide mankind
with enhanced understanding of the inner workings of stars, galaxies, and the gaseous medium between stars and galaxies, an
enhanced understanding that can be achieved in no other way.

In this paper, I will first describe a representative astrophysical problem that has occupied much of my research effort over
the past four years and then describe the mode of operation that
most efficiently utilizes both computer resources and human resources. Next, I will address the obstacles that the astrophysicist encounters in attempting to satisfy his truly immense need
for computer time. Finally, I shall suggest ways in which the
astrophysicist's needs can best be met; these will be of both the
ideal and the attainable kind.

The appendix contains a list of papers that describe several
astrophysical problems, the solutions to which would not have
been obtained without the existence of the large scale computers
in use at the time of solution.

II. A REPRESENTATIVE ASTROPHYSICAL PROBLEM - THERMAL PULSES

Following the exhaustion of hydrogen at its center, a star in
the range 3-9 solar masses $(M_\odot)$ transforms from an ordinary main
sequence star to a red giant. The interior consists of a rapidly
contracting and heating core capped by a hydrogen-burning shell
and a rapidly expanding and cooling envelope. Rapid core contraction is halted by ignition of helium at the stellar center.
Then, while burning helium in its core, the star moves away from
the giant branch and pulsates as a Cepheid. When its central
reservoir of helium is exhausted, the star again becomes a red
giant, but this time it possesses a much more complicated interior structure and manifests a much wider variety of fascinating
phenomena.

Depending on the initial main sequence mass of the parent star,
the core of the star contains initially from 0.5 to 1.0 $M_\odot$ of
matter that is primarily in the form of carbon and oxygen left
behind by the helium-burning core during the Cepheid stage.
Typical densities in a 'C-O' core range from a few times
10^9 gm/cm^3 to a few times 10^4 gm/cm^3 and temperatures are on the

111

order of a few hundred million degrees Kelvin. The radius of the core is on the order of the radius of the Earth. Neutrino losses maintain the core at nearly a constant temperature throughout. Except for the high temperatures at its edge, the core looks for all the world like a young white dwarf in the initial stages of its cooling phase. At the edge of the core is a thin region of nearly pure helium with a slight admixture of the mass 14 isotope of nitrogen. Roughly thirty percent of the helium is primordial; that is, the star was born with it. The other seventy percent has been left behind by a very thin region that burns hydrogen above the outer edge of the helium zone. The N^{14} is partially primordial but is predominantly a consequence of the conversion of primordial C^{12} and O^{16} in the hydrogen-burning shell. Typical temperatures and densities in the hydrogen-burning shell are 50-80 x 10^6 $^{\circ}K$ and 1-10 gm/cm^3. The mass of the hydrogen-burning region is incredibly small, ranging from 10^{-5} $M_{\odot}$ when the C-O core is of mass near $1M_{\odot}$ to 10^{-8} $M_{\odot}$ when the C-O core is of mass near 1.4 $M_{\odot}$.

The rest of the star is spread out over a huge volume the radius of which is on the order of the distance from the Sun to the Earth. Temperatures in this rarified envelope drop to a few thousand degrees at the photosphere and densities drop to 10^{-13} gm/cm^3 at the photosphere.

Instabilities of at least three kinds occur. The first of these is a coronal "evaporation" of mass from the surface that is related in origin to the solar wind. The second is a pulsational instability in the envelope of the star. The mode that is most frequently excited is the first harmonic radial mode and the periods that are exhibited range from years to a few decades. The driving mechanism for the pulsational instability is quite similar to that which drives Cepheids, except that the thermodynamic properties of the hydrogen ionization zone rather than those of the helium ionization zone are the primary contributors to the driving.

The third instability originates in the helium zone between the hydrogen-burning shell and the C-O core. During most of the second giant branch phase, this zone is inert, in the sense that nuclear transformations occur therein with negligible frequency. However, thanks to the high temperature sensitivity of helium-burning reactions and to the heat-flow characteristics of the helium zone, the helium zone becomes thermally unstable when temperatures and densities within it reach critical values. Then, nuclear burning "runs away", injecting energy at tremendously high rates (typically at ten million times the sun's luminosity and a thousand times the star's surface luminosity). Most of the injected energy is deposited in the helium zone, raising temperatures and pressures there to three or four times those prevailing prior to the onset of the instability. The huge deposit of thermal energy forces matter in the helium zone to expand and cool, thereby quenching the instability.

During the ensuing relaxation phase of the thermal pulse, matter at the hydrogen-helium interface is pushed out to such low temperatures and densities that hydrogen-burning reactions effectively cease occurring. At the same time, a region of convective instability growing outward from the leading edge of the helium zone joins up with a region of convective instability that covers most of the envelope. The mixing currents that are characteristic of convective regions then carry throughout the envelope products of helium-burning that have just been made in the helium zone. These products include C^{12}, Ne^{22}, many light elements from Mg^{25} to A^{36}, and the so-called "s-process" elements that are the consequence of successive neutron captures on Fe^{56} and its neutron rich progeny.

Eventually, all of the excess energy initially deposited in the form of thermal energy is converted into potential energy. The helium-burning reactions are extinguished and matter sinks back inward until the hydrogen-burning reactions are rekindled.

113

The star then embarks on another extended period of quiescent nuclear burning. Typically, a thermal pulse runs its course in a few years to several decades, while the interpulse phase can last from a few hundred years to several thousand years.

III. COMPUTER REQUIREMENTS

Storage requirements are not negligible. A complete model of a star in the thermally pulsing phase requires from 1000 to 2000 mass zones. That a large number of zones is necessary is obvious from the ranges in temperature (5×10^8 $^{\circ}$K to 3000 $^{\circ}$K), density (2×10^9 gm/cm^3 to 10^{-13} gm/cm^3), pressure (10^{27} dynes/cm^2 to 10^{-2} dynes/cm^2), and luminosity (-10^5 $L_{\odot}$ to 10^7 $L_{\odot}$) encountered and from the fact that difference equations become a poor approximation if state variables vary from one zone boundary to the next by over, say, ten percent. Furthermore, variations in temperature and luminosity are not monotonic, changing in sign at several locations in the star. In regions of varying nuclear composition and in regions of partial ionization additional demands for faithful representation can be met only by very fine zoning.

To follow the nuclear transformations of relevance, it is necessary to specify approximately ten composition variables in each zone. Four state and structure variables are also needed. Solution of the time dependent difference equations by an implicit relaxation technique requires two models to be present at one time, thus increasing the total number of composition, state, and structure variables from 14 to 28. Solution of the equations themselves requires an additional set of a dozen matrix elements per mass shell. Additional assorted flags, checks, and backup redundancies bring the total number of variables per shell to about 50. Multiplying 50 variables per shell by 2000 shells gives 10^5 double-precision words.

Programs are large, typically containing 5,000 to 10,000 statements. The total memory requirements are such as to exceed the fast memory of the central processor in the main computer at most university installations.

The CPU time required to follow a single pulse plus the intervening interpulse phase naturally varies from one computer to the next. On an IBM 360/75, a single time step requires roughly 2 minutes for convergence and on a CDC 6600, convergence can be achieved in roughly one minute. Since about 2000 time steps are involved, this means that roughly 3 solid days of computing on a 360/75 are required to follow just one complete pulse plus interpulse phase. Pulse amplitude builds up slowly, approaching a limit cycle only after 20 to 30 pulses. Hence, in order to examine the character of the limit cycle, a computing time of about two months on a 360/75 is necessary.

This two months of computing time is not production in the ordinary sense of the word. Each pulse is an adventure in itself; new areas in the code are continually being explored by the model star. This means that constant rewriting, debugging, and babysitting are involved. Further, each pulse brings an increase in the range of physical conditions encountered; additional nuclear reactions may have to be considered and items such as the equation of state may have to be revised. New criteria for rezoning must be invented and implemented. The two months of CPU time might conceivably be obtained over a three or four year interval and be accompanied by constant and sustained effort in interactive programming and code checking on the part of the astrophysicist.

IV. THE STRUGGLE FOR COMPUTER TIME

In most instances, the astrophysicist finds himself in a university environment. This is to be expected since, on casual inspection, solutions to many of the problems he attacks have little immediate applicability to problems faced by industry in supplying society with needed implements or to problems faced by government laboratories in building weapons and finding new sources of energy. In fact, however, the mathematical and physical structure of the problems tackled by the astronomer-astrophysicist have many things in common with problems of current interest in government and industrial laboratories and the schemes developed by astrophysicists to, for example, handle the logistics of large arrays of data or solve large sets of difference equations by relaxation, have applicability far beyond the purposes for which they were devised. Nevertheless, for whatever reasons, the astrophysicist tends to be in a university environment. What problems does he face in this environment?

His first task is to negotiate with administrators at several levels in an effort to buy computer time at a rate substantially below the standard rate. Interestingly enough, the standard price for an hour of computer time is nearly independent of the particular campus and, even more astonishingly, is almost independent of the specific type of central processor on campus, be it an IBM 360/75, a CDC 7600, or whatever. If we suppose that the average standard price for an hour of time on machine X is about $500 and that 2 months of time on machine X will lead to a publishable paper, then, at the standard pricing rate, that paper will cost about three quarters of a million dollars. No matter how talented, an astrophysicist can hope to obtain from government science agencies no more than perhaps one-tenth of such a sum (allocated to computing) over, say, a three-year period. He is forced to be a beggar on a very large scale.

Supposing that he has been successful in convincing the local research board to finance his venture, can he actually obtain the time granted by this board on the local campus central computer? The answer is usually an emphatic NO! At a typical large university, the central computer must serve perhaps 20,000 students and 2,000 faculty members. The staff of the computing center is faced with the task of satisfying as many of these clients as possible and of seriously offending as few of them as possible. The result is that algorithms for determining job priority preferentially favor jobs which require the least amount of CPU time and the least amount of memory. The standard algorithm insures that 20,000 students learn to program a computer while the research scientists (this includes students who are working with the scientists) gnash their teeth and grind their knuckles wondering why all that computer power is going to waste. If, from time to time, the scientists are successful in persuading the relevant directors to suspend the normal algorithm and to permit jobs with large time and memory requirements to run preferentially, then 20,000 students gnash their teeth and grind their knuckles, wondering why they aren't getting their tuition's worth. In the end, while classes are in session, the 20,000 students who are learning to program a computer win and the research scientists and their students go begging. Only on weekends when the weather is nice and during official vacation periods does the student pressure relax sufficiently for the standard algorithm to be suspended with impunity and for large jobs that tax the full capability of a large computer to be run.

Needless to say, the research scientist would also benefit from days in the sun and from vacations with his family. In order to preserve his mental, emotional, and physical health as well as to solve his research problem he is forced to look elsewhere for a solution. On a typical campus with strong science and engineering programs he might expect to find what are known as dedicated computers. These are computers financed by government agencies to further progress in areas of practical significance. Also on campus is a computer devoted to administrative data processing (for payrolls, sorting grades, scheduling classes, etc.). It is for me a continuing source of amazement that the computing power available on many campuses for administrative data processing exceeds the power available for the 20,000 students whom the university serves and the 2,000 faculty members who do the research that enhances the fame of the university.

It is frequently true that the dedicated computers and the ADP computers are idle for extended periods. Does this mean that the beggar astrophysicist who offers to profitably use this idle time finds surcease for his miseries? Perhaps for a short while, but only for a short while. All computing installations are staffed by human beings and human beings have an incredibly well developed territorial instinct. Resistance to an "outside" user is usually insurmountably formidable and can be overcome only when overwhelming pressure is brought to bear by some understanding administrator (there are such, thank goodness) who can control the purse strings of the particular installation affected. But even if access to the computer is granted to an outsider, human nature and the weight of numbers eventually conspire to deprive the outsider of effective access. Whereas for several years the computer may have idled for eight hours every night and have been shut down every weekend, suddenly urgent systems changes become necessary and new but important problems appear, crying for solution. The dedicated or administrative workload rises to fill the once idle hours. Under the most favorable circumstances, the outsider may have made a detectable impact on his problem before the proprietary instincts of the host installation have been sufficiently awakened to prevent him from using their computer further.

Let it not be forgotten, however, that the outsider has had to transform data and programs that are intelligible to the central campus processor into forms that are intelligible to the dedicated or ADP computer, and this is frequently a non-trivial process, consuming much of his time and the time of several consultants. This is due to the fact that the central computer and the dedicated computer have probably been constructed by competing manufacturers who have deliberately made their instruments as incompatible with one another as possible and to the fact that

the systems programmers at any one installation insist on constructing systems with features entirely different from the systems in use at any other installation.

Having exhausted the possibilities at home, the astrophysicist
then looks to the national center or the government laboratory
blessed with a large, fast, state-of-the-art computer. Extended
negotiations are the prelude to an invitation to visit and to use
the host computer. In the case of a government laboratory, security clearance must be obtained and this may require months of
waiting. In the case of a national center, a proposal must be
submitted for scrutiny by a panel of external consultants who are
experts in fields other than astrophysics. Proprietary instincts
are again aroused and the prospective outside user is granted
only a limited amount of computer time which may or may not permit him to make some small progress in solving his scientific
problem.

Then follow conversations between consultants on campus and
consultants at the laboratory to determine the best format for
placing data and programs on tape for transporting to the laboratory. Matters are complicated not only by the fact that the
nature of tape drives used on the campus computer and tape drives
used on the laboratory computer are different, but word size
employed by the two computers are different, and the systems programmers at the two installations have invented reading and writing schemes that are very clever but very different.

Having obtained a grant of computer time and hoping that the
data and program transportation and conversion problems have
been solved, the astrophysicist must now find the funds to transport himself to the national center or governemnt laboratory.
It is amusing to discover that it is sometime easier to obtain
$1000 to spend for two hours of computing on campus than it is
to obtain half that amount to travel to a laboratory or center
which will supply $100,000 worth of computing time.

119

Somehow the funds are found and the astrophysicist arrives at the host installation for, say, a two-week visit. His first shot at the host machine occurs only after several hours of conversation with consultants provides him with packages of job control language that permit him to load, compile, and run. Further assistance is necessary to actually transfer the information on his tapes onto disk files in a usable form. His first attempt at program compilation reveals that the laboratory compiler and, in fact, the entire laboratory system are totally different from those at home. Common statements are used differently and subroutine communication is different. The program that fit into fast core and ran satisfactorily on the home machine in single precision, can work only in double precision on the laboratory machine and requires extended core memory; thousands of EXP's must be converted into DEXP's and the outsider must invest time in a crash course on the use of extended core. By now it is clear that considerable program rewriting and editing will be necessary and the visitor must next invest further time in learning the editing language used locally. There are hundreds of words to learn, and symbols that mean one thing at home mean another at the laboratory. For example, at home, S = search, but, at the laboratory, S = scratch (with disastrous consequences).

Suppose, by some miracle, that the program which once worked at home actually begins to work on the host machine before the visitor's departure. Extending the visit is out of the question since the visitor has classes to teach at home and there is a limit to the amount of pinch hitting he can expect from even his most sympathetic colleagues at home. The next obstacle the visitor discovers is that the machine is saturated between 8 a.m. and 6 p.m. during weekdays and time for long runs becomes available only at night and on weekends. This would be alright if the visitor did not have a plane to catch in a few days or if his programs were truly production programs. So, he works on through supper and into the wee hours of the morning, keeping his weary eye on the computer output and diddling with the several hundred parameters he has built into his programs to deal with contingencies that inevitably arise. Stumbling to bed at four a.m., desperately hoping that at least two out of the five hour-long jobs he last submitted will work, is he comforted by the possibility of sleeping until noon? Of course not, for he has made appointments to talk later that morning with several of his hosts. After all, he is a guest, and does have the responsibility of describing the nature of the work he is doing under laboratory or center auspices.

Finally, plane time arrives and the exhausted visitor returns home with tapes that hopefully contain his last results. On arriving home he collapses, falling prey to a dread disease that his weakened and ravaged body can no longer combat. Six months later he may be sufficiently recovered to search for other alternatives.

One alternative might be extended visits. However, in many, if not in most cases, programs are in continuous evolution, requiring daily editing of an hour or two's duration over a period of several years and neither the host installation (which pays people to do things other than astrophysics) or the home institution (which pays people to do many things other than compute) can afford extended visits.

V. HOW TO EASE THE PAIN

The ideal solution would be interactive access by remote terminal to a state-of-the-art computer in some government or industrial laboratory which will guarantee rapid turnaround for editing and debugging large number-crunching programs (a debug run might require an hour of CPU time) and which will guarantee an amount of computer time sufficient to solve specific problems in a reasonable length of real time. Ideally, the user would access

the campus central processor from his office or home by phone and
the campus machine would provide the link to the laboratory computer. In the best of all possible worlds, a high-baud line
would also permit output to be printed on a fast and silent
printer in the user's office or home.

The major snag in achieving the ideal solution is the necessity
of convincing the industrial or government laboratory to provide
remote access to its computers and to guarantee large chunks of
time on these computers to astrophysicists whose expensive pastime
does not contribute in any obvious and tangible way to the major
mission of the industry or laboratory. Is it possible to con-
vince large industrial concerns or government agencies that understanding the evolution of stars and the formation of the elements
that make up our immediate world is of transcending importance,
ranking with the understanding of God's Word as revealed to the
authors of the Bible and the Koran? It might be easier to per-
suade the industrialist and the Internal Revenue Service that the
charitable donation of large quantities of computer time to in-
digent astrophysicists should be tax-deductible.

Although the ideal solution is an enticing goal, I suspect
that, for the foreseeable future, the astrophysicist will continue to move programs and data from one machine to another, computing at any one installation only as long as it takes the staff
of the host installation to become fully aware of his presence.
What then can be done to ease the pain of each move?

An effort should be made by directors of computing centers to
encourage the creation and adoption of standardized or universal
languages and procedures. That is, the scientist should be able
to use exactly the same job control language at installation A on
brand X machine as he uses at installation B on brand Y machine.
Every installation should be encouraged to support a universal
editing language so that the scientist need not be forced to learn

a new language each time he must move to a new installation. A standardized way of handling data bases should be introduced so that a tape written by brand X machine at installation A can be read at once by brand Y machine at installation B, without the need for lengthy and time-consuming consultations between consultants and the user. Finally, it would be a great help if the schemes for accessing extended core memory were standardized so that the entire structure of a code need not be rewritten for use at different machines at different installations.

The contents of the software black boxes that interface between the machines at any installation and the envisioned universal high level languages, and the black boxes that interface between the machines and the standardized procedures for data handling and transmission need not be revealed to the scientist. Just as he is now everlastingly grateful to the brilliant and energetic persons who conceive, design, and build those indispensable black boxes called digital computers, the peripatetic astrophysicist would be undyingly grateful to the brilliant and energetic persons who might design and maintain the software black boxes that would permit him to transport his problems from one installation to the next with a minimum of pain.

A final plea to all computing center directors. Please construct and enforce scheduling algorithms that permit some negotiated fraction of total available CPU time to be used to attack problems that can be solved in no other way than on fast computers with large core memories. It can be done, and I am happy to report that my own institution is blessed with administrators and computer center directors who, as a matter of course, make provision for such usage.

APPENDIX

CLASSIC PAPERS OR REVIEW DESCRIPTIONS OF

ASTROPHYSICAL PROBLEMS REQUIRING LARGE SCALE COMPUTERS

1. Galactic and Cluster Dynamics

Toomre, A. and Toomre, J., Astrophysical Journal, 178, 623 (1972). Galactic Bridges and Tails.

Arseth, S. J. and Lecar, M., Annual Review of Astronomy and Astrophysics, 13, 1 (1975). Computer Simulations of Stellar Systems.

2. Nucleosynthesis

Truran, J. W., Cameron, A. G. W., and Gilbert, A., Canadian Journal of Physics, 44, 563 (1966). The Approach to Statistical Equilibrium.

Wagoner, R. V., Fowler, W. A., and Hoyle, F., Astrophysical Journal, 148, 3 (1967). On the Synthesis of Elements at Very High Temperature.

Truran, J. W., Arnett, W. D., and Cameron, A. G. W., Canadian Journal of Physics, 45, 2315 (1967). Nucleosynthesis in Supernova Shock Waves.

Blake, J. B. and Schramm, D. W., Astrophysical Journal, 179, 569 (1973). Neutron Exposure of r-Process Material.

3. Stellar Structure and Evolution

Hayashi, C., Hoshi, R., and Sugimoto, D., Progress of Theoretical Physics Supplement Number 22, 1 (1962). Stellar Evolution.

Schwarzschild, M. and Härm, R., Astrophysical Journal, 145, 496 (1966). The Helium Flash.

Kippenhahn, R., Thomas, H. C., and Weigert, A., Zeitschrift für Astrophysik, 61, 241 (1965). Central Hydrogen and Helium Burning in a Star Five Times the Mass of the Sun.

Iben, I. Jr., Annual Reviews of Astronomy and Astrophysics, 5, 571 (1967). Stellar Evolution Within and Off the Main Sequence.

Iben, I. Jr., Annual Reviews of Astronomy and Astrophysics, 12, 215 (1974). Post Main Sequence Evolution of Single Stars.

Iben, I. Jr., Chapter 24 in Computers and Their Role in the Physical Sciences, ed. by Fernback, S. and Taub, A. H. (Gordon and Breach, New York), 1970. The Role of the Computer in Astrophysics.

4. Thermal Pulses

Schwarzchild, M. and Härm, R., Astrophysical Journal, 150, 961 (1967). Hydrogen Mixing by Helium-Shell Flashes.

Weigert, A., Zeitschrift für Astrophysik, 64, 395 (1966). Evolution with Neutrino Losses and Thermal Pulses.

Iben, I. Jr., Astrophysical Journal, 196, 525 (1975). Thermal Pulses; p-capture, α-capture, and s-process Nucleosynthesis; and Convective Mixing in a Star of Intermediate Mass.

5. Stellar Acoustical Pulsations

Christy, R. F., Astrophysical Journal, 144, 108 (1966). A Study of Pulsation in RR Lyrae Models.

Cox, J., Cox, A. N., Olsen, K. H., King, D. S. and Eilers, D. D., Astrophysical Journal, 144, 1038 (1966). Self Excited Radial Oscillations in Thin Stellar Envelopes.

Stobie, R. S., Monthly Notices of the Royal Astronomical Society, 144, 485 and 511 (1969). Cepheid Pulsation.

Wood, P. R., Astrophysical Journal, 190, 609 (1974). Models of Asymptotic Giant Branch Stars.

Stellingwerf, R. F., Astrophysical Journal, 195, 441 (1975). Modal Stability of RR Lyrae Stars.

Cox, J. P., Reports on Progress in Physics, 37, 563 (1974). Pulsating Stars.

6. Mass Transfer in and Evolution of Binary Systems

Kippenhahn, R., Kohl, K., and Weigert, A., Zeitschrift für Astrophysik, 65, 251 (1967); 66, 58 (1967). Evolution of Close Binary Systems.

Paczynski, B., Acta Astronomica, 16, 231 (1966); 17, 193 (1967). Evolution of Close Binaries.

Plavec, M., Kriz, S., Harmanec, P., and Horn, J., Bulletin Astronomical Institutes of Czechoslovakia, 19, 24 (1968). Evolution of Close Binaries.

Moss, D. C., Monthly Notices of the Royal Astronomical Society, 153, 41 (1971). The Evolution of Contact Binary Systems of Moderate Mass.

Plavec, M., Ulrich, R. K., and Polidan, R. S., Publications Astronomical Society of the Pacific, 85, 769 (1973). Mass Loss from Convective Envelopes of Giant Components in Close Binary Systems.

Bath, G. T., Astrophysical Journal, 173, 121 (1972). Time-Dependent Studies of Dynamical Instabilities in Semi-detached Binary Systems.

7. Nova and Supernova Explosion

Starrfield, S., Sparks, W. M., and Truran, J. W., Astrophysical Journal, 192, 647, 1974. CNO Abundances and Hydrodynamic Models of the Nova Outburst.

Colgate, S. A. and White, R. H., Astrophysical Journal, 143, 626 (1966). The Hydrodynamic Behavior of Supernova Explosions.

Thanks to Ronald F. Webbink and Peter R. Wood for help in constructing this list.

TURBULENCE AND NUMERICAL WIND TUNNELS

Harvard Lomax

Chief, Computational Fluid Dynamics Branch
Ames Research Center, NASA, Moffett Field, California 94035

ABSTRACT

The possibility of computing realistic three-dimensional,
unsteady fluid flows is considered. Particular attention is paid
to flows that might exist in wind-tunnel experiments at transonic
Mach numbers and high Reynolds numbers. Portions of such flows
that are essentially inviscid or have very low levels of vorticity
can be computed both efficiently and reliably. The object is to
approach the problem of computing those portions that are domi-
nated by turbulence and, as a result, have very high levels of
vorticity. An elementary study of the unsteady Navier-Stokes
equations shows that the difficulties of computing turbulence lie
in the problem of resolving the effects of the nonlinear convective terms which thoroughly mix the kinetic energy content of the
flow through a wide range of length scales, forcing foreseeable
finite-difference computations of turbulence to rely heavily on
statistical properties, assumptions, and/or approximations in at
least two space directions. An attempt is made to examine various
aspects of turbulence modeling by investigating some simple
examples based on the analysis of one- and two-dimensional equations that have nonlinear terms similar to those appearing in the
Navier-Stokes equations, and harmonic solutions with a large
spread of wave numbers. Results for high Reynolds number, two-
dimensional flow simulations found by calculating the full Navier-
Stokes equations with turbulence modeling are discussed. Finally,
recent experience with flow simulation is called upon to predict
future challenges and opportunities in numerical analysis and
possible future computer designs and capabilities.

INTRODUCTION

The aspect of a "numerical wind tunnel" has been raised at various times in the past few years and it is a very live issue today. Although there are a great many flows of practical interest that can or might be computed but are not generated by moving airplanes and are not therefore associated with wind tunnels, we will nevertheless focus our discussion on aerodynamic simulations. They are among the most difficult.

Most intelligent discussions on the matter are constrained by the agreement that computers will not replace wind tunnels, rather they will supplement them. Numerical simulation can quite reasonably be counted on to replace some experiments, suggest others, and provide interpolations that can expand our knowledge using whatever tests are carried out. Several articles have been published giving rather general overviews of the subject (refs. 1-7). In one of them (ref. 5), the objectives of computational aerodynamics are listed as follows:

• To provide flow simulations that are either impractical or impossible to obtain in wind tunnels or other ground-based experimental test facilities

• To lower the time and cost required to obtain aerodynamic flow simulations necessary for the design of new aerospace vehicles

• Eventually to provide more accurate simulations of flight aerodynamics than wind tunnels can

Of these, only the third is really arguable and that only in degree. Four major problem areas arise in accomplishing these objectives (listed in order of increasing difficulty in the author's opinion):

a. treating complicated geometries

b. providing efficient and reliable algorithms

c. building better computers

d. modeling turbulence

The latter two are stressed in reference 5. Each is touched upon in the following discussion, starting with a consideration of turbulence.

Anyone even superficially acquainted with the computation of turbulence can skip the first four sections. They are intended to provide a plausibility argument for the following comments quite well known to those acquainted with the subject:

• The direct calculation of high Reynolds number turbulence is impossible on any present or foreseeable computer.

• The details of the statistical structure of small-scale turbulence may be computable in one direction (e.g., normal to a surface) but not in the other two.

• In regions of massive separation, only the large-scale structure can be computed; the effect of small scales must be modeled or neglected.

Despite these limitations, there is reason to believe that many useful and important flows containing turbulence can be computed with an accuracy acceptable for use in airplane designs. This belief depends to a great extent on the following two hypotheses: the location and resolution of separation lines are by far the most crucial aspect of an aerodynamic simulation; away from the separation lines, only the statistics of turbulence need be computed. The analysis of representative one- and two-dimensional equations helps to give confidence to the latter of these assumptions. Recent calculations of transonic and supersonic flow using time-averaged models are also quite encouraging.

ON THE EQUATIONS FOR UNSTEADY FLUID FLOW

Our discussion is principally concerned with that part of the dynamics of fluid flow that encompasses the phenomena of turbulence. All of the basic concepts of turbulence are expressed mathematically in the terms on the left side of equation (1):

$$\left.\begin{array}{l}(\rho u)_t + (\rho uu)_x + (\rho uv)_y + (\rho uw)_z + p_x \\ (\rho v)_t + (\rho vu)_x + (\rho vv)_y + (\rho vw)_z + p_y \\ (\rho w)_t + (\rho wu)_x + (\rho wv)_y + (\rho ww)_z + p_z\end{array}\right\} = V \quad (1)$$

where u, v, and w designate the x, y, and z velocity components; t, ρ, and p designate time, density, and pressure; the
subscripts denote partial derivatives; without imposed surface and
volume forces, V designates those terms proportional to the viscosity (subsequently called viscous terms). Equations (1) are
referred to as the equations of motion (ref. 8, p. 137). Of
course, to actually determine the velocity distributions, one must
add equations for the rate of change of energy and mass of the
fluid, but these are not required for the discussion that follows.

Any observation of turbulent motion leads intuitively to the
concept of scales of motion. In such observations one sees a
thorough mixture of large and small scales or eddies. We replace
this qualitative concept with a quantitative one that expresses
these scales in terms of frequencies or wave numbers. In such
terms, the major difficulties that occur in analyzing flows with
turbulence are summarized in Table 1.

TABLE 1.- *Factors Leading to the Difficulties in Analyzing Turbulent Flows*

1. For high Reynolds numbers, a very wide spread occurs between k_M, the largest wave number, and k_1 the smallest wave number (e.g., $k_M \geq 10^4 k_1$).
2. The nonlinear velocity interactions in equation (1) constantly mix the amplitudes of the wave components and constantly redistribute their effects throughout the entire frequency range — referred to as the energy cascade.
3. Most of the energy is carried in the low-frequency components; most of the energy is removed or dissipated through the high-frequency components (by the action of V in eq. (1)).
4. The extremely important phenomenon of "flow separation" can drastically affect the low-frequency motion, but it is inti-mately related to the high-frequency behavior.

A classical way to attack equation (1), in view of the difficulties outlined in Table 1, is to replace the dependent variables
with the sum of a mean and fluctuating component so that the integral of the fluctuating component over some relatively large time
interval is zero. The literature is full (see, e.g., ref. 9) of
detailed descriptions of this approach. A good summary that makes
use of mass-averaging and a slowly moving mean flow is given in
references 10 and 11. If we replace the terms in equation (1)
with their mass-averaged values, the only modification to the left
side is to add the three lines:

$$\left. \begin{array}{l} \overline{(\rho u'u')}_x + \overline{(\rho u'v')}_y + \overline{(\rho u'w')}_z \\ \overline{(\rho v'u')}_x + \overline{(\rho v'v')}_y + \overline{(\rho v'w')}_z \\ \overline{(\rho w'u')}_x + \overline{(\rho w'v')}_y + \overline{(\rho w'w')}_z \end{array} \right\} \qquad (2)$$

which are the derivatives of the nine Reynolds stresses. The
time-averaged equations are still an exact representation of the
Navier-Stokes equations, but they have the six additional unknowns
displayed in expression (2). The manner in which these terms are
to be evaluated is referred to as the problem of closure. Closure
is the basis for most of the extensive literature on turbulence
modeling.

A more recent approach to the attack of the range-of-scale
problem in equation (1) is to employ space averaging rather than
time averaging. This has the advantage of making some of the
subsequent approximation required for numerical simulations less
restrictive and retains the phase relationships in the large-scale
structure. To maintain these advantages, the approach requires
the development of an unsteady solution of the large-scale motion,
but this may be expensive to calculate. A summary of this (often
referred to as the subgrid scale method) and the time-averaged
method is given in references 12 and 13.

The subject of turbulence can also be approached through the
study of vorticity dynamics. By far the most extensive analysis
of this subject pertains to incompressible flow. The

incompressible form of equation (1) can be written (by simply setting $\rho = 1$) in terms of the velocity vector $\underline{u}$ as

$$\frac{D\underline{u}}{Dt} + \nabla p = \text{viscous terms} \tag{3a}$$

where D/Dt is the substantial derivative. Since, for the incompressible case, $D\rho/Dt = 0$, continuity of mass gives $\nabla \cdot \underline{u} = 0$, and the pressure can be expressed in terms of the velocity components by the Poisson equation:

$$\nabla^2 p \equiv p_{xx} + p_{yy} + p_{zz} = -[(u^2)_{xx} + (v^2)_{yy}$$
$$+ (w^2)_{zz} + 2(uv)_{xy} + 2(vw)_{yz}$$
$$+ 2(uw)_{xz}] \tag{3b}$$

Alternatively, equations (3) and (4) can be written in terms of a vorticity vector $\underline{\omega}$ and a stream function vector $\underline{\psi}$ such that

$$\frac{D\underline{\omega}}{Dt} - (\omega \cdot \nabla)\underline{u} = \text{viscous terms} \tag{4a}$$

and

$$\nabla^2\underline{\psi} = -\underline{\omega} \tag{4b}$$

where the velocity field is recovered by the relation

$$\underline{u} = \nabla \times \underline{\psi} \tag{4c}$$

Of course, all the difficulties listed in Table 1 arise in the calculation of incompressible flows and they occur in analyzing either equations (3) or (4). The vorticity equations (4) have also received extensive analysis from the time-averaged point of view, and various aspects of vorticity dynamics have been related to and interpreted in terms of the Reynolds stresses (see refs. 9 and 14).

Another quite instructive approach to turbulence analysis lies in the procedure of tracing vortex filaments (see refs. 15 to 18). In this case, equations (4b) and (4c) are combined by the Biot-Savart law to form

$$\underline{u}(\underline{r},t) + \frac{1}{4\pi} \int \frac{(\underline{r} - \underline{r}') \times \underline{\omega}(\underline{r}',t)d\underline{r}'}{|\underline{r} - \underline{r}'|^3} = \underline{v}(\underline{r},t) \quad (4d)$$

where $\underline{v}$ is an irrotational velocity field that satisfies the irrotational boundary conditions.

ON THE DIRECT CALCULATION OF UNSTEADY VISCOUS FLOWS

By direct calculation, we mean the numerical computation of solutions to equations (1), (3), or (4) without introducing and modeling the Reynolds stress terms in expression (2). Stated in another way, we mean finding "exact" solutions for those Reynolds stress terms themselves. Of course, if the calculations employ some form of finite-difference approximation, there will be some error, but we assume this truncation error can be given proper physical interpretation and bounded below some satisfactory level.

Consider first the direct calculation of turbulence. It is usually agreed that to be turbulent a flow must have

(a)   Unsteady random vorticity fluctuations

(b)   Strong mixing and dissipation of kinetic energy   } (5)

(c)   Three-dimensional interactions

This description is based on observation. On the other hand, turbulence has been defined as the general solution to the Navier-Stokes equations (ref. 19). From this point of view, many of the systematic experimental studies of turbulent flow amount to the classification of possible "statistically stable" asymptotic solutions (ref. 20) of the nonlinear equations given by (1), (3), or (4) which fall in categories described by (5). Such being the case, the question arises:

Why not build a computer big enough and fast enough to make direct calculations of the Navier-Stokes equations? (6)

and be done with it. To answer this question, we return to Table 1 and discuss its consequences regarding numerical simulations.

133

Consider one of the simplest possible flow simulations that satisfies all the requirements in (5), the problem of computing isotropic, homogeneous (statistically invariant to rotation and displacement of a reference-measuring base) incompressible turbulence in a box. Specifically,

Find the incompressible, isotropic, homogeneous flow in a cube for which the boundary conditions are periodic, and the initial conditions are given by an appropriate, divergence-free, velocity field. (7)

We know (or hypothesize) *a priori* something about the solution to problem (7). In particular, after some length of time, its kinetic energy, $E = (1/2)(u^2 + v^2 + w^2)$, varies with k in a manner similar to that shown in figure 1 (curve a). The "significant" energy is described in a range of about 10 wave numbers and it is fully dissipated by molecular viscosity. If the initial energy content covered a broader spectrum, intermediate curves such as b, c, and d would be anticipated, with wave number spreads

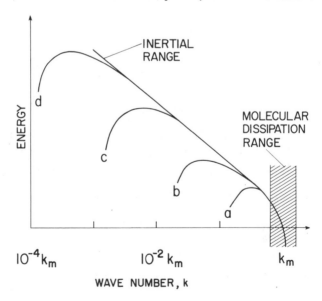

Figure 1. Energy spectrum in typical turbulent flows.

of 100, 1000, and 10,000, respectively. An experimental E vs. k distribution for pipe flow that clearly shows a 10^4 spread is given in reference 21.

The answer to the question in (6) for problem (7) can be determined by studying Table 2. Remember the constraint that the effect of molecular viscosity must be computed, not modeled. Remember also that the calculation must be time-dependent so that additional storage is required for time-accurate methods. This means a data base 5 to 10 times the number of mesh points is required to carry along a time-dependent calculation in the two- and three-dimensional cases, and the entire data base must be modified at each time step. Table 2 shows that, for a three-dimensional simulation of problem (7), a CDC-7600 would be forced to resort to disk (low-speed) storage for a spread of only 31 frequencies, and the entire disk storage capacity of the ILLIAC IV would not be enough to compute a spread of 127 frequencies in three dimensions (see also ref. 22).

TABLE 2.- *Numbers of Equispaced Mesh Points Required in One, Two, and Three Dimensions to Compute Various Scale Ranges by Spectral Methods.*

Approximate scale range	k_M, maximum frequency	Number of mesh points		
		One-dimensional	Two-dimensional	Three-dimensional
	7	16	256	4×10^3
10	15	32	1.0×10^3	32×10^3
	31	64	4.1×10^3	260×10^3
	63	128	16×10^3	2.1×10^6
100	127	256	65×10^3	16×10^6
	255	512	262×10^3	130×10^6
	511	1024	1.1×10^6	1.1×10^9
1000	1023	2048	4.2×10^6	8.6×10^9

Problem (7) has been considered for a mesh size of 32^3 (ref. 23). It has also been programmed for a CDC-7600 and the

ILLIAC IV for a mesh of 64^3, but results for this mesh size are
not available at this time.

ON THE DIRECT CALCULATION OF NONLINEAR EQUATIONS

The previous section indicated that the direct calculation of
three-dimensional turbulence with scale ranges greater than around
100 in all directions is impractical on available computers. This
leads directly to considerations of turbulence modeling, which
amounts to approximating the small-scale structure that falls
within grid cells (discussed in the next section). When no exact
solutions are available to check numerical approximation, one can
proceed all the way to experimental comparisons to seek verification. The complexity and wide variety of possible flows makes
this less than totally satisfactory in turbulent simulations. One
alternative is to compute "exact" solutions to equations that have
similar nonlinear and scale-spread properties but are amenable to
present computer power, and then to compare these results with
approximate solution found by modeling the small-scale structure.

Numerical solutions to one- and two-dimensional forms of the
Navier-Stokes equations have large and fairly large scale spreads,
respectively, and are not difficult to compute. No attempt is
made to suggest that these are solutions to turbulent flows in the
sense of (5) (see, e.g., ref. 24). They do, however, appear to
have an inertial range, and they can be used to test models that
have been proposed for the three-dimensional simulations.

One-Dimensional Equation

The classical Burgers equation is a one-dimensional representation of the interaction between the nonlinear-inertial terms and
the linear viscous terms in the incompressible Navier-Stokes
equation. It can be written:

$$u_t + uu_x = \nu u_{xx} + P(x,t) \qquad (8)$$

$$\text{cascade} \quad \text{dissipation} \quad \text{production}$$

where the terms responsible for various energy phenomena are identified. Applying periodic boundary conditions at $x = 0$ and L
and defining the total energy to be

$$E(t) = \frac{1}{L} \int_O^L \frac{u^2}{2} \, dx \qquad (9a)$$

one can show that, if u is continuous and $P = 0$,

$$\frac{dE}{dt} = - \frac{\nu}{L} \int_O^L (u_x)^2 \, dx \qquad (9b)$$

for finite ν. The case of most interest occurs when $\nu \to 0$, which
corresponds to a very high Reynolds number. In the limiting case,
$Du/Dt = 0$ and a Lagrangian analysis leads to an "exact" numerical
solution from any initial condition. The procedure is essentially
the classical method of characteristics. A typical time history
from a continuous starting solution grows into steepening waves
that eventually become discontinuous. A dissipation line then
starts and forms a trace in the xt plane. The rate of energy
dissipation across this line is

$$\frac{dE}{dt} = - \frac{(\Delta u)^3}{12L} \qquad (9c)$$

where Δu is the strength of the discontinuity.

The development of equations (9b) and (9c) is the principal
motivation for this section. Comparing the two equations, we note
that an effective viscosity can be identified in the "high" Reynolds number flow, the strength of which *depends only on the
large-scale structure.*

The total energy distribution found in the solution of
$Du/Dt = 0$ with $u(x,0) = \sin t$ can be calculated (as mentioned
above). In this case, the dissipation line forms at $t = 1$, at
which time the energy begins to decrease. The asymptotic decay
rate is $E_t \sim 1/t^3$. An inertial range forms after the decay has
started; and, in this one-dimensional study, $E \sim k^{-2}$ in the
inertial range.

Note that the problem just discussed is extremely special. No randomness is suggested. In fact, there is not even an out-of-phase component since the solution is always of the form $\Sigma\ b_n(t)\sin nx$ for $0 \leq x \leq L$. However, if one were given nothing but the wave number structure of repeated numerical experiments, one would detect an abrupt change in the dissipation rate (transition), a cascading of energy through a frequency range (mixing of energy at various scales), and a dissipation rate that can be correlated with large-scale structure (eddy viscosity).

Two-Dimensional Equations

In the past few years, many numerical solutions of the incompressible two-dimensional Navier-Stokes equations have been published. Of particular interest here are those that apply to isotropic, homogeneous cases, and might be used to provide information about the existence and form of an inertial range.

Some recent studies are discussed in references 25 and 26. All of these used Fourier expansions on a uniform grid in both Cartesian directions. Very recent results by Fornberg suggest that an inertial range may be detectable on a 64 × 64 grid and that the k^{-4} (i.e., $k^4E \sim$ const) power law applies (see ref. 27). However, the latest word on this subject is found in the article by Orzag published in this volume.

The two-dimensional Navier-Stokes equations have also been solved by using equations (4) to trace the vorticity without the use of a fixed grid (refs. 17 and 18). In the two-dimensional case, the second term on the left of equation (4) vanishes; this has two effects:

• It eliminates "vortex stretching," which is generally considered to be an essential part of three-dimensional turbulence.

• It greatly simplifies the analysis for cases representing very high Reynolds numbers.

The vortex tracing approach has received very little attention to date, probably for two reasons: its apparent lack of

generality to three-dimensional compressible flows and its unconventional (relative to the popular finite-difference Taylor series
analysis) approach to accuracy considerations. There is good reason to believe that the effects of both compressibility and three
dimensionality can be modeled in vortex tracing calculations, but
much work needs to be done in this area.

ON MODELING TURBULENCE

The philosophy of modeling can be demonstrated by considering
again the inviscid form of Burger's equation:

$$\frac{du}{dt} + \frac{1}{2} \frac{d(u^2)}{dx} = 0 \qquad (10a)$$

Setting $u = \bar{u} + u'$, where $\bar{u}$ is the (time or subgrid scale) mean
and u' is the fluctuating flow component, this equation can be
reduced, using the standard approximations of time or space
filtering, to

$$\frac{d\bar{u}}{dt} + \frac{1}{2} \frac{d(\bar{u}^2)}{dx} + \frac{1}{2} \frac{d(\overline{u'^2})}{dx} = 0 \qquad (10b)$$

The simplest and most widely used model of the Reynold's stress
term is to set

$$\frac{d}{dx} (\overline{u'^2}) \approx \frac{d}{dx} \left(\nu' \frac{d\bar{u}}{dx} \right)$$

where ν' is referred to as the eddy viscosity. Typically, ν'
is a function of the mean flow; for example, the Smagorinsky model
is to set

$$\nu' = L^2 \left| \frac{d\bar{u}}{dx} \right|$$

where L is some reference length. Simple numerical experiments
that use this model to find approximate solutions to Burger's
equation show that the energy in the large scale has reasonable
accuracy even when the small scale is quite incorrect.

The hope for three-dimensional modeling is that the dissipation of some components of the small-scale flow structure will
have no "practical" effect on the large-scale flow. Consider next

the problem of modeling turbulence near a solid boundary where
the flow is definitely neither isotropic nor homogeneous. For
high Reynolds numbers, the resulting large spread in scale and the
contents of Table 2 taken together show immediately that any significant small-scale effects can be *computed only in one direction*, the other two must be modeled simply because of the lack of
high-speed computer capacity. So long as the flow remains
attached, the preferred direction would logically be taken along a
normal to the surface, and some thin-layer theory naturally
evolves.

ON COMPUTING FLOWS ABOUT BODIES USING TURBULENCE MODELING

To make sense out of any turbulence simulation, we must
specify rather precisely our practical requirements. Clearly, we
cannot compute the flow exactly; the question really is: what is
the least information that must be computed to provide a "satisfactory" simulation? As a talking point for our discussion of
"numerical wind tunnels," let us impose the requirement that the
pressure can be calculated with "sufficient" accuracy on a wing
with

(a) a turbulent layer near the surface,
(b) one or more shock waves interacting with the
    turbulent layer, and
(c) separation caused by the shock, the trailing
    edge, or both.

$$(11)$$

The situation is illustrated in figure 2 which, at first
glance, appears entirely conventional. One sees an inner viscous
boundary layer coupled to an outer inviscid flow, and this has
been the basis for computing the flow about wings for many years.
There is nothing surprising in this — the classical boundary-layer
concept is a perfectly sound principle of fluid mechanics. However, subtle differences from most of the "usual" numerical simulations exist. These are caused by (a) strong shock-boundary-
layer interaction, (b) the existence of a viscous separation
point, (c) the separated region itself, and (d) the flow is both

140

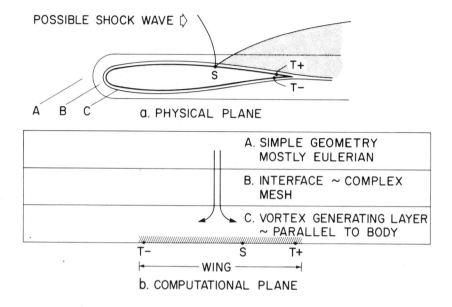

Figure 2. Regions of computational difficulty in realistic, high-Reynolds-number flows.

unsteady and three-dimensional. Most of these difficulties are relegated to the problem of computing the interface region (B), but it should be pointed out that region (C) cannot be computed by means of typical boundary-layer theories because of the separated flow.

It is gratifying to remark that the calculation of the outer flow (A) in figure 2 has definitely reached the predictive stage (assuming, of course, that the inner regions are correctly provided). This is evident from the many results that have been published (e.g., refs. 28 and 29) on the study of transonic flows using the Euler equations or their small-perturbation approximations. In this discussion, our concern is for regions (B) and (C).

The generally accepted structure of the inner layer in figure 2 is shown in figure 3, where a log scale is used to plot a "typical" turbulent-boundary-layer profile. The point of interest

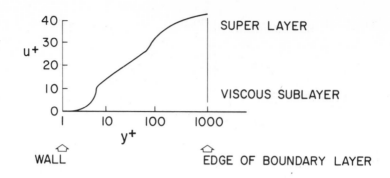

Figure 3. Typical turbulent-boundary-layer profile.

is the scale spread in the distance normal to the surface — it covers at least three orders of magnitude.

A standard approach used to compute flows with turbulent boundary layers is to

(a) assume that profiles such as that shown in figure 3 exist but do not vary greatly along directions parallel to the surface in distances commensurate with one boundary-layer thickness and

(b) assume that the correct details of the normal profile can be computed in an exponentially stretched mesh.

$$\left.\begin{array}{c}\\ \\ \\ \\ \\ \\ \\ \\ \\ \end{array}\right\} \quad (12)$$

This approach is illustrated in another way in figure 4 by using the smallest scale as the reference length. The mesh aspect ratio is shown to be at least 1000, clearly in accordance with the layer concept mentioned above.

An instructive way to view the consequence of statement (12) is to make use again of the concept that wave number can be used to represent scale. In this light, figure 5 illustrates in another way the basic nature of the above approach. Using second-order differencing schemes and 50 mesh intervals along both span and chord directions, one can resolve (appropriate clustering can be used to some advantage) about 10 harmonics with acceptable

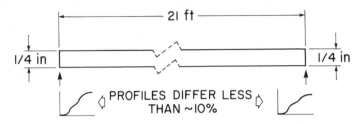

Figure 4. Mesh aspect ratio for innermost region of turbulent-boundary-layer calculations.

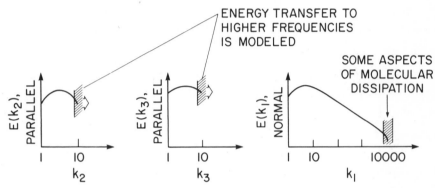

Figure 5. Resolvable energy spectrums for turbulent thin-layer calculations.

accuracy. It is clear that, in these two directions, the small-scale turbulence is at the complete mercy of the turbulence model. Only in the direction normal to the surface can any realistic attempt be made to compute some details of the statistics of a small-scale turbulence structure.

The above is simply an argument for the need of a turbulence model in the region of a boundary layer. Such models exist and even rather simple ones appear to give acceptable results if the flow does not separate. This leads us to the two vital hypotheses that must be demonstrated if we are to rely on numerical simulations of a flow similar to that sketched in figure 2, a flow that contains a region of massive separation in which the vorticity generated near the surface suddenly departs from it and occupies a region far outside a conventional boundary layer. One necessary hypothesis is that all of the important effects of turbulence in regions of massive separation are determined by resolving only the large-scale statistical properties of the turbulent flow, but resolving them in all three space directions. The other is that the location of the lines where separation occurs can be determined by a combination of a preceding thin-layer model and a succeeding massive-separation model.

As yet, the validity of the above hypothesis has not been demonstrated. The usefulness of vortex-tracing techniques in the massive separation region, or even at the separation point, is still an open question. The possibility of modeling an inertial range is still being investigated and has not been settled even for two-dimensional cases. The closure models for the thin-layer regions are the object of intensive studies. Clearly, we have a long way to go.

However, some encouraging results have been computed for a range of Mach numbers, high Reynolds numbers, and geometric conditions (see refs. 30 and 31). In these calculations, a form of the Navier-Stokes equations was used for all three regions in figure 2. Differences in treating the three regions occurred only in the mesh spacing and parameters that varied according to distance from the body surface. Relatively simple eddy viscosity (or algebraic) turbulence models and second-order hyperbolic marching schemes were used. Both trailing-edge separation and shock/boundary-layer interactions were calculated. The computed results agreed in all cases qualitatively, and in many cases quantitatively, with experiment. A typical result for a case with no separation is shown in figure 6. Further details can be found in reference 31.

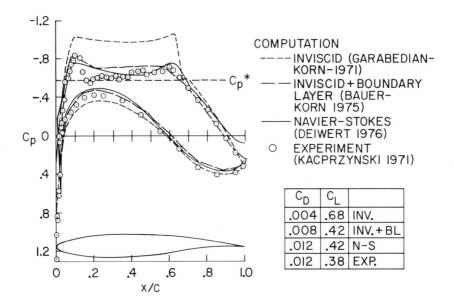

Figure 6. Comparison between theory and experiment for high-Reynolds-number transonic flow.

ON FUTURE DEVELOPMENTS IN NUMERICAL METHODS

Calculation of unsteady, nonlinear three-dimensional flow is still in its infancy due, for the most part, to the lack of computer power. It appears, in fact, that simulations of three-dimensional flows with realistic geometries await the next generation of computers even with thin-layer turbulence modeling. However, based on our experience with two-dimensional problems, we can anticipate certain challenges that will face the numerical analyst in his efficient use of whatever computers become available.

First, present indications are that three-dimensional flows will make extensive use of the technique referred to as "splitting or factorization" (see refs. 32 and 33). This concept permits one to cast a time-dependent set of partial differential equations into the form

$$u^{n+1} = A_1 A_2 \ldots A_j u^n + C_\alpha + \text{error } (a)$$

or

$$u^{n+1} = \prod_{j=1}^{J} A_j u^n + C_\alpha + \text{error } (a)$$

(15a)

where u is a vector composed of all dependent variables at all interior mesh points and C_α is a vector containing the effect of the boundary conditions. The composition and nature of the error term is, of course, vitally important and can be quite complicated to analyze. For our purposes, however, we will consider that the A_j can be determined so that error (a) is "satisfactory."

Under these conditions, the crucial part of equation (15a) is finding a suitable factored matrix string. The A_j matrices may be the result of explicit or implicit operations along different directions or on different terms in the same direction. They may result from second, third, fourth, or higher-order spatial differencing, from interpolation polynomials or from spectral methods. They may arise from vortex-tracing approximations or even from embedded analytic formulas.

Clearly, the formulation of a proper πA_j requires a sophisticated knowledge of both the mathematics and the physics of the problem and the latter is probably the most important. However, conceding that a πA_j with a satisfactory error bound can be found, we can form

$$B_n = \prod_{j=1}^{J} (A_j)_n$$

and write

$$u^N = \left[\prod_{n=1}^{N} B_n \right] u^O + C_b + \text{error } (b)$$

(15b)

where C_b again holds boundary condition effects.

Now it is well known that an acceptable accuracy in advancing u^n to u^{n+1} does not guarantee any accuracy in advancing u^O to

u^N. This surfaces the familiar problem of numerical stability and, in particular, the problem of stiffness. A major job of the numerical analyst is to avoid parasitic eigenvalues or misaligned eigenvectors in πB_n by an appropriate choice of A_{nj} while maintaining the required accuracy in u^N.

Clearly, a *goal* of the numerical analyst is to provide the A_{nj} so that u^N and its transient values are sufficiently accurate and so that the time steps involved are never limited by numerical stability bounds. As an example, a *goal* would be to converge a solution from u^O to u^N in 20 steps if the transient phenomena were unimportant. Of course, the attainment of such a goal for a simulation involving embedded shocks and slip surfaces is another matter, and it may be impossible to achieve.

The above comments can be given some substantiation by citing recent experience in calculating flows with shock/boundary-layer interaction using algebraic turbulence models. Published results (refs. 30, 34, and 35) were computed using factored operators in which the stability boundary was severely limited in sweeping through the operator calculating the flow in the inner mesh (C in fig. 2). By further factorization of this operator, the parasitic eigenvalues could be isolated and their stiffness removed without affecting the accuracy. Figure 7 shows some computer timings for several Mach and Reynolds numbers. Generally, computing times were reduced by nearly two orders of magnitude by the improved factorization. Details will be reported by MacCormack (ref. 36).

The problem of three-dimensional geometry is another one that will be challenging. The difficulty is not to provide the geometry of the surface, although that is not trivial, but rather to construct a (noncollapsing) mesh that surrounds it and on which accurate, nonlinear calculations can be carried out. At the present time, some technique for computing an interface (region B in fig. 2) that connects the inner region (closely tied to the geometry because of the turbulent thin-layer models) with the

147

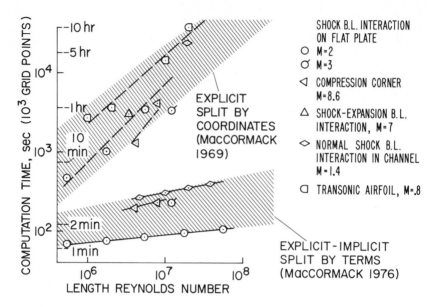

Figure 7. Effect of recent improvements in algorithms for time-averaged Navier-Stokes computations.

outer region (that has a simple mesh construction and is governed by the Eulerian equations) appears to be the most promising.

The complexity of these challenges will undoubtedly be increased by certain constraints imposed by future computer architectures. The very large data bases and very fast computing times involved in three-dimensional calculations will undoubtedly affect the nature of the algorithms that can be used. This is discussed briefly in the next section.

ON FUTURE DEVELOPMENTS IN COMPUTERS

It is not difficult to estimate some of the requirements for a computer that will meet the needs for making three-dimensional, finite-difference, fluid-flow calculations, assuming that these calculations will provide reasonably good resolution of large-scale motion about complicated geometries coupled with thin-layer results at the surface. Taking 100 as an estimate for the number of points (undoubtedly clustered) in each of the three directions and 20 as the average number of variables (including a space

148

metric and predictor-corrector storage requirements) that must be stored at each point, we arrive at a typical data base of about $W = 20{\times}10^6$ words. Taking a floating-point-operation count of about 50 operations per word in advancing one time step, and $N = 300$ time steps per case, we can estimate that

$$\frac{NPW}{F} \approx \frac{300,000{\times}10^6}{F}$$

seconds will be required to compute one case, where F represents the number of floating-point operations that can be computed in 1 sec. If we take $2{\times}10^6$ as the approximate value of F for a typical code operating on the CDC-7600, we see that a computer about 500 times faster than a CDC-7600 is required to compute one of our projected three-dimensional cases in about 5 min.

Now a value of $F = 10^9$ floating point operations per second for the next generation computer is not unreasonable if one considers various combinations of pipelines, overlapped, and parallel architectures. It appears that by far the biggest difficulty is the manipulation of the immense data base having on the order of 10^7 words, all of which go through the arithmetic units each time step. Assuming that the operating system manages several problems at once, these data will undoubtedly be staged through two or more levels of memory, each with its own transfer rate and access time. It seems clear that the data will be stored in pages and it is crucial that these pages can be moved to and from the memory hierarchies in each of three "directions" with similar transfer rates. In other words, we are faced with the data transpose problem on a very large scale. This problem alone may point to a computing facility designed especially for fluid-dynamic problems. In any event, it appears that the data management of three-dimensional problems presents the most serious challenge to the design of the next computer, and it will have repercussions on the development of future operating systems and numerical algorithms.

REFERENCES

1. Emmons, Howard W., Critique of Numerical Modeling of Fluid-Mechanics Phenomena. *Annual Review of Fluid Mechanics*, *Vol. 2*, 1970, pp. 15-36.

2. Fox, D. G., and Lilly, D. K., Numerical Simulation of Turbulent Flows. *Reviews of Geophysics and Space Physics*, *Vol. 10*, No. 1, 1972, pp. 51-72.

3. Orszag, S. A., and Israeli, M., Numerical Solution of Viscous Incompressible Flows. *Annual Review of Fluid Mechanics*, *Vol. 6*, 1974, pp. 281-317.

4. Krause, Egon, Application of Numerical Technique in Fluid Mechanics. *Aeronautical Journal*, Aug. 1974, pp. 337-354.

5. Chapman, D. R., Mark, H., and Pirtle, M. W., Computer vs. Wind Tunnels for Aerodynamic Flow Simulations. *Astronautics and Aeronautics*, *Vol. 13*, No. 4, April 1975, pp. 22-30, 35.

6. Moretti, G., Computations of Unsteady Flows — A Realistic View of the State of the Art and of Perspectives for the Future. *Unsteady Aerodynamics*, *Vol. 2*, edited by R. B. Kinney, July 1975, pp. 435-452.

7. Gessow, Alfred, and Morris, Dana J., A Survey of Computational Aerodynamics in the United States. Presented to the AGARD Fluid Dynamics Panel, London, England, Oct. 9, 1975.

8. Batchelor, G. K., An Introduction to Fluid Dynamics. Cambridge University Press, 1967.

9. Tennekes, H., and Lumley, J. L., A First Course in Turbulence. The MIT Press, 1972.

10. Rubesin, M. W., and Rose, W. C., The Turbulent Mean-Flow, Reynolds-Stress, and Heat-Flux Equations in Mass-Averaged Dependent Variables. NASA TM X-62,248, March 1973.

11. Cebeci, T., and Smith, A. M. O., Analysis of Turbulent Boundary Layers. *Applied Mathematics and Mechanics*, *Vol. 15*, 1974, Academic Press.

12. Rubesin, M. W., Sub-Grid or Reynolds Stress Modelling for Three-Dimensional Turbulence Computations, in *Aerodynamic Analyses Requiring Advanced Computers*, Part I, NASA SP-347, March 1975, pp. 317-339.

13. Reynolds, W. C., Computation of Turbulent Flows. *Annual Review of Fluid Mechanics*, *Vol. 8*, 1976.

14. Mollo-Christensen, E., Physics of Turbulent Flow. *AIAA Journal*, *Vol. 9*, No. 7, July 1971, pp. 1217-1228.

15. Rosenhead, L., Formulation of Vortices from a Surface of Discontinuity. *Proceedings of the Royal Society A*, *Vol. 134*, 1931, pp. 170-192.

16. Chorin, A. J., Numerical Study of Slightly Viscous Flow. *Journal of Fluid Mechanics*, *Vol. 57*, Part 4, 1973, pp. 785-796.

17. Clements, R. R., and Maull, D. J., The Representation of Sheets of Vorticity by Discrete Vortices. *Prog. Aerospace Sci.*, *Vol. 16*, No. 2, 1975, pp. 129-146.

18. Sarpkaya, T., An Inviscid Model of Two-Dimensional Vortex Shedding for Transient and Asymptotically Steady Separated Flow Over an Inclined Plate. *J. Fluid Mech.*, *Vol. 68*, Part 1, 1975, pp. 109-128.

19. Bradshaw, P., The Understanding and Prediction of Turbulent Flow. *Aeronautical Journal*, July 1972, pp. 403-418.

20. Orszag, S. A., Lectures on the Statistical Theory of Turbulence. Flow Research Rept. 31, March 1974.

21. Laufer, J., The Structure of Turbulence in Fully Developed Pipe Flow. NACA TR 1174, 1954.

22. Case, K. M., Dyson, F. J., Frieman, E. A., Grosch, C. E., and Perkins, F. W., Numerical Simulation of Turbulence. Stanford Research Institute Technical Rept. JSR-73-3, Nov. 1973.

23. Orszag, S. A., and Patterson, G. S., Numerical Simulation of Three-Dimensional Homogeneous Isotropic Turbulence. *Phys. Rev. Letters*, *Vol. 28*, 1972, pp. 76-79.

24. Batchelor, G. K., The Theory of Homogeneous Turbulence. Cambridge University Press, 1959.

25. Herring, J. R., Orszag, S. A., Kraichan, R. H., and Fox, D. G., Decay of Two-Dimensional Homogeneous Turbulence. *J. Fluid Mechanics*, *Vol. 66*, 1974.

26. Fornberg, B., A Numerical Study of 2-D Turbulence. Private Communication, 1975.

27. Saffman, P. G., On the Spectrum and Decay of Random Two-Dimensional Vorticity Distributions at Large Reynolds Number. *Studies in Appl. Math.*, *Vol. 50*, No. 4, 1971, pp. 377-383.

28. Ballhaus, W. F., Some Recent Progress in Transonic Flow Computations. Presented at the von Karman Institute, Lecture Series on Computational Fluid Dynamics, March 15-19, 1976.

29. Jameson, A., Transonic Potential Flow Calculations Using Conservation Form, Proceedings AIAA 2nd Computational Fluid Dynamics Conference, June 1975, pp. 148-161.

30. Deiwert, G. S., Computation of Separated Transonic Turbulent Flows. AIAA Paper 75-878, 1975.

31. Deiwert, G. S., On the Prediction of Viscous Phenomena in Transonic Flows. Proceedings of the Project SQUID Workshop on Transonic Flow Problems in Turbomachinery, Monterey, Ca, Feb. 1976.

32. Yanenko, N. N., The Method of Fractional Steps, Springer-Verlag, Berlin, 1971.

33. Lomax, H., Recent Progress in Numerical Techniques for Flow Simulation. To be published in the AIAA Journal.

34. Hung, C. M., and MacCormack, R. W., Numerical Solutions of Supersonic and Hypersonic Laminar Flows Over a Two-Dimensional Compression Corner. AIAA Paper 75-2, 1975.

35. Baldwin, B. S., and MacCormack, R. W., Interaction of Strong Shock Wave with Turbulent Boundary Layer. *Lecture Notes in Physics*, *Vol. 35*, Springer-Verlag, 1975, p. 132.

36. MacCormack, R. W., An Efficient Numerical Method for Solving
the Time-Dependent Compressible Navier-Stokes Equations. To
appear as NASA TM X-73,129, 1976.

GENERAL PURPOSE PROGRAM FOR FINITE ELEMENT ANALYSIS
SOME COMPUTATIONAL CONSIDERATIONS

Pedro V. Marcal

Marc Analysis Research Corporation
Palo Alto, California 94306

ABSTRACT

A review is made of the basis for a general purpose program for finite element analysis. Two factors affecting the implementation of general purpose programs are discussed. The first is computational efficiency. The assembly and solution of the master stiffness equations were found to be the critical operations in terms of computing requirements. The second factor is program reliability. It was found that with the large number of problem types that can be handled, program reliability becomes a statistical matter and special procedures need to be developed to improve program reliability.

INTRODUCTION

In this paper we review current developments of general purpose programs for finite element analysis. Though these programs emphasize the structural application areas, the finite element technology, on which they are based, is general enough to handle most physics problems and should be regarded as a general numerical tool in the physical sciences (e. g. see [1] for some applications of the finite element method to problems in non-structural areas).

In the following, we shall discuss the finite element technology on which the general purpose programs are based, examine the various computer-science problems that exist and consider some aspects of these problems in detail.

BASIS FOR GENERAL PURPOSE PROGRAMS

In this section we will take the nonlinear finite element formulation of [2] as the point of departure.

The nonlinear equilibrium equation obtained by the principle of virtual work is:

$$\{P\} = \int_V [B]^T \{\sigma\} \, dV \qquad (1)$$

where

$\{P\}$ is the equivalent force at the nodes,

$[B]$ is the increment of displacement to increment of strain transformation,

$\{\sigma\}$ is the stress and

V is the integration over an element.

The displacement strain transformation matrix $[B]$ is a function of the initial geometry, plus the current displacement. The stress vector $\{\sigma\}$ is a function of current displacement and the constitutive relation. Both quantities are, in general, nonlinear with respect to the equivalent force vector $\{P\}$. It is thus preferable to linearize the equation of equilibrium and then deal only with linear matrix equations.

Rewriting in incremental form, we have:

$$d\{P\} = \int_V d[B]^T \{\sigma\} dV + \int_V [B]^T [D] \ [B] dV d\{u\} + 0(I)$$

$$= ([k_o] + [k_G]) \ d\{u\} + 0(I) \qquad (2)$$

where

$[D]$ is the instantaneous stress strain relation

$\{u\}$ is the displacement at the nodes

$[k_o]$ is the small displacement element stiffness

$[k_G]$ is the geometric element stiffness

$0(I)$ is the residual load correction applied

to the incremental equation to account for

any deviation of the current results from

the nonlinear equilibrium equations.

The second line of (2) shows that the geometric nonlinear terms can be collected into a geometric element stiffness matrix $[k_G]$. The two stiffness matrices are not separated except in buckling (Eigenvalue) problems.

This equation is written at the element level, but may be summed directly to account for any structure made up of finite elements or subzones. The equation could have been written for dynamic nonlinear behavior without loss of generality [3].

It can be seen from (2) that a program can be written at the matrix manipulation level to implement this equation in a general form, i.e., programs can be written to evaluate the expressions in (2) without being too concerned with the form of [B] and [D], which will be dictated by the specific problem at hand. We call such programs general purpose programs. A program which has a selection of modules to account for different geometries, i.e., different [B],is said to have an element library. A program which has a selection of modules to account for different constitutive behavior, i.e., different [D],is said to have a material library[4] A program which has a selection of procedures to manipulate the resulting equation (2) for different physical problems is said to have a library of procedures.

In a program developed by the author and his colleagues [2] and called the MARC Program, the following library selection was found to be necessary to cover most of the field of structural mechanics:

Element Library:	50 elements
Material Library:	35 materials
Procedures Library:	15 procedures

Because these three separate libraries can be combined in any manner providing it makes physical sense, a general purpose program becomes a tool of widespread application. It is this generality which gives general purpose programs their strength and enhances their use in industry.

The reader may quickly get a feel for the number of different structural types of problems that can be solved by noting that a single combination from each of the libraries in the MARC general purpose program [2] can account for 50 x 35 x 15 =26,000 different structural types, whereas the combination of a selection of three from each library results in a combinatorial calculation which can account for approximately 10^{10} different structural types. It should also be noted that this last combination of three from each library is not a rarity but is quite representative of current industrial application.

1. COMPUTATIONAL EFFICIENCY

The flexibility and power of general purpose programs is easily recognized. However, its implementation raises many new questions as to the efficiency of such programs, as well as to their reliability. In this section we shall discuss these two aspects of the computational task.

The question of how best to achieve computational efficiency is quite complex and depends on the computing resources available, the programming skills,and languages used. It is difficult to assess computational efficiency in absolute terms. Instead, we will identify here the operations required by (2). Noting that the equations in (2) are formed in turn for each element and that each node will have its own label, we interpret the combination of equations for the whole structure by the direct stiffness method as one of the 'merge-sort' type. Because special efforts are made to relabel each node to minimize the band width of the resulting stiffness matrix [5] the 'merge-sort' problem becomes a banded one and for large problems requires a large amount of I. O. Some programs such as the SAP [6] program take advantage of the banded nature of the problem by writing all the element stiffnesses out on a tape and then taking passes to assemble the stiffness matrix for blocks of nodes at any one time.

Another solution such as that adopted for NASTRAN involves regeneration of element stiffnesses for the assembly of the stiffness matrix for each node. The philosophy being that it is cheaper to perform computations than to retrieve from the backing store. Of course each of the solutions turns out to be good for some range of problems but inadequate for others. We note here the need for flexibility given by several approaches an an adaptive selection of each. By similar arguments we may note the need for several approaches in each of the critical computing areas. The other area requiring computational efficiency is the solution of the linear symmetric and positive definite stiffness matrix resulting from the assembly of (2). The Gauss elimination procedure is favored. Two slightly different methods are used in organizing the data transfer from core to disc during the solution process. The first is to store blocks of nodes with a full bandwidth and to operate on this without regard to embedded zeros. The second is to pack the matrix and only to operate on non-zero data [7]. Care is taken in both procedures to ensure that sequential I. O. is used so that computing can be balanced against I. O.

As we examine the two computationally critical procedures of assembly and solution for large problems of the order of 5,000 to 10,000 degrees of freedom and a half bandwidth of 1,000 to 2,000 degrees of freedrm, we note that the assembly and related calculations have a C. P./I. O. ratio of about 1 in 10 where as the solution procedure has a C. P. to I. O. ratio of about 1 in 1.5. A proposal by Irons [8] combined the stiffness generation, assembly and solution procedure in what is now known as the wavefront solver. This procedure still has the limitation imposed by available core but does defer the time when the size of a problem results in large I.O. Many other solutions to the finite element computational problem become possible with hardware which allows multiple simultaneous access to disk together with multiple parallel processors. None of these possibilities have been fully explored to date.

The second problem of importance to be addressed is that of program reliability. Griffin [9] has divided the reliability question into two parts, i.e., that of verification and qualification. The problem of verification is that of ensuring that the program performs as intended. The problem of qualification is that of ensuring that the model used by the program corresponds to the real physical world. As noted elsewhere, the problem of qualification can only be solved by constant use and comparisons with experiment. A general purpose program can only be qualified for a fraction of its problem solving capacity. Therefore, it is important that this qualified base be used as the basis of extensive verification to ensure the integrity of the program.

The problem of verification can be recognized as a statistical one. By an examination of the flow sequence, it is estimated that it takes about 15 main program modules to obtain the solution of (2). Data is processed continuously from module to module and each result depends on the previous result. In the case of a nonlinear problem the results are passed through about 70 modules. To estimate the probability of error in running a new problem with all the usual assumptions of unbiased distribution of errors, we assume an error probability of 1 in 10,000 for each module. Then for a new linear problem we obtain a reliability of 0.0015 and for a new nonlinear problem we obtain a reliability of 0.007. A reliability of 1 in 10,000 appears to be reasonable for a well used program. Indeed it is certain that any new code added to the program will have a much lower reliability. It is unlikely that this reliability can be raised significantly by testing of individual modules, since it would require 10,000 tests to find 1 error. What appears to be required is some automatic testing of the whole program system along the lines of the systematic testing that computing hardware is subjected to. This should be coupled with instrumentation to examine the results both to its accuracy and to its computing costs.

Finally, in closing, attention is drawn to the fact that with such large scale generation and processing of data, inadequate attention has been paid to pre and post-processing of data in order to ensure the accuracy and ease of preparation of input data and also to ensure the digestion and presentation of output data in a form where the human senses can rapidly appreciate its significance. The introduction of computer graphics holds much promise for this area. Much needs to be done. Perhaps it may be possible to develop general purpose programs for pre and post-processing which recognize the human being's ability to think in qualitative terms and the inability to think in detailed quantitative terms. Thus, input and output data should be reduced to its absolute minimum and a picture should be regarded as worth a thousand words.

REFERENCES

1. Zienkiewicz, O. C., The Finite Element Method in Engineering Science, McGraw-Hill, 1971.

2. Hibbitt, H. D., Levy, N., and Marcal, P. V., "General Purpose Programs for Nonlinear Finite Element Analysis", Proc. Session on General Purpose Programs, ASME Winter Annual Meeting, New York, 1970, pp. 98-122.

3. McNamara, J. F. and Marcal, P. V., "Incremental Stiffness Method for Finite Element Analysis of the Nonlinear Dynamic Problem", Proc. ONR Symposium on Numerical and Computer Methods in Structural Mechanics, Urbana, Illinois, Sept. 1971.

4. Marcal, P. V., "Some Current Finite Element Models for Material Behavior", Proc. U. S. - Japan Seminar on Strength and Structure of Solids, Oct. 1974, abstracts reprinted in *Int. Journal of Fracture 1975, Vol. II*, p. 675.

5. Cuthill, E. and McKee, J., "Reducing the Bandwidth of Sparse Symmetric Matrices", Proc. 1967, National Conference of Association for Computing Machinery.

6. Wilson, E. L., Bathe, K. J., Peterson, F. E., Dovey, H. H., "Computer Program for Static and Dynamic Analysis of Linear Structural Systems", Report No. EERC 72-10, College of Engrg., Berkeley, 1972.

7. Melosh, R. J., Bamford, R. M., "Efficient Solution of Load-Deflection Equations", Proc. ASCE, *Vol. 95, ST4,* April 1969.

8. Irons, B. M., "A Frontal Solution Program for Finite Element Analysis", *Int. Journal Numerical Methods in Engineering, 1970, Vol. II*, pp. 5-32.

9. Griffin, D. S., "The Verification and Acceptance of Computer Programs for Design Analysis", Proc. Session on General Purpose Programs, ASME Winter Annual Meeting, 1970, pp. 143-150.

CASE STUDIES IN RELIABLE COMPUTING

W. M. McKeeman

University of California at Santa Cruz

ABSTRACT

The meaning of reliability in computing is discussed.
Various techniques for achieving it are presented by example.
The examples are taken from numerical analysis, systems program-
ming and a commercial environment.

> "Assembly of Japanese bicycle require
> great peace of mind."
> > in Robert M. Pirsig's
> > Zen and the Art of
> > Motorcycle Maintenance

0. INTRODUCTION

To paraphrase Webster, something is reliable to the extent
our experience allows us to place confidence in it. Thus when we
use the adjective "reliable", we are in fact ultimately describing a state of mind. The question is what technique can we use
to achieve it?

There have been many proposals relating to the art of
computer programming. Taken together and applied to a particular
programming task, they provide , to the mind of this author,
grounds for considerable confidence. We shall attempt to impart
both some of the techniques and some of the confidence through
the examples that form the body of this paper.

The examples are taken from numerical analysis, from systems
programming, and from a commercial environment. The techniques
vary widely. The lack of coherence in the literature on the
subject has, in fact, been the source of a certain amount of

criticism. Polya was probably reacting to similiar criticism
when he wrote, in his popular book, How to Solve It, that "This
sort of study, called heuristic by some writers, is not in fashion nowadays but has a long past and, perhaps, some future".

To some extent the variety of technique is due to the fact
that so many different complex processes are involved. A thousand people may be cooperating to a single end; a single programmer may be choosing among a thousand implementation alternatives;
a user may be leafing through a thousand pages of documentation;
a maintenance programmer may be staring at a thousand lines of
code; an operating system may be bringing one of a thousand
active segments into memory, and so on. All must be done with
efficiency, and with reliability as the objective. All depend
on the existence of some regularity and structure to reduce the
space of possible choices.

In the first example we are interested in achieving a
reasonable specification of numerical quadrature and then refining it into a working program. The emphasis is on the efficiency
and reliability of the quadrature, and as well the same two
properties for the process whereby it is specified and written.
We use Wirth's technique of stepwise refinement. The essential
point is that the program exists as a sequence of forms, each
"correct" at the level of understanding being discussed, and each
easily related to the neighbors in its sequence. The sequence
progresses from arbitrarily chosen convenient notations towards
an implemented programming language. To show that the program
has some particular property one must first establish that
property somewhere in the sequence, and then argue that it is
preserved across the remaining steps. It allows us to understand
the program naturally, rather than in terms of a meaningless
little covey of computer integers which really are codes for the
actual properties of the problem.

In the second case we are interested in constructing a

symbol table module of some generality. It is to be used in a number of translators for scientific programming languages. In some space is critical. In others, time. All are to be easy to bring up, test and certify. Here the essential point is long-term viability as a component. The emphasis is on functional specification and bringing the parameters to the "front panel", so to speak. We use the data structure axioms of Guttag to define the function; then superimpose the access method to give the performance.

Finally we consider a mass produced commercial product which contains a computer. Each delivery potentially requires a different program. Here the problem is masses of similiar programs which must be maintained by customers with no computer expertise. To add to the difficulty, the computer inside the product will be changed in the field to that of a different manufacturer several times during the product life. Many techniques are used here, the principle approach being that of emulation and simulation using linguistic levels to separate functions.

1. QUADRATURE

We wish to devise a procedure Int to compute definite integrals. The problem is specified in Form 1.

$$Int(f,a_0,a_1) = \int_{a_0}^{a_1} f(x) \, dx$$

Form 1

The idea is to successively refine Form 1 (through forms 2,3,...) until the last form contains a computer program. At each stage we must be sure that we have not lost the essence of the challenge although we may very well modify the content of the specifications along the way.

The problem, as stated, is actually much too hard. We must

restrict the choice of f to some tractable family of functions F. There will be different solutions for different families, but since a good deal of the analysis can proceed without our knowing the specific properties of F, we leave it undefined, restating the problem in Form 2.

$$\text{For } f \in F$$
$$\text{Int}(f,a_0,a_1) = \int_{a_0}^{a_1} f(x) \, dx$$

Form 2

Rice [1] claims there are 1,000,000 useful solutions to the above and has proposed a metalgorithm on the space of those solutions. A quadrature formula for a given function f is a weighted sum

$$(a_1-a_0) \sum_{i=1}^{N} w_i \, f(x_i)$$

where

$$\sum_{i=1}^{N} w_i = 1$$

and each

$$x_i \in [a_0,a_1].$$

Let $Q_{a_0}^{a_1} f$ be the set of all such formulas. The quadrature problem for f is to pick a formula that approximates the integral of f. Suppose the allowed tolerance is ε. Then we have a new statement in Form 3.

166

Given a_0, a_1, ε and also $f \in F$, pick

$\mathrm{Int}(f, a_0, a_1, \varepsilon) \in Q_{a_0}^{a_1} f$ such that

$\left| \mathrm{Int}(f, a_0, a_1, \varepsilon) - \int_{a_0}^{a_1} f(x)\ dx \right| \leq \varepsilon$

Form 3

The value of Int may depend on (a finite number of) values of f as well as any general properties of the family F. For reasons of efficiency we would expect the computed values of f to be restricted largely to those used in the quadrature summation.

We now wish to broaden the specification to deal with a new kind of difficulty. It is usually expensive to compute the integrand. We may therefore accept an approximation much less accurate than the rounding level of the computer. Suppose the error in f is bounded by a noise limit ϕ. Then we can state the problem in terms of a new function g as shown in Form 4.

Given a_0, a_1, ε, $f \in F$, ϕ, and g such

that $\left| f\text{-}g \right| \leq \phi$ on $[a_0, a_1]$,

pick $\mathrm{Int}(g, \phi, a_0, a_1, \varepsilon) \in Q_{a_0}^{a_1} g$ such that

$\left| \mathrm{Int}(g, \phi, a_0, a_1, \varepsilon) - \int_{a_0}^{a_1} f(x)\ dx \right| \leq \varepsilon$

Form 4

And, finally, we mention that any finite quadrature can be "fooled" by a rapidly varying function which "hits" the sample points x_i with the same values as some other function, but differs in between. For example, if the sample points are x_1,

$x_2 \ldots x_n$ then the polynomial

$$(x-x_1)^2 \ (x-x_2)^2 \ \ldots (x-x_n)^2$$

is zero on the sample but has a positive integral. Thus we need to have specified a length, λ, which is an upper bound on distance between sample points. The user is guaranteed that no sample points will be further apart than λ. Used above so that $\lambda < \min(x_{i+1}-x_i)$ would force the samples closer and avoid the spurious "hits".

The integral program is then finally specified in Form 5.

Given $a_0,a_1,\varepsilon,f \in F,\phi,\lambda$ and

g such that $|\ f-g\ | \leq \phi$ on $[a_0,a_1]$,

pick $\mathrm{Int}(g,\phi,\lambda,a_0,a_1,\varepsilon) \in Q_{a_0}^{a_1} g$ such that

$|\ \mathrm{Int}(g,\phi,\lambda,a_0,a_1,\varepsilon) - \int_{a_0}^{a_1} f(x)\ dx\ | \leq \varepsilon$

Form 5

In order to be reliable, Int must estimate its own error as well as the integral. That is, we expect Int to be two-valued. Expanding the final two lines of Form 5 we have Form 6.

Let $(I,E) = \mathrm{Int}(g,\phi,\lambda,a_0,a_1,\varepsilon)$.

Then $I \in Q_{a_0}^{a_1} g$,

and $|\ I - \int_{a_0}^{a_1} f(x)\ dx| \leq E$

Form 6

We know, a priori, that E is bounded from below:

$$\phi(a_1-a_0) \leq E.$$

The confidence of the user is understandably increased if, in addition,

$$E \leq \epsilon.$$

If it is not, the user is at least warned to be suspicious of I.

The result so far is to inject a note of realism into the program: there is only so much it can accomplish. The user must make the tradeoff on accuracy vs. cost (via ϵ), and the estimate of accuracy of the integrand (via ϕ), and the variability of the integrand (via λ), and the determination of appropriateness of the integrand (even though the definition of F may be no more precise than that given above!). The user must also be prepared for an occasional report of failure (via $E > \epsilon$).

Nor can we hope for a very sharp result on efficiency.

Suppose Int takes N samples to approximate $\int_{a_0}^{a_1} f(x)\, dx$. By the mean value theorem, if f is continuous, there is a point $\xi \in [a_0,a_1]$ such that $\int_{a_0}^{a_1} f(x)\, dx = (a_0-a_1)\, f(\xi)$. That is, there is a quadrature formula that needs only one sample for an exact result.

The problem reduces to picking the rule from $Q_{a_0}^{a_1}g$; that is, picking the sample points x_i and weights w_i. We make the following assumptions:

(1) The existence of ϕ makes the use of high order rules inefficient.

(2) The variance in the derivatives of f makes uniform sampling intervals inefficient

The reasons for making the assumptions is beyond the scope of this paper; the question is how we proceed having made them.

The basic approach is, given some quadrature on $[a_0, a_1]$, to refine it and compare the results. We assume the two values are successive terms in a convergent sequence, and that the error in the sequence is related to the difference of the values. We either accept the refinement, or subdivide the interval and repeat the process on the halves. Once the process terminates we have a series of value pairs (I_j, E_j) such that

$$(I, E) = (\sum_{j=1}^{n} I_j, \sum_{j=1}^{n} E_j) = Int(g, \phi, \lambda, a_0, a_1, \varepsilon)$$

The objective is to minimize n subject to the constraint

$$E \leq \varepsilon.$$

Let P be a pool of unprocessed intervals (that is, intervals for which I and E have not been computed). Then the algorithm will proceed as follows. Select an interval from P; refine the estimate for it; either accept the refinement or split the interval and put the parts back into P for later processing. The body of procedure Int is given abstractly in Form 7.

Initialize(P);
while ¬ Empty(P) do
begin
    I := Refine(Next_interval(P));
    if Acceptable(I) then Accumulate(I)
    else Save(Split(I), P)
end

Form 7

The intervals in P may contain considerable information, partly as an adjunct to making the acceptance decision, and partly to avoid recomputation of previously used values.

Acceptance can come for one of two reasons. Either the difference in estimate between the interval and its refinement is small, implying the actual error is small, or the algorithm is running into difficulty with ϕ. In the former case the actual error will be much less than the required tolerance. The excess is left in an error pool, relaxing the requirements and hence the amount of computation needed, for subsequently processed intervals.

We finally must deal with the characteristics of F. The algorithm Refine generally depends on the number of well-behaved derivatives of the integrand. The selection Next_interval determines the order of interval processing. A FIFO discipline gives a strictly left-to-right depth-first order. A LIFO discipline processes all intervals of a given width before proceeding to any smaller ones. LIFO is better, primarily because the "easy" intervals are done first, leaving extra error tolerance available for "hard" intervals, thus allowing them to pass acceptance with less subdivision. LIFO, on the other hand, uses a great deal more storage than FIFO, hence a compromise is in order: LIFO early, FIFO when the pool is nearly full.

The process continues, but our discussion ceases here. The end of the trail of forms is an algorithm such as Lyness' [2] SQUANK, written in Fortran incorporating the various decisions noted above.

The value of the approach is clarity. Decisions are made and recorded in a formal notation, but long before the intrusion of the limitations of contemporary programming languages confuse us and obscure our thoughts.

2. SYMBOL TABLES

A compiler must associate each occurrence of an identifier with its collected attributes. The attributes may include the name itself, type information, machine address, cross references and so on. The information is held in the symbol table.

An entry is made into the symbol table when an identifier is

171

declared. Attributes are entered as they become available. When an identifier is used the symbol table is interrogated for information needed for translation. If a new scope is entered in the program being translated, declarations within the inner scope control. Upon exit from a scope (e.g. upon encountering the end of a procedure) the entries for the locals are discarded, serving the dual purpose of freeing symbol table space and "uncovering" any previous use of those symbols in outer scopes.

The symbol table module carries out these functions in a compiler. The module is almost totally self contained, being accessed only through a short list of entries and sharing no common data structures with the rest of the compiler.

We are interested in implementing a symbol table module of some generality. We expect it to be used for a variety of popular programming languages (say Algol, Fortran and PL/1). We expect it to be used in a variety of environments (say for student programs and large production programs, and on small computers and large computers). We not only want the module to be reliable and efficient, we want the process of adapting it to a new environment to be reliable and efficient.

The symbol table is, from the viewpoint of the user, the set of access functions. They are briefly described in Table 2.1 .

Our first task is to define the access functions precisely and formally. We use the data structure axioms of Guttag [4].

Each access function that changes the symbol table must be considered to have a (new) symbol table as its value. The inputs to the access function consist of identifiers, attributes, and attribute classes (an attribute class might be "type", an attribute in that class might be "fixed"). The sets forming the domains and ranges of the access functions are described in Table 2.2 . They are used to describe the functionality of the access functions in Table 2.3 . Standard abbreviations for elements of the sets are also given in Table 2.2 . They are used in the axioms in Table 2.4 .

TABLE 2.1: Symbol Table Access Functions

INIT	a function that creates an initial (empty) symbol table
ENTR	a function that creates a new local naming scope in a symbol table
LEAV	a function that discards the most local naming scope from a symbol table
DECL	a function that enters a new identifier into the symbol table having first determined the identifier is not already in the local scope
ATTR	a function that sets an attribute for an identifier having determined that it has been declared in the local scope and not previously received an attribute of this type
RCRD	a function, called by DECL and ATTR, that actually records information in the symbol table
RTRV	a function that retrieves a particular type of attribute from the symbol table for a specified identifier

TABLE 2.2: Domains and Ranges of Symbol Table Access Functions

St	a symbol table
Sts	the set of all symbol tables
Id	an identifier
Ids	the set of all identifiers
Class	an attribute class
Classes	the set of all attribute classes
Attr	an attribute
Attrs	the set of all attributes
Empty	a particular member of Attrs signifying the absence of attribute information

TABLE 2.3: Functionality of Symbol Table Access Functions

INIT:	→ Sts
ENTR:	Sts → Sts
LEAV:	Sts → Sts
DECL:	Sts × Ids → Sts
ATTR:	Sts × Ids × Attrs → Sts
RCRD:	Sts × Ids × Attrs → Sts
RTRV:	Sts × Ids × Classes → Attrs

TABLE 2.4: Symbol Table Axioms

1 LEAV(INIT) = compiler_screened_error

2 LEAV(ENTR(St)) = St

3 LEAV(RCRD(St, Id, Attr)) = LEAV(St)

4 DECL(INIT, Id) = compiler_screened_error

5 DECL(ENTR(St), Id) = RCRD(ENTR(St), Id, Empty)

6 DECL(RCRD(St, Id_1, Attr), Id_2) =
   if Id_1 = Id_2 then duplicate_declaration
   else RCRD(DECL(St, Id_2), Id_1, Attr)

7 ATTR(INIT, Id, Attr) = compiler_screened_error

8 ATTR(ENTR(St), Id, Attr) = undeclared_identifier

9 ATTR(RCRD(St, Id_1, $Attr_1$), Id_2, $Attr_2$) =
   if Id_1 = Id_2 and CLASS($Attr_1$) = CLASS($Attr_2$)
   then duplicate_attribute
   else if Id_1 = Id_2 and $Attr_1$ = Empty
   then RCRD(RCRD(St, Id_1, $Attr_1$), Id_2, $Attr_2$)
   else RCRD(ATTR(St, Id_2, $Attr_2$), Id_1, $Attr_1$)

10 RTRV(INIT, Id, Class) = undeclared_identifier

11 RTRV(ENTR(St), Id, Class) = RTRV(St, Id, Class)

12 RTRV(RCRD(St, Id_1, Attr), Id_2, Class) =
   if Id_1 = Id_2 and CLASS(Attr) = Class then Attr
   else if Id_1 = Id_2 and Attr = Empty
   then undefined_attribute else RTRV(St, Id_2, Class)

The axioms are, in fact, a catalog of things that can happen. Axioms 1,4, and 7 are statements about the behavior of an empty symbol table. A correctly functioning compiler will never allow such a situation to occur since it will (perhaps automatically) generate a block entry for the outermost scope. Axiom 2 states that leaving a block cancels the preceding entry. Axiom 3 states that all of the information in the local scope is discarded upon leaving a block.

Axiom 5 states that we may set an entry in the symbol table once we have determined, via axiom 6, that it is not already there. Axiom 8 notifies us that we cannot set an attribute on an identifier before it is declared. Axiom 9 provides for setting new attributes in the symbol table once it has determined that no previously entered attribute of the same class is already there.

Axioms 10 - 12 provide for the retrieval of attributes from the symbol table. Axiom 11 states that any scope can be accessed on retrieval; contrast it with axiom 5 which terminates the search upon encountering a block entry. Axiom 10 is the limiting case indicating failure to find any information about the identifier. Axiom 12 retrieves the attributes if they are there or signals the fact they are undefined.

The mechanism just defined is very general. It allows arbitrarily many nested scopes, each scope with arbitrarily many identifiers, each identifier with arbitrarily many classes of attributes (actually a stack of stacks of stacks). That is, of course, asking too much in a software engineering sense. The best that can be provided is "variable but limited". In the case of classes of attributes, the number is fixed for most programming languages, hence the module need provide no variability at all in any given implementation. Furthermore, the access functions are symbol-table-valued but a single data structure (the symbol table) represents the before and after values. And, finally, the implementation of the access functions may be optimized for space, or time, or just plain simplicity.

To make the discussion explicit, the Algol program in Table 2.5 will be used as a sample program to be translated.

TABLE 2.5: Sample Program for Translation

---

begin comment an Algol program;
   integer A,B;
   A := 1;
   begin
      integer C,A;
      A := B := C := 2;
      begin
         A := 3;
      end;
      begin
         integer A;
         A := 4;
      end;
      A := 5;
   end;
   A := 6;
end;

From the viewpoint of the symbol table the compilation process is a sequence of access function calls which can be described linguistically by the grammar in Table 2.6 .

TABLE 2.6: Compiler/Symbol Table Communication

---

program = INIT block
block = ENTR actions LEAV
actions = declare | set_attribute | retrieve_attribute | block
declare = DECL Id
set_attribute = ATTR Id Attr
retrieve_attribute = RTRV Id Class

The specific example in Table 2.5 gives the sequence of access function calls in Table 2.7 .

TABLE 2.7: A Test Sequence

INIT   ENTR   DECL   A   DECL   B   ATTR   A   integer   ATTR   B   integer
RTRV   A type   ENTR   DECL   C   DECL   A   ATTR   C   integer   ATTR   A
integer   RTRV   A   type   RTRV   B   type   RTRV C type   ENTR   RTRV
A   type   LEAV   ENTR   DECL   A   ATTR   A   integer   RTRV   A   type
LEAV   RTRV   A   type   LEAV   RTRV   A   type   LEAV

The symbol table module can be tested by itself. A sequence such as that in Table 2.7 is used, together with a minimal driver program. Passing such tests before dealing with the complexity of module integration increases our confidence in the resulting compiler.

The underlying data structure is displayed in Figure 2.1.

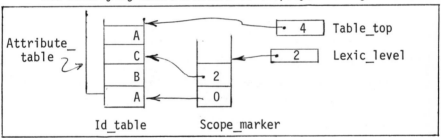

Figure 2.1: Linear Access Method: Symbol Table Configuration

The state of the data structure is that reached after the compiler has finished the first five lines of the program in Table 2.5 . Id_table holds the identifiers A,B,C and A. Scope_ marker signifies the first two are in the outer scope and the rest are local. The variables Table_top and Lexic_level point to the next available cell in their respective tables. Attributes are held in another table but are accessed via the same pointer that locates identifiers in Id_table.

A simple linear search algorithm is given in Table 2.8 . It is beyond the scope of this paper to attempt a proof of

177

equivalence between it and the axioms.

TABLE 2.8: PL/1 Symbol Table Module

INIT:
```
  procedure;
    declare Table_limit fixed static initial (100),
      Table_top fixed,
      Id_table(0:Table_limit) character(32) varying;
    declare Lexic_level_limit fixed static initial (10),
      Lexic_level fixed,
      Scope_marker(0:Lexic_level_limit) fixed;
    declare Index fixed, Sb fixed;
    Lexic_level = 0; Table_top = 0;
    return;
```

ENTR:
```
  entry;
    /* Make sure program is not too deeply nested */
    if Lexic_level = Lexic_level_limit then call ERROR;
    Scope_marker(Lexic_level) = Table_top;
      /* point to first local */
    Lexic_level = Lexic_level + 1; /* increase nesting level */
    return;
```

LEAV:
```
  entry;
    /* compiler checks for extra scope exits */
    Lexic_level = Lexic_level - 1;
    Table_top = Scope_marker(Lexic_level);
    return;
```

DECL
```
  entry(Id);
    declare Id character(32) varying;
```

178

```
        /* first check for duplicate declaration */
        Sb = Scope_marker(Lexic_level - 1);
        Index = Table_top;
        do while (Index > Sb);
            Index = Index - 1;
            if Id = Id_table(Index) then call ERROR;
        end;
        /* check for table overflow*/
        if Table_top = Table_limit then call ERROR;
        /* enter new id */
        Id_table(Table_top) = Id;
        call RCRD(Table_top, Empty);
        Table_top = Table_top +1;
        return;

ATTR:
    entry(Id, Attr);
        declare Attr fixed;
        Sb = Scope_marker(Lexic_level - 1);
        Index = Table_top;
        do while (Index > Sb);
            Index = Index - 1;
            if Id = Id_table(Index) then
            do;
                /* Record attribute */
                call RCRD(Index, Attr);
                return;
            end;
        end;
        call ERROR; /* undeclared identifier */
        return;
```

```
RTRV:
    entry(Id, Class) returns(fixed);
        declare Class fixed;
        Index = Table_top;
        do while (Index > 0);
            Index = Index - 1;
            if Id = Id_table(Index) then
                return(ATTRIBUTE(Index, Class));
        end;
        call ERROR;   /* Undeclared identifier */
        return(0);
    end;
```

If we wish a module with identical behavior but faster (and occupying more memory), we can superimpose a hash access on it without affecting the previous data structure. The extended data structure is shown in Figure 2.2 .

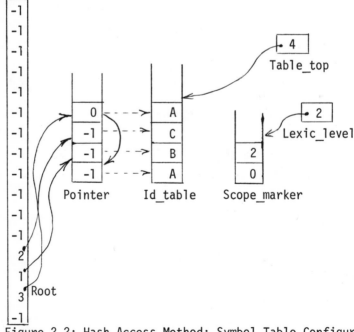

Figure 2.2: Hash Access Method: Symbol Table Configuration

The corresponding module is given in Table 2.9 .

TABLE 2.9: PL/1 Symbol Table Module Using Hash

```
INIT:
    procedure;
        declare Table_limit fixed static initial(100),
            Table_top fixed,
            Id_table(0:Table_limit) character(32) varying;
        declare Lexic_level_limit fixed static initial(10),
            Lexic_level fixed,
            Scope_marker(0:Lexic_level_limit) fixed;
        declare Hash_size fixed static initial(15),
            Root(0 : Hash_size) fixed,
            Pointer(0:Table_limit) fixed;
        declare Index fixed, Sb fixed, K fixed;
        Lexic_level = 0;  Table_top = 0;
        do Index = 0 to Hash_size;
            Root(Index) = -1;
        end;
        return;


ENTR:
    entry;
        /* make sure program is not too deeply nested */
        if Lexic_level = Lexic_level_limit then
            call ERROR;
        Scope_marker(Lexic_level) = Table_top;
        Lexic_level = Lexic_level + 1;
        return;


LEAV:
    entry;
        /* compiler checks for extra scope exits */
        Index = Table_top;
```

```
Lexic_level = Lexic_level - 1;
Table_top = Scope_marker(Lexic_level);
do while (Index > Table_top);
    Index = Index - 1;
    K = HASH(Id_table(Index));
    Root(K) = Pointer(Root(K));
end;
```

DECL:
```
entry(Id);
    declare Id character(32) varying;
    /* first check for duplicate declaration */
    K = HASH(Id);
    Index = Root(K);
    Sb = Scope_marker(Lexic_level - 1);
    do while (Index > = Sb);
        if Id = Id_table(Index) then call ERROR;
        Index = Pointer(Index);
    end;
    /* check for table overflow */
    if Table_top = Table_limit then call ERROR;
    /* enter new id */
    Id_table(Table_top) = Id;
    call RCRD(Table_top, Empty);
    Table_top = Table_top + 1;
    return;
```

ATTR:
```
entry(Id, Attr);
    declare Attr fixed;
    Sb = Scope_marker(Lexic_level - 1);
    Index = Table_top;
    do while (Index > = Sb);
        if Id = Id_table(Index) then
```

```
    do;
        /* record attribute */
        call RCRD(Index, Attr);
        return;
    end;
    Index = Pointer(Index);
end;
call ERROR; /* undeclared identifier */
return;


RTRV:
    entry(Id, Class), returns(fixed);
        declare Class fixed;
        Index = Root(HASH(Id));
        do while (Index ¬ = -1);
            if Id = Id_table(Index) then
                return(ATTRIBUTE(Index, Class));
            Index = Pointer(Index);
        end;
        call ERROR; /* undeclared identifier */
        return(0);
    end;
```

A few comments are in order. We have a formal definition of the symbol table access. Guttag presents a method of refining it into a program. We chose instead to leap to the answers. There are two; neither has been tested; neither has been proven equivalent to the definition. But they can be. Once done (and corrected) the initial goal is met. We have a module which is simple. And with minor changes we have one that is fast. This is achieved by separating the access function from the lookup method and leaving the symbol table structure untouched as we modify the lookup.

3. CUSTOMIZED SOFTWARE

A manufacturer ships 1000 items a month, each containing a
minicomputer. Each customer wants a different program in his.
Even if the manufacturer can do the programming the maintenance
problem becomes eventually insurmountable. It is a problem that
is likely to occur often in the next few years.

We propose to solve the problem by implementing a software
support system that involves a large segment of the corporate
population. Essentially, instead of hiring programmers, we shall
turn the normal everyday activities of others, in sales and field
support, into the equivalent of programming. At the same time we
solve some intercorporate communication problems.

The support system is a powerful (but not necessarily large)
computer. It can be resident within the corporation or a generally accessible time sharing service. In any case it must be
available, via CRT terminal, over normal dial-up telephone service.

Work is initiated by the salesman. For him the terminal is
a sales aid. He establishes contact with the support system and
begins in specification mode. What he sees is a menu-selection
style program which leads the salesman and the customer through
the product definition. Such decisions as sequencing, insertion
of messages, choice of configuration and so on are asked and
answered. Upon completion of the run the support system has a
complete description of the sale stored in its data base.

The menu selection program is prepared by the systems
programming staff. Properly done, it itself is table driven.
That is, a change in the specification mode operation requires
only a change in the tables that drive it.

Having defined a product, the salesman switches to demonstration mode. The customer can then exercise the product via
simulation from the support computer. Such changes as are

necessary can then be entered back in specification mode, and so on until the customer is satisfied.

The salesman then switches to contract mode where a custom tailored document is prepared for signature at the sales site. See Figures 3.1 and 3.2 .

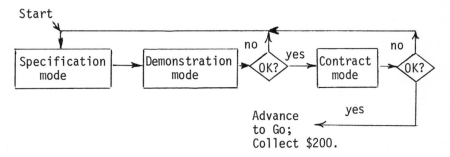

Figure 3.1: Support System in Sales Environment

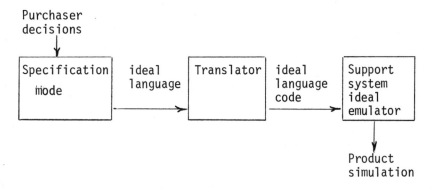

Figure 3.2: Data Flow During the Sales Effort

Since the terminal defines what is to be sold, the salesman never sells non-deliverable products. And he knows immediately when a new feature is available because it appears on the menu.

When the product is ready for shipment the internal program is ready in the data base of the support system. No programmer is needed.

When the product fails in field service, it may be due to

any one of a number of causes, including foreign equipment
attached to the product (e.g. the central computer of the customer). The field maintenance people can dial into the support
system which simulates the product for the foreign equipment and
simulates correctly functioning foreign equipment for the product. If the error is in the internal program of the product, an
updated version can be downline loaded and the customer is back
on the air.

As one might guess, it is a non-trivial task to get such a
system going. We describe an approach that seems feasible below.
Many parts of it have been tested, but there is no complete
system such as this in operation known to the author.

The internal software in the product separates into two
categories: that which is constant for all deliveries and that
which changes under customer demand.   In the former category
are such things as device drivers, memory managers and so on. In
the latter are messages, sequencing of the various product actions and the like. They are separated into two languages. The
former may as well be written in the assembler or, if available,
a high-quality systems language for the mini. The latter, however, are to be written in an invented ideal language for the
application. The ideal language should have high-level primitives (such as OPEN_CASH_DRAWER) but otherwise be low level, even
to the point of being an assembly language.

The customized program is translated into a compact interpretive code to be loaded into the memory of the mini. Among the
constant code for the mini is an emulator for the ideal language
code. Thus the actual operation of the product involves a fetch
of interpretive code, followed by an indexed branch to the
emulated ideal language op-code, and back to the fetch cycle
again. For programs of any real size, the combined emulator and
interpretive code is less consumptive of memory than straight
assembly code for the same functions.

Generally speaking not every customer will want every

service so the building of the constant code is also customized
in that only selected parts are combined for any particular
customer.

If main memory in the product is a critical resource, the
interpretive code is more easily overlaid from a secondary memory
since it can be designed to be relocatable (or even address
insensitive). The hot code can also be overlaid with the usual
precautions.

The interpretive code is not, of course, actually written by
programmers. It is assembled from the salesman's specification
of the product.

The demonstration of the system for the customer during the
sales visit requires another emulator for the ideal language be
written, on the support system. Then it can act like the mini in
driving the terminal. The need to simulate some product actions
makes this emulator somewhat more complex but it is written in
the support system higher level language, reducing the extent of
the problem.

Finally, the systems programmers must prepare the underlying
programs in the mini assembler. For them the host system provides a cross-assembler, a mini emulator and a real-time environment simulator. All mini code is tested on the host. Since the
actions of the product probably depend on real time events, they
must be simulated. Real-time protocols are described by the
programming staff in an event language acceptable to the real-
time event simulator. This subsystem is outlined in Figure 3.3 .

The ultimate disaster, changing the type of minicomputer,
causes little problem. All of the customized code remains the
same. It is only the constant code that need be rewritten (as
well as most of the tools).

In summary, the problem can be attacked by building a
comprehensive set of tools that are designed to enhance the overall ability of the product team to operate and communicate. They
are expensive. But when the amount of programming reaches a

certain level, something like this must be done.

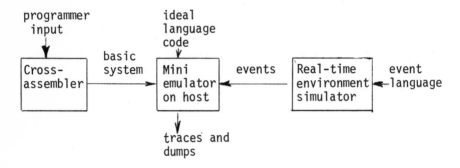

Figure 3.3: Data Flow in Programmer Support System

One might ask exactly where the leverage was obtained. In the first place all development was taken onto a large computer where sophisticated diagnostic tools can be built, thereby increasing the productivity of the programmers. Secondly, the middleman is gone between the customers' needs and the code produced. Thirdly, each problem is matched with a simple language. In contrast we might use a very complex language (like PL/1) for something. Or we might use assembler for everything. Finally, and most important, the inherent structure of the problem is captured in the menu selection. There is variability but it is strictly controlled and, in the final analysis, simple enough to understand. It is from this that our confidence derives.

4. CONCLUSIONS

Three quite different problems were partially solved. The tools used were also very different. Those presented here by no means exhaust the interesting techniques appearing in the literature with increasing frequency.

It brings to mind a plaint of yesteryear. "Why wasn't it specified? And why don't you document it?" We didn't know how.

And we are now beginning to find out.

REFERENCES

[1] Rice, John R., "A Metalgorithm for Adaptive Quadrature," *J. Assoc. Comp. Mach. 22,* 1975, 61-82.

[2] Lyness, J. N., "SQUANK, Algorithm 379," *J. Assoc. Comp. Math. 16,* 1969, 483-495.

[3] McKeeman, W. M., "Symbol Table Access,"in Compiler Construction, An Advanced Course, Lectures Notes in *Computer Science 21,* (F. L. Bauer and J. Eickel,Editors) Springer-Verlag, 1974, 253-301.

[4] Guttag, John V., "The Specification and Application to Programming of Abstract Data Types,"Ph.D. Thesis, University of Toronto, Department of Computer Science (1975).

DESIGN OF LARGE HYDRODYNAMICS CODES

Steven A. Orszag*

Department of Mathematics
Massachusetts Institute of Technology
Cambridge, Massachusetts   02139

ABSTRACT

This paper explains how machine architecture, problem size, and computing algorithms affect the design of hydrodynamics codes. An analysis is given of the design of the KILOBOX code designed for the CDC 7600 to study two-dimensional turbulence, two-layer ocean dynamics, and other problems. KILOBOX typically uses $(1024)^2$ Fourier modes to represent each two-dimensional field. It uses three levels of storage (small core memory, large core memory, and disk) and proper design is critical for efficient use of the computer. Some of the particular design considerations are: (i) buffering schemes between the three storage levels; (ii) memory layout to permit efficient access to needed quantities; (iii) choice of numerical algorithm; (iv) code optimization; and (v) system cost algorithm.

_____*Work supported by the Office of Naval Research under Contract No. N00014-72-C-0355, Task No. NR 066-233.

1. INTRODUCTION

Design of computer codes, like so many other arts, is perhaps best explained by describing one's own personal experiences.
In this paper, the author makes no attempt to discuss the whole
field of numerical hydrodynamics but concentrates on some noteworthy features of problems he has worked on. The problems discussed here all involve in one way or another turbulence and
transition in incompressible fluids.

Before discussing the problems of code design, let us
briefly survey the physics of the problems in order to understand
why their numerical solution is hard. Ideally, one would like to
run numerical calculations of geophysical or laboratory scale
flows with realistic flow parameters. For example, a realistic
study of small-scale turbulence in the ocean may require study
of a flow with root mean square (rms) turbulent velocity v of
100 cm/s, a large eddy size L of 10^4 cm and a small eddy size
ℓ of 1 cm. The Reynolds number of this flow is $R = vL/\nu = 10^8$,
where the kinematic viscosity ν of water is about .01 cm^2/s .

In order to simulate this flow numerically while treating
all dynamically important scales accurately, it is necessary to
resolve the whole range of scales between 1 cm and 10^4 cm so that
at least 10^4 degrees of freedom are required in each of the
three space directions. Consequently, about $(10^4)^3 = 10^{12}$
degrees of freedom (grid point values, Fourier modes, etc.) must
be used at each instant of time to describe the flow field. However, the dynamical problem of fluid motion is an initial value
problem so that to be useful the calculation should proceed for
some dynamically significant time like the large eddy circulation
time which is about $L/v = 100s$. But numerical considerations
(stability and accuracy) limit time steps to about $\ell/v = 10^{-2}s$
so that at least 10^4 time steps must be used to calculate through
one large eddy circulation time. Even if our computer code required only 1 machine cycle per degree of freedom per time step

192

we would then require 10^{16} cycles to complete our calculation. A more realistic estimate is 10^{21} cycles to compute the flow described above. Even with the anticipated computer speed improvements expected in the next decade or so 10^{21} operations is far beyond realistic projections.

The basic problem which led to the outrageous estimate above is the large range of scales in turbulent flows. Turbulence theory (Orszag, 1976) provides estimates for the way that the required resolution scales with Reynolds number. These estimates are given in Table 1.

TABLE NO. 1

Reynolds Number Scaling of Two-Dimensional and Three-Dimensional Homogeneous Turbulence

	Two Dimensions	Three Dimensions
Range of spatial scales	$R^{1/2}$	$R^{3/4}$
Number of operations per run	$R^{3/2}$	R^3
Estimated number of operations at $R = 10^8$	10^{15}	10^{21}

There are still other difficulties involved in numerical calculations of high Reynolds number hydrodynamics. These include:

(i) Boundary layers. A boundary layer is a thin region near a body where the flow changes rapidly. It is obviously necessary to resolve such a region and this requires high resolution near the body. In itself this is not a serious difficulty so long as the boundary layer is laminar (not turbulent); it suffices to use a nonuniform grid or mapping to resolve the boundary

layer. However, boundary layers are a serious problem if they
are turbulent (even if the flow outside the boundary layer is not
turbulent); in this case there are small scale motions streamwise
along the boundary layer and resolution requirements are very
severe and mappings and nonuniform grids do not help much.

(ii) Shocks. Another region of rapid change is a shock
wave in a compressible flow. Problems with complicated shock-
shock or shock-body interactions, while probably tractable, are
still very difficult.

(iii) Boundary conditions. Appropriate boundary conditions,
especially at outflow boundaries where fluid leaves the computational domain, are sometimes unknown.

(iv) Flow geometry. If a complicated body is part of a
flow calculation, finite element methods should be considered.
The complications are great.

(v) Fluid physics. Sometimes even the basic flow equations
are not completely agreed upon. A case in point is two-phase
flow, which is of considerable importance in reactor safety
studies, where some of the most commonly used sets of evolution
equations lead to ill-posed initial-value problems.

(vi) Three space dimensions plus time. In most turbulent
flows, it is not reasonable to approximate the flow by reducing
the number of space dimensions from three to two or one. Basic
features are lost when the dimension is deflated.

By now the reader should be convinced that the turbulence
problem is beyond grasp of foreseeable computers. While this is
partly correct, there are problems that can be solved so long as
the right questions are asked.

In Table 2 we list six representative computer codes for
turbulence and transition studies that we have developed. In
addition to the principal applications, some design characteristics are also given. Notice that all these programs were designed to run on a CDC 7600 computer so they should give an idea
of the flexibility of this machine. In the next section we

analyze the design of one of these codes: KILOBOX, which is the
1024x1024 two-dimensional turbulence code developed in 1975.

TABLE NO. 2

Examples of Turbulence and Transition Codes

Date	Application[1]	Resolution[2]	Total Storage	CPU Time/ time step[3]	Time/ run[3]	Reynolds Number
1971	3-D HIT	32×32×32 FM	400K	3s	10 min	$R_\lambda \sim 40$
1972	2-D HIT	128×128 FM	100K	7s	10 min	$R_\lambda \sim 1000$
1973	3-D SFT	32×32×33 FM,CP	400K	4s	20 min	$R_\lambda \sim 10^4$
1974	3-D FPT	257×33×8 GP,FM,CP	700K	9s	1 hr	$R_x \sim 10^6$
1975	2-D HIT	1024×1024 FM	6M	48s	10-30 hr	$R_\lambda \sim 10^4$
1976	3-D HIT SFT	128×128×128 CP,FM	25M	3 min	20 hr	$R_\lambda \sim 100$

[1] HIT: homogeneous isotropic turbulence; SFT: shear
  flow turbulence; FPT: flat plate transition

[2] GP: grid points; FM: Fourier modes; CP: Chebyshev
  polynomials

[3] CDC7600 computer time

[4] R_λ: microscale Reynolds number; R_x: x-Reynolds number

---

2. DESIGN OF KILOBOX

KILOBOX is a two-dimensional turbulence code that has been
designed to provide information on the following physical

problems:

(i) Inertial range energy spectrum of two-dimensional homogeneous isotropic turbulence. In the so-called enstrophy-cascade
inertial range (see Orszag, 1976), theories predict that the
energy spectrum E(k) is proportional to either k^{-3} (with some
logarithmic corrections) or k^{-4} . Earlier numerical computations with a 128x128 resolution computer code could not distinguish between these theoretical predictions (Herring, Orszag,
Kraichnan & Fox 1974). Some calculations with analytical theories suggested that a 1024x1024 code could resolve these inertial
range questions; this was the original motivation for KILOBOX.

(ii) Backwards-cascade energy-transfer inertial range. It
has been predicted by Kraichnan (1967) that two-dimensional turbulence could support an inertial-range spectrum E(k) $\propto k^{-5/3}$
in which energy transfer is from small eddies to large eddies.
In addition, this backward cascade implies a pile-up of energy
at the lowest wavenumbers. This leads to an intermittent excita-
tion in the largest scale of motion, another feature in need of
understanding. A high resolution computer code (like KILOBOX) is
needed to solve these problems because the backward-cascade range
must terminate at intermediate wavenumbers and enough resolution
must still be available for an enstrophy-cascade and dissipation
range at still higher wavenumbers.

(iii) Subgrid scale modelling of two-dimensional turbulence. KILOBOX can provide controlled tests of subgrid scale
two-dimensional turbulence modelling, which is an essential part
of global circulation models of the atmosphere and ocean.

(iv) Two-layer ocean dynamics. KILOBOX is designed so that
it can be easily modified to run as a two-layer high-resolution
mesoscale ocean model.

(v) Other applications include particle dispersion dynamics
in two-dimensional turbulence, predictability of turbulence,
studies of random surface waves on the ocean, etc.

In our discussion of the design of KILOBOX we shall discuss

the following five problems:

    (i)   Mathematical formulation

    (ii)   Numerical algorithms

    (iii)   Memory management

    (iv)   Code optimization

    (v)   Graphics and output

Mathematical formulation

The equations of motion of two-dimensional incompressible hydrodynamics are

$$\frac{\partial \zeta(x,y,t)}{\partial t} + \frac{\partial(\zeta,\psi)}{\partial(x,y)} = \nu \nabla^2 \zeta(x,y,t) \qquad (1)$$

$$\zeta(x,y,t) = - \nabla^2 \psi(x,y,t) \qquad (2)$$

where ζ is the vorticity and ψ is the streamfunction. The velocity field (u,v) is related to the streamfunction by

$$u = \frac{\partial \psi}{\partial y} \quad , \quad v = - \frac{\partial \psi}{\partial x} \ .$$

In order to simulate homogeneous turbulence, periodic boundary conditions are applied to (1)-(2):

$$\zeta(x \pm 2\pi, y \pm 2\pi, t) = \zeta(x,y,t)$$
$$\psi(x \pm 2\pi, y \pm 2\pi, t) = \psi(x,y,t) \ . \qquad (3)$$

These boundary conditions simulate the absence of real boundaries in such a flow.

The mathematical problem is to solve (1)-(3) as an initial value problem with $\psi(x,y,0)$ or $\zeta(x,y,0)$ specified as a given (random) function of x and y .

Numerical algorithms

The usual procedure to solve partial differential equations like (1)-(3) is to use finite differences. However, we have found it much more efficient and accurate to employ spectral methods in which the basic flow variables are expanded in suitable orthogonal series (see Orszag and Israeli, 1974 for further references and details).

With periodic boundary conditions, it is appropriate to expand in Fourier series:

$$\zeta(x,y,t) = \sum_{k,p} \hat{\zeta}(k,p,t)e^{ikx+ipy}$$
$$\psi(x,y,t) = \sum_{k,p} \hat{\psi}(k,p,t)e^{ikx+ipy} \tag{4}$$

where k, p are integers. If these expansions are substituted into (1)-(2) and coefficients of exp(ikx+ipy) are identified, the results are

$$\frac{\partial\hat{\zeta}}{\partial t}(k,p,t) = N(k,p,t) - \nu(k^2+p^2)\hat{\zeta}(k,p,t) \tag{5}$$

$$\hat{\zeta}(k,p,t) = (k^2+p^2)\hat{\psi}(k,p,t) \tag{6}$$

where the nonlinear term is given by

$$N(k,p,t) = \sum_{k_1,p_1} [k_1 p - kp_1]\hat{\zeta}(k_1,p_1,t) \\ \cdot \hat{\psi}(k-k_1,p-p_1,t) \tag{7}$$

In order to solve (5)-(7) on a computer it is necessary to restrict the infinite range of wavenumbers $-\infty < k < \infty$, $-\infty < p < \infty$ to the finite range $-K < k < K$, $-P < p < P$. In KILOBOX, the cutoffs are typically chosen as $K = P = 512$ so that a total of 1024x1024 Fourier modes are retained in the expansions (4).

The evaluation of the convolution sums in (7) is done efficiently by use of the fast Fourier transform and a discrete form
of the convolution theorem.

KILOBOX is also designed to solve (1)-(3) alternatively
using a pseudospectral (or collocation, see Orszag and Israeli,
1974) method, as opposed to the spectral method (5)-(7). The
advantage of the pseudospectral method is that it is about a factor two more efficient than the spectral method. Pseudospectral
solution of (1)-(3) requires 5 real or conjugate symmetric
Fourier transforms on a 2Kx2P field per time step, while spectral
solution of (5)-(7) requires 10 Fourier transforms per time step.

Time stepping in KILOBOX is done using a fractional step
method in which the nonlinear terms are included using a leapfrog
time step and the viscous terms are included using a Crank-
Nicolson implicit time step. If the rms turbulent velocity of
the flow is v , then it is our experience that the scheme is
stable provided that the time step Δt satisfies

$$\Delta t < \frac{1}{2Kv}$$

where we assume $K = P$. Technically, the stability limit is
$\Delta t < 1/(kv_{max})$ where v_{max} is the largest velocity in the field
but $1/(2Kv)$ seems to work well in practice.

Memory management

KILOBOX normally runs on the CDC 7600 computer at the
National Center for Atmospheric Research in Boulder, Colorado.
This machine has available to the user approximately 54000 words
of fast small core memory (SCM), 460000 words of slower large
core memory (LCM), and very large, very slow disks.

System charges are proportional to

$$C = (CPU + \frac{1}{3} PPU) \times (10 + \frac{SCM}{4096} + \frac{LCM}{32768})$$

where CPU is the central processor time, PPU is the peripheral
processor time, SCM is the required small-core memory, and LCM
is the required large-core memory.

KILOBOX requires enormous amounts of storage because each
dynamical field involves over 10^6 separate data at each time step
when K = P = 512 . It turns out that the most efficient way to
solve the problem (lowest 'cost' C) is to minimize SCM, minimize
LCM and store nearly all variables on disk, thereby increasing
PPU so that CPU << PPU . While this is cheapest in terms of C ,
it is also a disastrous use of the computer resource (which is
supported by the National Science Foundation so C is not real
dollars). With this scheme, an hour of real computation may tie
up the computer for up to 8 hours if no other user was available
to compute in a multiprogrammed mode. It is only slightly more
costly in terms of C to write an efficient code that balances
the use of all the available resources: CPU, PPU, SCM, LCM, and
disk. With this kind of code PPU $\doteq$ 1.9 CPU but since two
peripheral units can be engaged at once, the real computing time
is essentially all compute (CPU) time rather than input-output
(PPU) time.

The idea is to use disk for temporary storage of complete
dynamical fields, LCM for storage of partial fields, and SCM for
work areas. Transfers between LCM and disk are done asynchro-
nously while the CPU is engaged in other computations so that
about 93% of all disk transfers are fully covered by other computer operations. Transfers between LCM and SCM are done very
efficiently so long as blocks of words are transferred; typical
transfers between LCM and SCM in KILOBOX involve at least 128
words. The total time spent on data transfers between LCM and
SCM is about 1% of the total computer time.

The data stored on disk must be accessed in several different ways. Sometimes it must be accessed as a function of the
x-coordinate, sometimes as a function of the y-coordinate. In
order to facilitate this kind of array access we made a

preliminary study of several kinds of blocking arrangements. By experimentation with the disks we discovered that disk access and transfer efficiency is very much degraded when block sizes are smaller than about 10,000 words long. In order to keep typical block sizes at least this long, we chose a blocking scheme that changes as the calculation proceeds. In contrast to our earlier codes (see Table 2) that used a fixed blocking arrangement, we found that we could decrease PPU times by about 20% by implementing this variable blocking procedure.

One further complication with the disk access and blocking procedure is the data layout. The Fourier components $\hat{\zeta}(k,p)$ or $\hat{\psi}(k,p)$ in (4) must satisfy constraints so that the physical space fields $\zeta(x,y)$ and $\psi(x,y)$ are real:

$$\hat{\zeta}(k,p) = \hat{\zeta}(-k,-p)^*$$
$$\hat{\psi}(k,p) = \hat{\psi}(-k,-p)^*$$

(8)

In addition, for technical programming reasons, it is convenient to store the arrays in the modified order

$$\hat{\hat{\zeta}}(k,p) = \begin{cases} \hat{\zeta}(k,p-P) & 0 \leq k < K \\ \hat{\zeta}(k-2K,p-P) & K \leq k < 2K \end{cases}$$

This layout is shown schematically in Fig. 1 in which the effect of the reality constraints is indicated. In Fig. 2 we indicate how the independent variables A-I are stored in KILOBOX; notice that the memory layout in Fig. 2 has only half the number of degrees of freedom as that in Fig. 1.

Code optimization

The basic dynamical and data management parts of KILOBOX were first written in FORTRAN. After debugging this code, it was

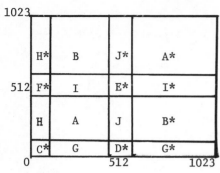

FIGURE 1: Schematic diagram of storage locations in the arrays $\hat{\zeta}(k,p)$ and $\hat{\psi}(k,p)$. The reality constraints (8) are indicated.

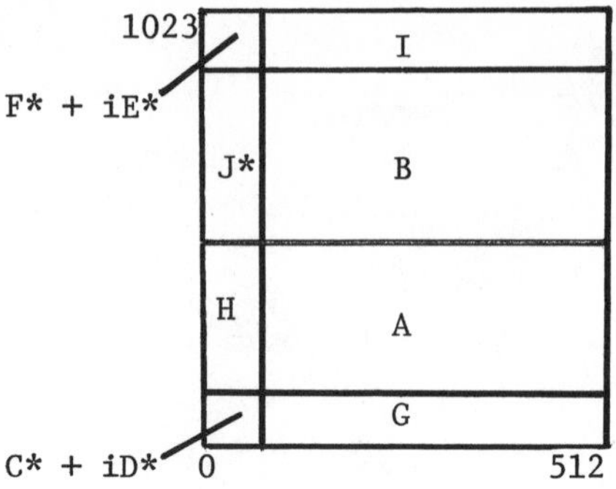

FIGURE 2: Schematic diagram of storage locations actually used for the independent variables in the arrays $\hat{\zeta}(k,p)$ and $\hat{\psi}(k,p)$. The reality constraints (8) are used to expand the array depicted in this Figure to the one depicted in Figure 1.

analyzed to determine which loops should be optimized in assembly language. The results of this optimization were quite striking, with speed improvements of a factor 3 or more being typical.

The fast Fourier transforms used to implement the spectral and pseudospectral equations have all been optimized for the 7600. A complex 1024-point Fourier transform requires about 7ms using this assembly language program. Overall, Fourier transforms alone require about 37s per time step in the 1024x1024 KILOBOX code versus a total time of about 49s per time step.

Some running times of KILOBOX are given in Table 3. The 1024x1024 KILOBOX requires about 30,000 words of SCM, 380,000 words of LCM, and 6,000,000 words of disk memory.

Graphics and output

One major difficulty with KILOBOX is extracting information. Since each dynamical field involves over 10^6 data points when K = P = 512 , a long tape is filled by data from just two time steps! For this reason, most data reduction is done on line with

TABLE NO. 3

Running times for KILOBOX (per time step)

Code[1]	CPU[2]	PPU[3]
PS	512×512	12s	19s
PS	1024×1024	49s	87s
S	512×512	26s	36s
S	1024×1024	102s	173s

[1] PS: Pseudospectral; S: spectral code
[2] CDC7600 processor time
[3] Peripheral time based on CDC819 disks.

only output at selected time steps (about once every 100 time steps) stored on permanent files.

Graphic output is another problem because of the huge amounts of data involved. In order to plot flow characteristics efficiently it is necessary to smooth the field and use an effective resolution of about 128x128. The programs to do this also run on-line and graphical output accompanies the computer runs.

Applications

To date, KILOBOX has only been applied to the study of inertial range spectra. Some important results that have been obtained are:

(i) Observation of departures from a k^{-4} inertial range spectrum in the direction of a k^{-3} spectrum.

(ii) Observation of a strong Reynolds number effect on enstrophy transfer as indicated by a Reynolds number effect on the skewness factor.

(iii) Observation of disagreements between the test-field model analytical theory of turbulence and the numerical simulations.

These results and others will be reported in detail elsewhere (Herring and Orszag, 1976).

The author would like to thank Mr. Earl Cohen (MIT '78) for

his careful programming of KILOBOX and his effective implementation of the complicated data management schemes involved. The computations with KILOBOX have been performed at the National Center for Atmospheric Research which is supported by the National Science Foundation.

REFERENCES

Herring, J. R., Orszag, S. A., Kraichnan, R. H., and Fox, D. G. 1974. Decay of two-dimensional homogeneous turbulence, *J. Fluid Mech. 66*, 417-444.

Herring, J. R. and Orszag, S. A., 1976. To be published.

Kraichnan, R. H. 1967. Inertial ranges in two-dimensional turbulence, *Phys. Fluids, 10*, 1417-1423.

Orszag, S. A. 1976. Lectures on the Statistical Theory of Turbulence, in Fluid Dynamics - Dynamiques des Fluides, ed. R. Ballan and J.-L. Peube, Gordon & Breach, London.

Orszag, S. A. and Israeli, M. 1974. Numerical simulation of viscous incompressible flows, *Ann. Rev. Fluid Mech. 6*, 281-318.

SOFTWARE TOOLS FOR COMPUTER GRAPHICS

R.L. Phillips
Computer, Information, & Control Engineering Program
and
Department of Aerospace Engineering
The University of Michigan, Ann Arbor, Michigan

ABSTRACT

Ten years of extensive research in computer graphics has
produced a collection of basic algorithms and procedures whose
utility spans many disciplines; they can be regarded as tools.
These tools are described in terms of their fundamental aspects,
implementations, applications, and availability. Programs which
are discussed include basic data plotting, curve smoothing,
contour line production, and manipulation of general 3-dimensional
objects. As an aid to potential users of these tools, particular
attention is given to discussing their availability and, where
applicable, their cost.

1. INTRODUCTION

Direct computer-produced graphical output, once considered a
luxury, is becoming relatively commonplace. The availability of
low cost plotters and display terminals is largely responsible
for the trend. Increased usage of computer graphics has given
rise to a need for application-oriented, non-research, graphical
software. It is the goal of this paper to point out and discuss
such software. The hope is that duplication of effort can be
avoided and that the use of non-general, low quality graphic software will be discouraged.

The software to be described here is of such generality,
widespread utility and ready availability so as to be classified
as a tool — a tool to be employed to the user's advantage and not
encumber him in his work. The paper, then, is a survey of sorts,
but a rather limited one. We shall not discuss any software in
the research stages, nor any software that is not readily available. Moreover, since device and system independence are also
valued attributes, vendor supplied packages, no matter how good,

will not be discussed. In what follows we shall discuss basic
line drawing packages, both for two and three dimensions, and
basic data presentation techniques, again for two and three
dimensions. Then certain data processing and enhancement methods
will be described, e.g. clipping and shading.

2. GRAPHICAL OUTPUT DEVICES

Our goal is to describe software whose operation does not
depend upon the device eventually used for graphic output. This
goal can almost, but not completely, be reached because at some
level the description of a point or a vector must be expressed in
a form compatible with the hardware. This is true whether we are
dealing with a sophisticated display terminal or a rudimentary
incremental plotter. For the former, a coordinate must be
expressed in the hardware coordinate system (regardless of the
system the user perceives) and then mapped into a series of characters which are transmitted to the terminal. This process is
usually straightforward, requiring a small amount of software
that can be produced by a non-expert programmer.

For a plotter, where the pen can move only incrementally and
along prescribed directions, the user-to-hardware mapping may be
slightly more complex. This is because a vector of arbitrary
position and orientation must be optimally mapped into the plotter
mode of operation. There are some excellent references on this
subject, e.g. (1) and (2).

It must be made clear that the problems of computer system
independence are quite distinct from those of output device independence. The former are operating system-imposed or deal with
data representation in the computer. We shall avoid discussing
all packages which limit portability because of system considerations.

3. BASIC GRAPHIC PACKAGES

3.1 Two Dimensional Packages

Just one level up from the device dependent interface is the
basic package of line drawing routines. Complete device

206

independence is easy to achieve at this level and there are
several packages available that do it well. Such a package provides the user with the fundamental move-draw capability, or for
those who are plotter oriented, the pen-up, pen-down primitives.
Packages at this level should transparently perform the mapping
from user to hardware coordinates; the user should only need to
supply information on data extrema. A method for handling textual
output, more convenient than that provided by, say, FORTRAN,
should be part of such a package. Finally, for those devices
that can support it, the package should provide a way of handling
graphic input, i.e. from a tablet or light pen. Packages in this
category may provide more capabilities, but the above are an
absolute minimum.

There are five packages known to the author that provide at
least these services, in most cases more. Three of them, however,
GINO-F (3), TCS (4), and DISSPLA (5) are program products and are
available for a not inconsiderable fee. GINO-F and DISSPLA carry
an initial investment of about $20,000 and since our goal is to
discuss graphics software for _everyman_, we will exclude these
packages from further discussion. TCS is not expensive ($500)
but it is tightly bound, both in concept and implementation, to
the Tektronix line of display terminals.

That leaves GCS (Graphic Compatability System) (6), which
was originally developed at West Point, and CKLIB (7), a system
from The University of Michigan. Both of these packages are
transportable, are well documented, and are available for a nominal handling charge. GCS offers many more capabilities than the
minimum set described above while CKLIB is a true low level
graphics package, which was designed with the expectation that
non-basic tasks would be carried out at a higher level.

3.2 Packages with Three-Dimensional Capability

Many packages do not make a significant distinction between
two and three dimensional graphics; the former is merely regarded
as a degenerate case of the latter. Indeed, a general

207

transformation matrix can be established which handles three
dimensions as easily as two. From a practical standpoint, however, a general three-dimensional package often forces the user
who works only in two dimensions to supply superfluous arguments
to subroutines and observe other coding conventions that simply
make extra work for him. Thus, one can make a case for relegat-
ing three dimensional operations to a separate package, which then
passes the planar projection of the desired image to a two-
dimensional package. This is the approach taken by CKLIB (7),
where a companion package MGLIB (8) is used for three dimensional
operations independently of any device or package. MGLIB even
has a rudimentary hidden line processing capability. GCS (6) also
offers three-dimensional operations but as an integral part of
the system. A system designed primarily for three dimensional
operations is ARCH-GRAPHICS (9). It was intended for use in
architectural design, but it is a true 3D package and offers
hidden line processing. It is available for a handling charge.

4.   DATA PRESENTATION (2-Dimensional)

4.1 Overview

One of the most useful applications of computer graphics is
data presentation, or graphing of data on an axis system. The
two dimensional graph is the most common qualitative and quantitative method of representing relations among data. Several
software tools have been developed to facilitate the data presentation process, ranging from automatic axis scale determination to passing smooth curves through the data points.

4.2 Automatic Scale Generation

If we impose the reasonable restriction that the scale to be
determined is "nice" or readable, the process of automatic scale
selection is not at all trivial. A scale obtained by dividing
the span of a variable by the corresponding axis length will
almost never satisfy this restriction. "Nice" scale intervals
will never have values like 0.125 or 1.1 but rather will be more
usable values like 0.1 or 2.0. Even where a "nice" interval of,

say 5, is used, corresponding axis labels like –1, 4, 9, etc., would not qualify as a readable scale. Tastes may differ on readability but there are some fundamental good practices that should be followed in scale selection.

Several algorithms have been published for automatic production of readable scales. They all produce acceptable results and we shall describe only one in some detail, the algorithm due to Lewart (10). The rules are simple — the scale intervals must be the product of an integer power of ten and one of a set of "nice" coefficients. Certainly this set should consist of at least 1, 2, and 5 but individual taste may allow perhaps 4 and 8 to be included. The next requirement is that axis labels must be integer multiples of the scale intervals. These requirements result in an axis whose extremes will embrace the data it represents. When the algorithm is applied to each axis the resulting graph is "efficient" — the data come as close as possible to filling the available plotting area. Figure 1 shows the results of applying this algorithm to a situation where a data zoom is performed on

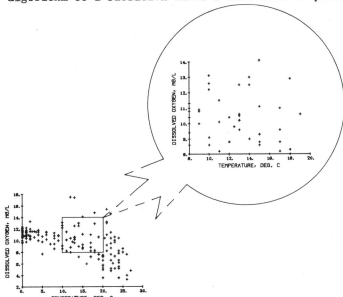

Figure 1.   Automatic Scale Generation.

the original graph. The algorithm, being general, can adapt to any situation. Comparable algorithms are described in (11) and (12).

4.3 Labelling with Software Characters

A common goal in the preparation of computer-produced data representations is to make them report-ready, i.e. no subsequent draftsman work should be required. If this goal is to be attained all text that appears on the graph should be of high quality. The usual stick figure software characters usually will not suffice for this; something more elegant is desired. The nonpareil of all software character fonts are those developed by Hershey (13). Complete font digitizations as well as several sophisticated typographic subroutines are available for the cost of mailing a tape. A sample of textual output using Hershey's fonts is shown in Fig. 2; nothing more need be said.

4.4 Curve Fitting

We shall make a distinction now between curve fitting, where one attempts to pass a smooth curve through all data points, and curve smoothing, where a smooth curve is passed through a neighborhood of all points according to some least squares criterion. The latter process is useful where the data is statistical or imprecisely known; this will be discussed in Section 4.5.

In a case where data are precisely known and no smoothing is required, one often wishes to join the data points with a continuous curve. The process is trivial, of course, if many intermediate data points can be calculated so that joining them by a straight line produces a sufficiently smooth curve. This is often not feasible however. It may be that the data are derived from an expensive computation, as in the solution of a set of nonlinear partial differential equations, or the original computational scheme is not available, such as data obtained from a table of thermophysical properties.

Without benefit of prior experience, one is tempted to try to produce a smooth curve by using either a global high order polynomial fit to all data points or to produce intermediate points by second or higher order interpolation. Neither approach is ever very successful; unwanted oscillations usually result. An excellent overview of these problems is found in Akima's paper (14) where he proposes a new scheme for curve fitting. His contribution was to devise a new way of locally computing slopes at each data point and using these slopes to construct a series of cubic

Invitation	COMMUNICATION	*Publication*
ECONOMY	*VERSATILITY*	**Quality**
CARTOGRAPHY	Standardization	TYPOGRAPHY
Γραμμα	Συμβολον	Αριθμος
Графика	СЛОЖНОСТЬ	Фонетика
Rotation	EXTENSION CONDENSATION	ROTATION
Syllabary	ΛΕΞΙΚΟΝ	Alphabet
Art	書道	Music
Meteorology	Wissenschaft	Astronomy
CHEMISTRY	Electronics	MATHEMATICS

Figure 2. Hershey's Software Character Fonts.

polynomials, continuous at each join. The program that implements this algorithm appears in (15). The author has not been
able to find a situation where Akima's method fails. It is inexpensive as well as accurate. Figure 3 demonstrates its
capabilities.

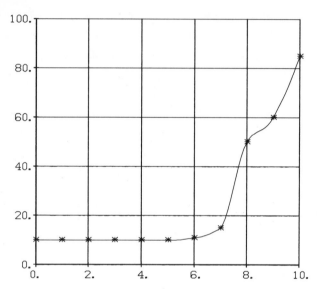

Figure 3.   Curve Fitting with Akima's Method.

In some instances Akima's method produces a curve of greater
curvature than may be desired, especially where the original data
is sparse. In this case one should consider the tension splines
of Cline (16). Cline develops a rigorous theory for these curves
but pragmatically we can imagine them to be flexible wires which
are passed through a series of eyelets (the data points) and made
as taut as one wishes by pulling on either end. The amount of
tension is under control of the user, which is at the same time
an advantage and drawback of the approach. It is not clear
a priori what value of tension is appropriate. Figure 4 shows
Cline's method using different amounts of tension on the same set
of data.

212

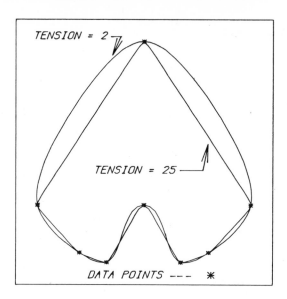

Figure 4. Application of Cline's Tension Splines.

4.5 Curve Smoothing

For data that is imprecisely known or statistical in nature
a curve fitting approach as described above would be inappropri-
ate. Rather, we wish to obtain some smooth, mean curve that
passes through the neighborhood of the data according to some
least squares criterion. Often, the curve obtained is to be
used for further computation such as differentiation or interpolation so it is important to perform the smoothing accurately.
Variations that are statistically significant must be accounted
for; thus, the method must be capable of recognizing trends.
There are, by the way, many nonlinear regression techniques that
have been developed in the statistical literature (17), (18) that
treat this problem, but to use them one must usually make some
assumptions about the functional form of the data. The method of
smoothing splines, however, requires no such assumptions and it
is this technique we discuss. Here a series of spline curves
are computed which join continuously at knots. Knots may or may
not coincide with data points; the number of them and their
position are selected by the program so as to produce a best fit,

213

subject to a least squares constraint. The user can supply
weighting factors to the original data so that outliers can be
eliminated from the smoothing process.

Two smoothing spline algorithms have been published in the
literature. The method of Powell (19) requires somewhat more
user judgment than one would like but seems to produce good results. Lyche and Schumaker (20) have described a method that is
based upon local procedures, but it is published in Algol and
involves a recursive procedure. Thus, the program cannot be
easily transliterated into FORTRAN. Results typical of Powell's
algorithms are shown in Fig. 5. Details on a third smoothing

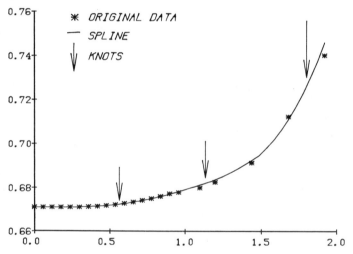

Figure 5. Application of Powell's Smoothing Splines.

spline algorithm have not been published but the routine that
implements it is available from Kahaner (21). This routine is
noteworthy because it allows the user to apply certain boundary
conditions to the resulting smooth curve. The other algorithms
do not allow this, a fact which may sometimes prove objectionable.

5.   DATA PRESENTATION (3 Dimensional)

5.1   Overview

Often one wishes to display bivariate data in the form of
a surface, a projection of the three dimensional representation

of the data. While this representation is seldom of any quantitative use it can provide valuable insight into the behavior of
complex datasets. Such a representation is shown in Fig. 6 where
the transfer function of an underwater sound signal is represented (22). The steps required to obtain a plot such as this
can be difficult, depending upon the original form of the data.
All possibilities will be discussed below.

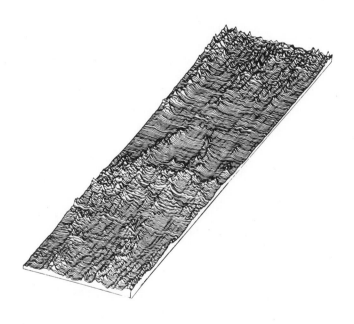

Figure 6. Representation of a Complex Dataset as a
Three-Dimensional Surface.

5.2   Interpolation on a Regular Grid

We are imagining a dataset, functional or tabular, Z(X,Y),
where Z is some altitude or third dimension associated with every
coordinate pair X,Y. If the data happen to have been derived on

a regular lattice, that is,Z is known at all points on a specified X-Y array, intermediate points can be obtained fairly
easily. It is not even necessary that the lattice spacing be
the same in the X and Y directions; it simply must be regular.
The production of intermediate points with the aim of plotting a
smooth surface can be approached as a simple bivariate interpolation problem. Unless the function Z(X,Y) is very benign, however,
straightforward interpolation schemes produce unreal values in
the vicinity of strong local variations. The most successful and
generally applicable algorithm for regular grid interpolation is
due to Akima (23). The method is, in fact, the bivariate analog
of the successful univariate scheme described in (15). The program has a simple interpolation entry point for deriving values
from a bivariate table, and a smooth surface mode, where a dense
array of interpolated points are returned for subsequent plotting.
The author has used these routines in many situations, always
with good results.

5.3 Interpolation from Scattered Observations

A more realistic case than that of Section 5.2 is where the
dataset consists of a table of Z values known only at irregular
and arbitrarily spaced X-Y coordinates. Most spatially distributed geographic data is in this category, as is experimentally-
derived bivariate data. The process of interpolating from
scattered observations to produce a regular grid is much more
challenging than the corresponding problem for regular data; over
100 papers have been published on the subject over the last 20
years. The problem stems from choosing an interpolation function that will not bias the data thus derived. Two interesting
and successful solutions to this problem have recently appeared.
One is due to Akima (24), who we have referenced twice already.
He again extends his "local procedure" scheme, to handle the
case of irregularly spaced initial data. The results are in
excellent agreement with test data presented in his paper.

Tobler (25) has recently produced another approach to this problem, which amounts to an iterative solution of the biharmonic equation in the vicinity of each data point. His program produces results equal to those of Akima, using the same data.

5.4   Surface Plotting

Once the dataset has been regularized, one can proceed to produce a plot of the surface it describes. Any method that is to be acceptable for our purposes must satisfy three criteria:

a)   user-specified perspective projections of the surface must be obtainable,

b)   hidden lines, e.g. the back of the surface, must be eliminated,

c)   one should be able to display the surface as viewed from any orientation, including from below.

There are dozens of surface plotting packages but only a few satisfy all these criteria. One that does is due to Williamson (26). It is acceptable in all three of the above respects but it might be criticized for its lack of generality. It is very much plotter oriented, expressing size variables in terms of inches rather than abstract user units. Another system which is acceptable in all respects was developed by Wright (27) and forms part of the impressive NCAR graphics package (28). Wright's program has many options for representing a surface, including cross-hatching and the production of stereo pairs. Figure 7 is an example of a surface produced by Wright's program.

5.5   Contour Plotting

Another method of representing bivariate data is by plotting contour lines, the locus of all points in the X-Y plane having equal Z-values or altitudes. Here the user specifies a set of Z values and the two dimensional grid (regular, of course) is searched for locations where this value exists. The points found are joined by straight lines, or perhaps curve fitting is applied to produce smoother contours. The NCAR library (29) contains several contour plotting routines, which produce plots

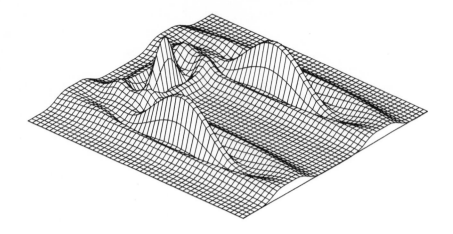

*Figure 7. Three-Dimensional Representation of a
Mathematical Function.*

with varying degrees of sophistication. An example of a plot with smooth contours, different line textures, and automatically placed labels is shown in Fig. 8.

Cederquist (30) has implemented a more modest contour package than NCAR's, but it is noteworthy for its efficiency, generality of application to any plotting device (it plots on a virtual device), and transportability to most operating systems.

6.   DATA PROCESSING AND ENHANCEMENT

6.1   Shading and Cross-Hatching

It is often the case that one wishes to automatically shade or cross-hatch a general two-dimensional polygon. This capability is frequently required for architectural applications, engineering drawings, and thematic cartography. The task is, given an n-sided simply connected polygon with no restrictions on concavity or convexity, find the intersection of a family of shading lines with the boundary of the polygon. The lines are then drawn with the proper angle and spacing. For cross-hatching this process is repeated for a different orientation, and perhaps spacing. A general shading routine should also permit variable spacing between shading lines so that arbitrary and unusual

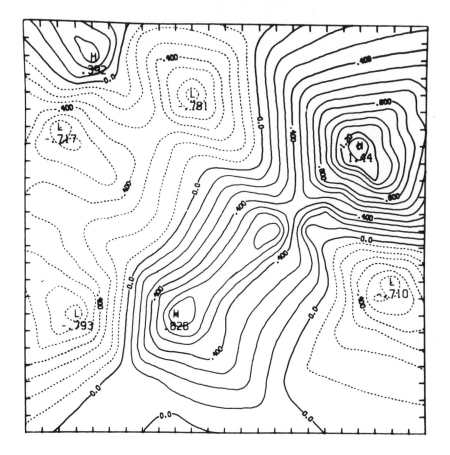

*Figure 8.   Contour Plot with Contours Smoothed by
Tension Splines.*

patterns can be obtained. Finally, it is desirable to be able to
shade a multiply connected region by specifying invisible, coin-
cident cut points that join inner and outer boundaries of a
polygon.

All of these desirable properties are displayed in Fig. 9,
which was produced by an algorithm originally suggested by
Dwyer (31) and implemented by Phillips (32). The algorithm uses
vector algebra for the computation of shading line intersections,
an operation that is simulated in (32) by the complex arithmetic
features of FORTRAN. A more elaborate example of shading is
shown in Fig. 10, a thematic map showing the location of water

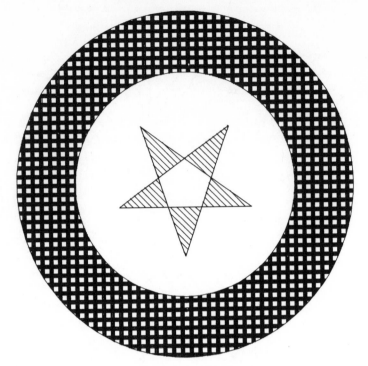

Figure 9.   Shading of Compound Polygons.

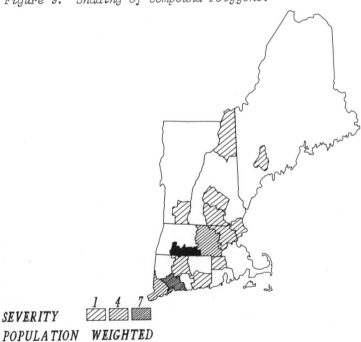

SEVERITY

POPULATION   WEIGHTED

Figure 10.   Use of Shading to Depict Pollution Patterns.

polluting industries in New England. Another shading program has been developed by Ison (33) which is capable of complex patterns such as bricks, soil patterns, etc. This package, however, seems unnecessarily oriented toward the digital plotter as an output device.

6.2 Windowing and Shielding

The process of methodically preventing some part of a graphical display from being plotted is known as clipping. This is often done when the user narrows his field of view in his coordinate space, e.g. zooming in for more detail, and the part of the picture falling outside that area is not to be seen. The boundaries of the narrowed field of view is called a viewport and can generally be formed by any polygon. Usually, however, the viewport is simply a rectangle, making the process of clipping straightforward (34), (35). The most general case involves any simply connected polygon, concave or convex. Moreover, the term window implies that the portion of a picture inside the viewport is to be seen, while the viewport acts as a shield if the picture outside it is to be visible. Behler and Zajac (36) have published an algorithm for treating this general case. The problem differs from the one of general shading in that it does not deal with a family of lines having common characteristics; here every line is a special case. An example of polygonal windowing is shown in Fig. 11. There the polygon is the lower peninsula of Michigan consisting of 370 points, which windows contour lines that have been computed on a rectangular grid that is much larger than the polygon. CKLIB (7) also contains a polygonal clipping routine, which uses complex arithmetic to solve the intersection problems.

6.3 Data Generalization or Caricaturization

It is often the case that a dataset that is to be graphically displayed is unnecessarily dense or detailed for the display device, or for the data transmission speed that is available. This situation occurs when dealing with cartographic data and for

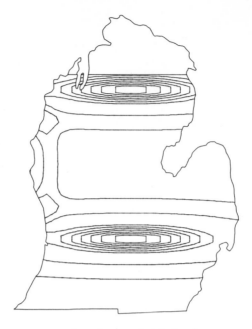

Figure 11.   General Polygonal Windowing.

data derived experimentally from seismographics, EKGs, etc. We
would like to be able to thin such datasets, but in a special
way—distinguishing features must be preserved. Thus, simple,
"every nth point" algorithms will usually fail, and one must look
for something better. Two such algorithms have been published in
recent years (37), (38).   They both involve passing a "tolerance
envelope" through the dataset, which determines how much thinning
can be tolerated. The greater the tolerance the more the
thinned dataset becomes a caricature of the original data. Data
generalization is useful not only for display efficiency but
also for producing a new dataset that is to be further used in
other graphical operations. For example, the polygonal windowing shown in Fig. 11 would have been less expensive, and probably
looked just as good, if the number of points in the Michigan outline had been reduced by 50%. Figure 12 shows varying amounts of
thinning applied to the Michigan outline using the method of (38).

Notice that distinguishing features are preserved, even for extreme thinning.

7. SUMMARY

A reader may find fault with this limited survey for having omitted several of his favorite graphics routines; this is inevitable. I have endeavored to discuss all packages of which I am aware (one could do no more) and with the important stipulations that the software is of proven utility, it can easily be installed on most machines, it is available (from the sources referenced), and the cost, if any, is nominal. Naturally, the author welcomes any revelations of other software that satisfies these constraints.

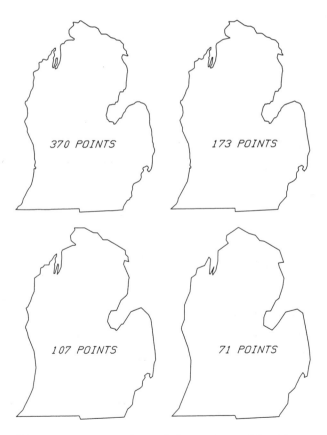

Figure 12. Examples of Data Generalization

REFERENCES

1. Stockton, F.G., Algorithm 162, "XYMOVE PLOTTING," *Comm. ACM, 6,* 161, April 1963.

2. McConalogue, D.J., Algorithm 66, "An Automatic French-Curve Procedure for use with an Incremental Plotter," *The Computer Journal, 14,* 207-209, 1971.

3. GINO-F User's Manual, Computer Aided Design Centre, Cambridge, England, 1972.

4. Terminal Control System User's Manual, Doc. No. 062-1474-00, Tektronix, Inc., Beaverton, Ore., 1975.

5. DISSPLA, Beginners/Intermediate Manual, Integrated Software Systems Corporation, San Diego, Cal., 1970.

6. Graphics Compatibility System (GCS) Programmer's Reference Manual, U.S. Military Academy, West Point, N.Y., 1974.

7. CKLIB Reference Manual, The University of Michigan, Ann Arbor, Mich., 1975 (contact R.L. Phillips, Dept. of Aerospace Engineering).

8. MGI User's Guide, The University of Michigan, Ann Arbor, Mich., 1972 (contact R.L. Phillips, Dept. of Aerospace Engineering).

9. ARCH:GRAPHICS, Architectural Computer Graphics System, Architectural Research Laboratory, The University of Michigan, Ann Arbor, Mich., 1975 (contact H. Borkin, College of Architecture and Urban Planning).

10. Lewart, C.R., Algorithm 463, "Algorithms SCALE1, SCALE2, and SCALE3 for Determination of Scales on Computer Generated Plots," *Comm. Acm, 16,* 639-640, October 1973.

11. Thayer, R.P. and Storer, R.F., Algorithm AS21, "Scale Selection for Computer Plots," *Applied Statistics, 18,* 206-208, 1969.

12. Herro, J.J., Program 00546B, "Optimum Scale for a Graph," HP-65 User's Library, Hewlett-Packard Co., Cupertino, Cal., 1974.

13. Hershey, A.V., "FORTRAN IV Programming for Cartography and Typography," NWL Technical Report TR-2339, U.S. Naval Weapons Laboratory, Dahlgren, Va., Sept. 1969.

14. Akima, H., "A New Method of Interpolation and Smooth Curve Fitting Based Upon Local Procedures," *J. ACM, 17,* 589-602, October 1970.

15. Akima, H., Algorithm 433, "Interpolation and Smooth Curve Fitting Based on Local Procedures," *Comm. ACM, 15,* 914-918, October 1972.

16. Cline, A.K., "Scalar- and Planar-Valued Curve Fitting Using Splines under Tension," and Algorithm 476, "Six Subprograms for Curve Fitting Using Splines Under Tension," *Comm ACM, 17,* 218-223, April 1974.

17. Draper, N. and Smith, H., *Applied Regression Analysis,* Wiley, New York, 1966.

18. Cuthbert, D. and Wood, F.S., *Fitting Equations to Data,* Wiley-Interscience, New York, 1971.

19. Powell, M.J.D., Subroutine VC03A, Harwell Subroutine Library, Atomic Energy Research Establishment, Harwell, Berkshire, England, 1967.

20. Lyche, T. and Schumaker, L.L., Algorithm 480, "Procedures for Computing Smoothing and Interpolating Natural Splines," *Comm. ACM, 17,* 463-467, August 1974.

21. Kahaner, D., Program ISPLIN, Los Alamos Scientific Laboratory, Los Alamos, N.M., 1975.

22. Cederquist, G.N., "The Use of Computer-Generated Pictures to Extract Information from Underwater Acoustic Transfer Function Data," Ph.D. Dissertation, The University of Michigan, 1975.

23. Akima, H., Algorithm 474, "Bivariate Interpolation and Smooth Surface Fitting Based on Local Procedures," *Comm. ACM, 17,* 26-27, January 1974.

24. Akima, H., "A Method of Bivariate Interpolation and Smooth Surface Fitting for Values Given at Irregularly Distributed Points," OT Report 75-70, U.S. Dept. of Commerce/Office of Telecommunications, Boulder, Colo., 1975.

25. Tobler, W., "Tuning an Interpolated Lattice," Dept. of Geography, The University of Michigan, Ann Arbor, Mich., 1976.

26. Williamson, H., Algorithm 420, "Hidden Line Plotting Program," *Comm. ACM, 15,* 100-103, February 1972.

27. Wright, T.J., "A Two-Space Solution to the Hidden Line Problem for Plotting Functions of Two Variables," *IEEE Transactions on Computers, C22,* 28-33, January 1973.

28. NCAR Software Support Library, Volume 3, NCAR-TN/IA-105, National Center for Atmospheric Research, Boulder, Colo., 1975 (contact T.J. Wright).

29. CONREC, CONRECQCK, CONRECSMTH, *op cit.*

30. Cederquist, G.N., "CONSYS- A Collection of Fortran Subroutines to Produce Contour Maps of Data Surfaces Defined on Rectangular Grids," Cooley Laboratory, The University of Michigan, Ann Arbor, Mich., 1974.

31. Dwyer, W.C., "Windows, Shields, and Shading," Proc. 6th UAIDE Meeting, Washington, D.C., 1967.

32. Phillips, R.L., "Subroutine SHADE," Department of Aerospace Engineering, The University of Michigan, Ann Arbor, Mich., 1972.

33. Ison, N.T., "An Algorithm to Shade a Plot," *Computer Graphics* (SIGGRAPH-ACM Quarterly), *7*, 10-23, 1973.

34. Newman, W.M. and Sproull, R.F., *Principles of Interactive Computer Graphics*, McGraw-Hill, New York, 121-126, 1973.

35. Jarvis, J.F., "Two Simple Windowing Algorithms," *Software-Practice and Experience*, *5*, 115-122, 1975.

36. Behler, B. and Zajac, E.E., "A Generalized Window-Shield Routine," Proc. 8th UAIDE Meeting, Coronado, Cal., 1969.

37. Douglas, D.H. and Peucker, T.K., "Algorithms for the Reduction of the Number of Points Required to Represent a Digitized Line or its Caricature," *The Canadian Cartographer*, *10*, 112-122, December 1973.

38. Reumann, K. and Witham, A.P.M., "Optimizing Curve Segmentation in Computer Graphics," *International Computing Symposium, 1973*, American Elservier Publ., New York, 467-472, 1974.

COMPUTERS AND QUANTUM CHEMISTRY

Isaiah Shavitt

Battelle Memorial Institute, Columbus, Ohio 43201
and Department of Chemistry, The Ohio State University,
Columbus, Ohio 43210

ABSTRACT

In its fifty years of existence quantum chemistry has had a
far reaching impact on the understanding and development of
chemistry. In its earlier years it mainly provided grossly
simplified models in terms of which chemical data could be
interpreted and correlated, but it is mainly in the last twenty
years, with the help of the computer, that quantum chemistry has
been emerging as an increasingly reliable quantitative and
predictive tool. The further development of these capabilities
is strongly tied to continued progress in computer technology.

The principal mathematical problem of quantum chemistry is
the solution of the Schrödinger equation, a partial differential
equation of the elliptic type whose eigensolutions provide the
energy levels and other properties of molecular systems. The
size of the systems which can be handled in a satisfactory
manner, and the obtainable accuracy, are severely limited by the
enormous computational problem of very high dimensionality ($3N$,
where N is the number of electrons) and complicated symmetry
conditions. Quantum chemistry has thus had ever increasing
demands for greater computer power. Its computational needs
have included both "number crunching" and extensive data
handling, and have contributed to the development of techniques
and algorithms useful in other fields.

Working in a field of research in which the principal
limiting factor is the power of the computer, quantum chemists
are anxious to have access to all the computer's resources, and

227

are keenly interested in the efficient operation of their programs. As sophisticated programmers, they are apprehensive about operating policies and system developments which limit their access to the computer's facilities, reduce their control over program execution, and encumber the system with efficiency-robbing features.

1. INTRODUCTION

The first quarter of this century saw a far-reaching revolution in our understanding of the physical laws governing our universe, encompassing such new concepts as quantization, relativity, and the dual nature of particles and radiation, and culminating in 1926 with the development of quantum mechanics. In the brief span of about five years following this development the implications of the new theory for the understanding and prediction of chemical phenomena were elucidated, and the basic mathematical approaches to approximate methods of solution of the relevant equations were developed and applied to some very small test systems (primarily the helium atom and the hydrogen molecule). An oft quoted statement of that period by Nobel Laureate P. A. M. Dirac (made in 1929) summarized the situation as follows:

"The underlying physical laws necessary for the mathematical theory of a large part of physics and the whole of chemistry are thus completely known, and the difficulty is only that the exact application of these laws leads to equations much too complicated to be soluble" [1].

For the last fifty years quantum chemists have been working to obtain increasingly accurate solutions to the quantum-mechanical equations for more and bigger chemical species. In the last 25 years they have had an increasingly powerful tool for this effort, the electronic digital computer.

Before the advent of the computer most of the effort to

apply quantum mechanics to chemistry had concentrated on the development of simplified approximate models which, while based on the general theoretical formalism, reduced that formalism to manageable proportions by radical surgery, removing many terms and replacing others by adjustable parameters. The parameters were determined by fitting the results of the model to observed experimental data, and the parameterized model was then used to predict other data and to explain and correlate a vast quantity of chemical knowledge. Many such models have been developed, varying in the types of approximations employed and in the way the parameters were determined, and each had its successes and failures. Taken together, they have had a tremendous impact on the development of chemistry in the last half century by providing a general framework to channel the chemist's thinking and to classify and organize his data. It is difficult indeed to imagine modern chemistry without the concepts and insights produced by these extremely simplified and even crude models. In partial recognition of the importance of these developments, Nobel prizes in chemistry were awarded to two researchers who were responsible for important work in this field, Linus Pauling (1954) and Robert S. Mulliken (1966).

It was only with the emerging use of electronic digital computers in scientific research about 25 years ago that the assumptions and simplifications of the so-called "semiempirical" treatments could begin to be subjected to rigorous tests. While it is still not possible to solve most problems of chemical interest to the desired degree of accuracy by ab initio methods — methods which do not drastically oversimplify the formalism and do not make use of adjustable parameters to fit experimental data — it is at least possible to determine the relative magnitude and importance of different terms in the solution process and to gauge the validity of various approximations. In this examination the semiempirical methods have been found wanting, many of their assumptions have been found unjustified, and some of their concepts lacked sound theoretical foundation. This is not meant to detract from their extreme and continuing importance for the development and understanding of chemistry, but to point out that they should be viewed more as elaborate interpolative schemes, with only a limited connection to an underlying theoretical foundation.

Having shown up the deficiencies and limitations of existing semiempirical models to an increasing degree, the introduction of electronic computers has also led to the modification and improvement of those models, eliminating some inconsistencies in the approximations and bringing back some previously ignored terms, culminating in the present proliferation of models known by such names as CNDO (complete neglect of differential overlap), INDO (intermediate neglect of differential overlap), and MINDO (modified intermediate neglect of differential overlap). Each of these has several varieties (e.g., CNDO/2, CNDO/S, MINDO/3, etc.), depending on parameterization and the type of phenomena they are most successful in correlating. These models have become sufficiently elaborate that the computer is now required for their application. A considerable number of widely circulating computer programs for their implementation are being used in the chemistry community, often by experimentalists with little quantum-mechanical background and even less previous exposure to computers. They find such calculations increasingly valuable as direct adjuncts to their experimental work, both guiding their experiments and helping to interpret the experimental results.

By far the greatest use of computers in quantum chemistry is in ab initio calculations, employing no adjustable parameters and introducing well-defined mathematical approximations (such as truncated expansions) in preference to physical approximations. Some calculations of this type, employing desk calculators, were carried out in the earlier days of quantum chemistry, but were necessarily limited to very small systems and to relatively low accuracy. The first pioneering attempts to utilize the power of

the computer for complete atomic and molecular calculations were
made by S. F. Boys at Cambridge University in the early 1950's
[2]. I had the good fortune of coming to Cambridge as a graduate
student in 1954 and joined Boys' group, using EDSAC at the
University Mathematical Laboratory.

EDSAC was the first automatic fully-electronic stored-
program digital computer to be put into service (in 1949), and
its capabilities are dwarfed by most of today's minicomputers
and even by some modern desk-top machines. It had an acoustic
delay-line memory containing 1024 17-bit words, with double-
precision (35-bit) arithmetic but no floating point. There was
a repertoire of 25 instructions (not including division), no
compiler, and a rudimentary assembler/loader (which was entered
electromechanically from a pre-wired set of uniselector switches).
While this assembler was only 41 words long (plus 15 words of
working space), it had decimal-to-binary address conversion and
fairly effective subroutine and relative addressing capabilities
[3]. Memory space was obviously at a premium, and great
ingenuity was called for in coding. Typical mathematical
subroutines were 30-50 words long. Execution time for most
instructions was about 1.5 ms. Those of us who used computers
in those days developed certain habits regarding tightness and
efficiency in coding which have become ingrained and very
difficult to shake off even in these days of megabyte stores
and nanosecond cycle times.

2. MATHEMATICAL PROBLEMS

The principal mathematical problem of quantum chemistry is
the solution of the stationary-state Schrödinger equation, a
a linear partial differential equation of the elliptic type
which can be represented in condensed form as

(1) $$\mathcal{H}\Psi = E\Psi .$$

In this, $\mathcal{H}$ is the Hamiltonian operator, a second-order linear

differential operator which represents the kinetic energy of the
particles (e.g., electrons) and the interactions between them.
Its eigenfunction Ψ is the desired <u>wave function</u> of the system,
which describes the motions of the particles as fully as allowed
by the laws of quantum mechanics, while the eigenvalue E is the
total energy.

For a system of N electrons moving in a field of K fixed
nuclei, the Hamiltonian can be written in the following form
(using a convenient system of "atomic" units):

$$(2) \qquad \mathcal{K} = \sum_{i=1}^{N} (-\tfrac{1}{2}\nabla_i^2) - \sum_{a=1}^{K}\sum_{i=1}^{N} \frac{Z_a}{|\underset{\sim}{r}_i - \underset{\sim}{r}_a|} + \sum_{i<j} \frac{1}{|\underset{\sim}{r}_i - \underset{\sim}{r}_j|} ,$$

where ∇_i^2 is the Laplacian operator for the coordinates of the
$\underline{i}$-th electron (represented by the vector $\underset{\sim}{r}_i$) and Z_a is the
atomic number of the $\underline{a}$-th nucleus (which is located at the point
defined by the vector $\underset{\sim}{r}_a$). The first term represents the kinetic
energy of the electrons (the nuclei are held fixed in the
solution of the electronic equation and their motion is handled
subsequently in a separate equation). The second term describes
the Coulombic attraction between the oppositely charged nuclei
and electrons, while the last term represents the repulsion
between the different electrons. Additional minor terms have
been left out in (2); they are usually treated separately by
perturbation methods.

The primary reason for the difficulty in solving the
electronic Schrödinger equation (1,2) is the dimensionality of
the problem. The independent variables are the coordinates $\underset{\sim}{r}_i$ of
the electrons, so that there are 3N such variables for an N-
electron problem. In some typical small molecules N=10 (water),
N=24 (ozone), N=42 (benzene). Additional difficulties are due to
the singularities in $\mathcal{K}$ whenever the coordinates of two particles
coincide, and particularly due to rather complicated symmetry
conditions on the wave function Ψ. The principal symmetry
condition requires that Ψ be <u>antisymmetric</u> in the coordinates of

the different electrons; this means that Ψ must change sign whenever the coordinates of any two electrons are interchanged. Additional conditions, too complex to be discussed here, are related to the spin property of the electrons, and are generally expressed in terms of an additional set of coordinates, one per electron, in Ψ. These spin coordinates are discrete, each having just two possible values.

The above description is necessarily very abbreviated and oversimplified (for a detailed treatment see, for example, the book by Slater [4]), but serves to point out some of the complexities. Exact analytical solutions are impossible except in some trivial cases, and approximate methods have to be used. Almost all of these are based on expansions in a basis of pre-selected functions, using variational and/or perturbation techniques for determining the expansion coefficients. Computational limitations generally preclude carrying such treatments to an entirely satisfactory level of convergence for all but rather small problems, and much of quantum chemistry is concerned with the generation and interpretation of inadequate approximations to the solutions of the Schrödinger equation.

The expansions used for the approximate solution are generally constructed in terms of a one-electron **basis set**, a set of functions $\{\chi_p\}$ of the coordinates of one electron. These are usually of the form

$$R(r)Y_{\ell m}(\theta,\phi) \; ,$$

where $R(r)$ is a radial function, $Y_{\ell m}(\theta,\phi)$ is a spherical harmonic, and (r,θ,ϕ) are polar coordinates defined relative to one of the nuclear positions as origin. Typically there would be several dozen such functions, about 2-20 of these centered on each of the various nuclei in the molecule. Typical forms of the radial functions involve exponentials,

$$r^{n-1} e^{-\zeta r} \; ,$$

or Gaussians,

$$r^{\ell} e^{-\zeta r^2} .$$

The basis functions $\{\chi_p\}$ are transformed linearly into an orthonormal set of <u>orbitals</u> $\{\varphi_i\}$,

$$(3) \qquad \varphi_i = \sum_p \chi_p c_{pi} ,$$

having certain desired properties. Products of such orbitals are used in the construction of N-electron functions Φ_r, either as direct approximations to Ψ or as a basis for the linear expansion of Ψ.

In order to satisfy the symmetry conditions on the resulting Ψ, each of the N-electron functions Φ_r is constrained to have as many of the desired symmetry properties as practical. Most importantly, it is constructed to be antisymmetric in the coordinates of the different electrons. This is usually accomplished through the convenient device of the <u>Slater determinant</u>,

$$(4) \qquad \Phi_{\underset{\sim}{i}} = \alpha \varphi_{i_1}(\underset{\sim}{r}_1) \varphi_{i_2}(\underset{\sim}{r}_2) \cdots \varphi_{i_N}(\underset{\sim}{r}_N) ,$$

where the "antisymmetrizer" α is a linear combination of permutation operators P_u, with parities σ_u, operating on the electron coordinates:

$$(5) \qquad \alpha = (N!)^{-\frac{1}{2}} \sum_{u=1}^{N!} (-1)^{\sigma_u} P_u .$$

The result of the operation of α on the product in (4) can be written as a determinant having elements $\varphi_{i_k}(\underset{\sim}{r}_j)$, with the electron index j running from 1 to N horizontally while the orbital index i_k runs from i_1 to i_N vertically. Obviously, α projects an antisymmetric function out of the product function on which it operates. Additional projection operators (for spin and spatial symmetry) are used as needed to satisfy other conditions. The resulting projected functions Φ_r are sometimes called <u>configuration functions</u>.

In the simplest and most common method of approximation, the self-consistent field (SCF) method, the wave function Ψ is expressed as a single term of the form (4), using a variational method to optimize the orbitals $\{\varphi_i\}$ so that the resulting function is as good an approximation of Ψ as is possible for this restricted form. A more accurate, but much more difficult approach is the configuration interaction (CI) method [5], in which Ψ is expressed as a linear combination of numerous orthonormal configuration functions,

(6) $$\Psi = \sum_r c_r \Phi_r \ .$$

Application of the variational method to optimize (6) leads to a matrix eigenvalue equation for the vector of coefficients c_r,

(7) $$\underset{\sim}{H} \underset{\sim}{c} = E \underset{\sim}{c} \ ,$$

where the eigenvalue E is the desired energy. The Hamiltonian matrix $\underset{\sim}{H}$ has the elements

(8) $$H_{rs} = \int \Phi_r^* \mathcal{H} \Phi_s \, d\tau \ ,$$

the integration being over the coordinates of all the electrons (including spin coordinates).

The matrix elements H_{rs} can be reduced by complicated procedures to linear combinations of basic integrals involving one or two electrons and two or four orbitals at a time. These in turn can be obtained by linear transformations from similar integrals in terms of the basis functions. The most difficult to compute of the latter are the electron repulsion integrals

(9) $$g_{pqrs} = \iint \chi_p^*(\underset{\sim}{r}_1)\chi_q(\underset{\sim}{r}_1)\frac{1}{|\underset{\sim}{r}_1 - \underset{\sim}{r}_2|}\chi_r^*(\underset{\sim}{r}_2)\chi_s(\underset{\sim}{r}_2)\,d\underset{\sim}{r}_1 d\underset{\sim}{r}_2 \ ,$$

which represent the electrostatic repulsion between two charge distributions, each of which is described by a product of two basis functions. Since the four basis functions in (9) may be centered on four different nuclei, the evaluation of the g_{pqrs} represents a formidable mathematical problem. This has once been

235

called the principal bottleneck of quantum chemical calculations
[6], but the bottleneck has been effectively broken by the use
of Gaussian-type basis functions instead of the previously common
simple exponentials. These Gaussians, first introduced by Boys
[7], while less effective than exponential-type basis functions
in terms of convergence rates, allow the evaluation of the
integrals in (9) in terms of the error function and related
incomplete gamma functions [8].

3. COMPUTATIONAL PROBLEMS

The principal steps in the variational solution of the
Schrödinger equation by the configuration interaction method can
be summarized as follows [5]:

1. Pick an appropriate basis set $\{\chi_p\}$. This choice is
based on accumulated previous experience, and is the most important factor in determining the accuracy of the resulting
solution.

2. Calculate the one-electron and two-electron integrals in
terms of the basis functions.

3. Choose a linear transformation from basis functions
$\{\chi_p\}$ to orthonormal orbitals $\{\varphi_i\}$. This is based on spatial
symmetry properties and on some preliminary calculations, such
as by the self-consistent field method. It has a most important
effect on the number of configuration functions Φ_r which have to
be included in the expansion (6) for adequate convergence.

4. Transform the basis-function integrals to orbital
integrals. For n basis functions this step requires about n^5
multiplications.

5. Choose and construct a set of configuration functions
Φ_r for the linear expansion of Ψ. Obviously, this step must
be carried out on the computer, since thousands of terms are
often involved.

6. Compute the Hamiltonian matrix $\underset{\sim}{H}$ (eq. 8). This involves
first determining the formula for each matrix element in terms

of the orbital integrals, and then substituting the necessary
integrals in these formulas to obtain numerical values.

7. Obtain one or more eigensolutions of the matrix eigenvalue equation (7).

8. Use these solutions to derive desired molecular
properties.

In many cases these steps have to be repeated many times for
different relative positions of the nuclei, in order to obtain
energy surfaces (or hypersurfaces) in terms of which the motion
of the nuclei can be treated.

An adequate basis set for a small molecule may typically
require about 20-80 basis functions, and hundreds of such
functions may be required for the adequate treatment of medium-
sized molecules. This can give rise to millions of basis-set
integrals g_{pqrs} (eq. 9), and the evaluation of each of these
requires a certain amount of analysis to determine the appropriate formula, as well as an appreciable amount of arithmetic.
The more sophisticated computer programs for this step can
exploit molecular symmetry and other relationships between the
basis functions to reduce the amount of computation appreciably.

The resulting large number of basis-set integrals have to be
collected into well organized structures and transformed to
orbital integrals. This step, being proportional to n^5 in computational effort (where n is the number of basis functions),
can be one of the most costly in the calculation, involving both
a large number of arithmetic operations (of order 10^{10} multiplications for a 100-function basis) and very extensive data manipulation. Again, sophisticated programs can utilize molecular
symmetry for some reduction in the computational effort [9,10].

The number of linearly independent configuration functions
Φ_r which can be constructed from a given basis set increases
approximately as the N-th power of the number of basis functions,
but an appropriate choice of the orbital transformation can
reduce the number of terms needed for adequate convergence by

many orders of magnitude. Even then, a satisfactory solution for a small molecule may require thousands or tens of thousands of terms, while medium-sized and larger molecules may call for millions of such terms even for a barely adequate solution. Current state-of-the-art capabilities allow up to about 50,000 such terms. The principal difficulty here is not just in the solution of a matrix eigenvalue equation of this order (which is difficult enough, but can be handled by iterative techniques [11,12], since the matrices are diagonally dominant and sparse and only one or a few of the lowest eigenvalues are required), but primarily in the computation of the millions of matrix elements.

Each matrix element H_{rs} requires derivation of the appropriate reduction formula to express it in terms of orbital integrals. These formulas depend on a detailed matching of the two configuration functions Φ_r and Φ_s in H_{rs} (eq. 8), and is complicated by the various symmetry adaptations used in constructing the functions. This is by far the most complex step in the calculation. A vast number of computer logical operations are involved in the derivation of the many formulas, and these formulas have to be represented in a suitably coded form for subsequent substitution of the integral values. This latter step involves a very difficult data management problem, since each of the millions of matrix elements requires integral values taken from almost anywhere in the huge arrays of hundreds of thousands or millions of orbital integrals. Ordinary record-oriented random-access mass storage is not very helpful in this operation, and a virtual-memory type of storage system would be hopelessly and horribly inefficient. Large auxiliary bulk core memories, such as Extended Core Storage (ECS) on CDC machines, which allow truly random access for one word or any number of words without record boundaries, are much more helpful. One interesting, but still somewhat cumbersome, solution to this problem, using record-oriented direct-access mass storage, is based on an ingenious sorting scheme [13] which has potential applications in other fields. It uses just two passes to sort the matrix element formulas into batches each of which refers to just one core-load of integrals.

4. THE QUANTUM CHEMIST AND THE COMPUTING ENVIRONMENT

It has been shown that quantum chemical calculations involve heavy utilization of all the different types of computer capabilities, including nonnumerical (logical and analytical) work, a vast amount of arithmetic, and extensive data manipulation. Graphics capabilities are also used, primarily for multidimensional plotting of the results [14].

The computer programs required for this work are large and complex, and involve a very considerable investment of effort and a high degree of sophistication. Much effort has been saved by the free exchange of programs among quantum chemists. This has been facilitated primarily through the Quantum Chemistry Program Exchange (QCPE), which has been operating since 1962 out of Indiana University [15]. It has provided tested and documented programs to many users, experienced and inexperienced alike, merely for the cost of copying and shipping.

Since large basis sets and numerous configuration functions are needed even for a barely satisfactory treatment of even small molecules, and since there is demand for the theoretical study of ever larger molecules and of systems of interacting molecules, the quantum chemist usually works near the limit of his computer's capabilities. He has an insatiable appetite for larger and faster computers, and his use of these machines easily expands to utilize all the resources made available to him. Ever since the beginning of the use of electronic computers in scientific research, quantum chemistry has been one of the heaviest users of computer time, and has contributed to the constant demand for increased computing power at universities and research laboratories.

Another result of the demands of his work is that the quantum chemist has always been greatly concerned with the efficiency of his programs and of their execution by the computer. While very happy with the increased flexibility and convenience of modern compilers and operating systems, he is nevertheless apprehensive about the apparently disappearing concern for efficiency among today's system programmers. Today's most powerful computers are about 10,000 times faster than EDSAC, and have 1000 times the central memory, in addition to mass storage and other new facilities, but we need these capabilities, and more, and are very unhappy with any reduction in speed and available resources due to system design. Today's systems and operating policies (particularly at universities) appear to be designed primarily for the handling of vast numbers of small jobs, and badly neglect the needs of those users who require as much memory and as much uninterrupted computing as possible. Furthermore, catering to many unsophisticated users and seeking to save them the burden of learning how to manage their storage needs and trying to help them as much as possible with debugging their programs, these systems become encumbered with a proliferation of efficiency robbing devices. One gets the impression that the system programmer believes he has an inexhaustible resource at his disposal, and that he can take over as much of it as he finds convenient for carrying out system functions and can generally ignore any questions of efficiency.

One simple (though rather limited) demonstration of this

Figure 1. (Facing page) Example of subroutine compilation on IBM 360 and 370 systems. (a) Source program. (b) Assembly-code listing of hand-coded object program. (c) Assembly-code listing of Fortran H Extended (OPT=2) compiled object program. Only executed statements are listed, in the order of execution (in the compiled program the prologue actually appears at the end and the save area and constants appear before the body).

(a)

```
FUNCTION ADD(A,B)
ADD = A + B
RETURN
END
```

(b)

```
ADD    ST   2,28(13)        Save R2
       LM   1,2,0(1)        Argument addresses to R1, R2
       LE   0,0(1)          Argument 1 to FR0
       AE   0,0(2)          Add argument 2 to FR0
       L    2,28(13)        Restore R2
       BR   14              Return
```

(c)

```
ADD       B    12(15)           Skip subroutine name
          :
          STM  14,12,12(13)     Save registers
          LR   4,13             Old save area address to R4
          LM   12,13,32(15)     Prologue address to R12, new
                                   save area address to R13
          ST   4,4(13)          Old save area address to new
                                   save area
          ST   13,8(4)          New save area address to old
                                   save area
          BR   12               Go to prologue
          :
PROLOGUE  LM   7,8,0(1)         Argument addresses to R7, R8
          LE   2,0(7)           Argument 1 to FR2
          STE  2,88(13)         Save argument 1
          LE   2,0(8)           Argument 2 to FR2
          STE  2,92(13)         Save argument 2
          B    104(13)          Go to body
          :
BODY      LE   6,88(13)         Argument 1 to FR6
          LE   4,92(13)         Argument 2 to FR4
          LER  0,6              Argument 1 to FR0
          AER  0,4              Add argument 2 to FR0
          STE  0,96(13)         Save result
          SR   15,15            Return code = 0 in R15
          LR   14,0(13)         Epilogue address to R14
          BR   14               Go to epilogue
EPILOGUE  LE   0,96(13)         Result to FR0
          L    13,4(13)         Old save area address to R13
          L    14,12(13)        Return address to R14
          MVI  12(13),255       Return marker
          LM   2,12,28(13)      Restore registers
          BR   14               Return
```

Figure 1.   (Legend on facing page.)

argument is provided by an examination of the compilation of a small subroutine by a typical "optimizing" compiler. A trivial Fortran function-type subroutine is shown in Fig. 1(a). It receives two floating-point arguments and returns their sum as the value of the function. An efficient rendering of this sub-routine as a hand-coded assembly program for the IBM 360 and 370 systems is shown in Fig. 1(b). The assembly program resulting from a compilation of the source program by the Fortran H Extended compiler at optimization level 2 is shown in Fig. 1(c), omitting all nonexecutable statements. A comparison of the resource requirements of the two assembly versions is given in Table 1; it reflects a ratio of about 9:1 in program length and about 5:1 in execution time. And this is supposed to be an optimizing compiler! Statistics for the same task on the CDC

TABLE 1

Comparison of compilation and hand coding of a trivial subroutine.[a]

Item	IBM 360, 370		CDC 6400, 6600	
	Compiled	Hand coded	Compiled	Hand coded
Executed instructions	27	6	16	7
Words fetched and stored	44	6	8	3
Branch instructions	5	1	2	2
Program length (words)	54	6	10	4

[a] The source program is shown in Fig. 1(a). The hand-coded and compiled object programs for the IBM computers are shown in Figs. 1(b) and 1(c), respectively. Compilation was carried out with the Fortran H Extended (OPT=2) compiler for IBM and with the Fortran Extended Version 4 (OPT=2) compiler for CDC. Note that in the CDC system register saving and restoration is done in the calling program, and is therefore not included in these statistics. The word length is 32 bits for IBM, 60 bits for CDC.

6000-series machines are also shown in Table 1. While not as extreme in this example as the IBM version, they also show appreciable waste.

The above subroutine is not a very typical example, of course, and was chosen purposefully to dramatize the results. Other examples could be found for which the IBM compiler's performance is far better than that of CDC. Both compilers are designed primarily for the optimization of inner loops and for longer-running subroutines in which the entry and exit overhead is less important. They also have to contend with multiple entry and exit capabilities and to provide debugging information. But one cannot escape the impression that the overall system design is insensitive to efficiency requirements.

For a look at another aspect of the problem, the above subroutine was loaded together with a main program which reads two vectors, adds them term by term (using the subroutine), and prints the sum vector. The total storage for the link-edited program in the IBM system, including system-supplied subroutines but exclusive of storage for the vectors, was over 25,000 bytes, or more than 6000 words (the length of the same program in the CDC system, exclusive of vector storage, was about 6700 60-bit words). And all this for a trivial undertaking! Furthermore, this does not include the big chunk of memory reserved for the resident part of the operating system. Now is this any way to run a railroad?

I have used a variety of computers and software systems since 1954, including some one-of-a-kind machines, the sequence of IBM machines 704, 709, 7090, 7094, 360, and 370, as well as the CDC 6000 series, among others. I sometimes feel that the optimum balance between software facilities and software efficiency (or as near to that balance as we are likely to get) was reached no later than the time of IBSYS Version 13 for the IBM 7094, though even in that product the operating system expropriated about a fourth of the computer's central memory for

its own use. I am not longing for the pre-compiler and pre-
operating system days, and I very much like and use many of the
facilities which modern software systems provide, but nevertheless, I am increasingly frustrated by the ever-expanding usurpa-
tion of computer resources by these systems. I do not believe
that this situation is unavoidable. It is primarily a matter of
attitude and philosophy of system design and implementation.
There appears to be much waste and fat in the present systems
which can be cut, and efficiency should not be downgraded.
Coding and resources designed to facilitate special features
should only affect those programs in which these features are
used or requested. It should be possible to eliminate the
generation of traceback and other debugging information when the
user no longer wants it. Lean systems, designed to be frugal and
modest in their demands for system resources, will serve the
computing community better and will not reduce the power of
multimillion-dollar machines by ridiculous amounts. I believe
that with the proper attitude this can be achieved.

At the present time I am concerned about the effects of
virtual memory systems. While extremely convenient in many
applications, they can reduce the running efficiency of some
programs by orders of magnitude, necessitating a complete re-
thinking and redesign of some algorithms, at the cost of considerable personal effort and some loss of program efficiency (see,
for example, the discussion of the calculation of the Hamiltonian
matrix $\underset{\sim}{H}$ in the previous section). These difficulties could be
ameliorated to some extent if the individual user were given at
least some control, when he wants it (and without operator intervention), over memory utilization and paging in his program.

Some quantum chemists are taking an interesting shortcut
around these problems. Rather than fight the system designer for
system resources, and fight computer-center policies which are
necessarily designed (particularly at universities) to serve
multitudes of small users and terminals to the detriment of

large-scale computing needs, they have found that a private, dedicated minicomputer can sometimes provide a cheaper and more effective way to serve their purpose. Since they can have full control over such a facility, they can set policies and make system changes to suit their own needs and to make a small machine go a long way. Such a system, the Harris SLASH 4 (originally Datacraft 6024/4), was installed late in 1973 in the Chemistry Department of the University of California at Berkeley under a National Science Foundation grant to two theoretical chemists, Professors Henry F. Schaefer and William H. Miller. It cost $130,000, and is about half as fast as a CDC 6400. Its main limitation is memory size (32,000 48-bit double-words), but it has a 56-million-byte disk and other peripherals. It can be left unattended to work on a problem for hours or days, including overnight, until it is solved, without running up all those expensive CP-second charges. It has been used very effectively in many research projects [16,17]. With the cheaper large memories now emerging and the consequent increase in the power of new minicomputers, this mode of operation may become more popular among researchers, particularly at universities.

At the other end of the scale, for some time there has been an effort, initiated by Professor Harrison Shull of Indiana University, to set up a national computation center dedicated to the needs of large computations in chemistry. Such a center, equipped with a very large computer, with hardware and software configurations and operating policies designed specifically to facilitate very large calculations, if made available to chemists throughout the nation, could significantly enhance research capabilities in all fields of chemistry, and particularly in quantum chemistry. A series of meetings and studies have been held on this proposal under the auspices of the National Academy of Sciences and with support from the National Science Foundation, beginning in 1965, and several reports have been issued [18-21]. These resulted in a recommendation by the National

Academy of Sciences to NSF and to the Energy Research and Development Administration to set up such a center, initially (phase 1) utilizing the computational facilities of a suitably equipped host laboratory, but advancing, after about three years, to its own dedicated state-of-the-art facility. This recommendation has been accepted in principle by the funding agencies, and steps are under way towards implementation [22].

The use of the largest and fastest computers not only enables bigger computations, but also tends to reduce costs for a given task, since these machines are more cost effective than medium-sized computers. It appears, in fact, that at present cost effectiveness is optimum at both ends of the scale, for the very big machines such as the CDC 7600 and the IBM 370/195, and for minicomputers such as the Harris SLASH 4 and SLASH 7, and is worst in the middle range of size and speed. (This evaluation reflects not only the band-pass characteristics discussed at this meeting by Dr. W. Wulf, but also the amount of data easily accessible, which can be critical for overall performance.)

5. SOME SUGGESTIONS

Reflecting the concerns discussed above, I would like to offer several comments and suggestions relating to hardware and software design which can increase efficiency or programming convenience, particularly in the type of applications I have described.

The most important factor, after the electronics, in determining a machine's efficiency and programmability is what has come to be known as the computer's architecture. This includes the overall logical structure of the machine, the type, number, and possible sizes of its functional units, the word structure, and the instruction repertoire. In these respects, each of today's computers has its strengths and its weaknesses. For example, the IBM 360 and 370 series has a fairly complete and effective instruction set and a flexible word structure, but the overall design has two annoying and efficiency-reducing features. One is the base register concept, and the other is the need to generate multiple versions of integer variables which are also used as subscripts for arrays of different word lengths. This latter problem has been solved very neatly on the Xerox Sigma computers by automatically offsetting indexing quantities in accordance with the word length referred to by the indexed instruction.

Two types of logical instructions which are extremely useful in the determination of formulas for matrix elements between configuration functions (eq. 8), but which I have not been able to find implemented on the same machine, are the population count and the content-dependent shift. The first of these (present on CDC machines) returns the number of one-bits in a word, and is most helpful in determining the number of orbital noncoincidences between two configuration functions. Since the matrix element vanishes whenever the number of noncoincidences exceeds two, a very rapid determination of this number allows quick disposal of such elements (which are the large majority of the elements in typical cases) and can contribute materially to the overall speed of the process. The content-dependent shift (present in a more limited form on UNIVAC machines) would shift the specified word left (or right) repeatedly, n bits at a time, until the leftmost (or rightmost) n bits are not all zero, and return the resulting shift count. This is very similar to what happens in floating-point normalization. A complete set of mask-controlled operations, such as those available on UNIVAC machines, would also be very convenient. All these features should be useful in other nonnumerical and list-processing applications.

A much more generally useful feature for many scientific applications would be hardware square roots and exponentials. These functions are ubiquitous in scientific calculations, and deserve special treatment. After all, even some $20-50 pocket calculators offer these features. Hardware implementation of the

square root is hardly more complicated than division. Not only
is hardware implementation much faster intrinsically than a
programmed subroutine, but it also saves all that register
juggling which typically accompanies subroutine calls and
returns. The available software implementations of the exponential, in particular, often confront the user with the choice
between inadequate single precission and the much more than
adequate, and therefore rather slow, double precision.

Another very useful hardware feature is an array processor,
such as is available on the UNIVAC 1100-series machines. This
can speed up some of our programs by an order of magnitude, and
appears to be a reasonable and flexible alternative to a machine
designed entirely around a vector concept, or to a parallel
processor machine in which all processors have to do exactly the
same thing at the same time.

Turning now to higher level languages, I was delighted when
the PL/I language description first appeared, since it seemed to
combine the best features of Algol, Fortran, and Cobol, with
unique additions of its own, and without some of the inefficiency-
inducing aspects of Algol. In connection with this last point I
would mention in particular the concept that complicating
features such as recursive subroutine capabilities, which are
only occasionally useful, are only supplied when specifically
asked for, rather than cluttering up everybody's programs all the
time. Unfortunately PL/I did not catch on very well, at least
partly, no doubt, due to limited availability and atrociously bad
initial implementation, but also due to programmers' inertia.

It has now been recognized that with the large investment in
existing programs, changes in programming usage are more likely
to be evolutionary rather than revolutionary, and attention has
focused on the gradual upgrading of Fortran. So far, unlike the
continuous modification and growth of operating systems, the
upgrading of Fortran has been extremely slow. Many attractive
features which have existed in some variants of Fortran for many

years have not yet made their appearance in standard Fortran.
(Some of these existed, for example, in MAD, the Michigan
Algorithmic Decoder [23], a Fortran-like language of the early
and mid 1960's which had many advantages over Fortran but has
disappeared for lack of sufficient backing.) Some such features
have been implemented in preprocessors, particularly those
devoted to structured Fortran [24], but it is difficult to understand the reluctance to make them part of standard Fortran [25],
particularly since this can generally be done without invalidat-
ing existing programs.

It now appears that the Fortran Standards Committee (X3J3)
has turned again in favor of incorporating the IF-THEN-ELSE
control structure in the current Fortran revision [26]. This is
indeed a very welcome development which can improve program
readability and facilitate better optimization, as well as speed
coding and debugging. A very useful addition to this revision,
in my opinion, would be a label-free looping structure such as
exists, for example, in Basic in the form of the NEXT I statement.
By using a distinctive loop initiation statement, such as
FOR I=1,N, this feature could coexist with the present DO loop
structure. It would greatly improve program readability (a distinctive ending for such loops, rather than the ubiquitous end
bracket of Algol, is particularly useful in this regard), as well
as eliminate the need to clutter up the program with numerous
statement labels which do not flag possible GO TO destinations.
The elimination of these labels should also facilitate compiler
optimization and avoid the inconvenience of having to select a
statement number for the terminating statement of a loop at the
time the opening statement is written, particularly when a major
part of the program may sometimes lie between these two
statements.

I am not an evangelist on the matter of GO TO's and statement labels. If a GO TO appears the convenient and natural way
to accomplish one's objective, by all means it should be used.

249

But one should have the means to avoid it when it is not the most natural and transparent way to control program execution. The proliferation and increasing popularity of structured Fortran preprocessors evidently shows that there is much desire for such features among programmers.

Another feature I would like to see is a "local" subroutine capability, which can be seen as an extension of the presently available, but too limited, statement-defined function. This would be a callable program element (function or subroutine-type) written and compiled as part of a surrounding subprogram, callable from within that subprogram only, and having available to it all variables which are defined in that subprogram. This can reduce program fragmentation and improve efficiency by reducing the need for long argument lists in many subroutine calls. (It can also reduce the inducement to place almost everything in COMMON blocks.)

A facility for programmer definition of in-line functions, such as Fortran macros, or even assembly macros in a Fortran program, if at all practical, would be quite useful.

On the other hand, unlike Dr. J. C. Browne, I am not particularly anxious for Fortran to handle complex data structures for me, primarily because of the inherent inefficiency. In fact, I use little of what Fortran now provides for accessing multidimensional arrays, preferring to linearize such arrays explicitly in many cases. The programmer knows more about his particular array structures and their accessing sequence during program execution than the compiler can realistically hope to find out, and can therefore be much more effective in handling it. In my own programs I prefer to use mapping functions implemented in the form of pointer arrays. For example, for the arrays of two-electron integrals g_{pqrs} (eq. 9), we need only store elements for which $p{\geq}q$, $r{\geq}s$, and $(pq){\geq}(rs)$. Furthermore, many combinations of p, q, r, s may be missing for reasons of space symmetry. Storage as a four-dimensional array would be extremely wasteful, but a compact one-dimensional storage scheme can be devised [5] using mapping functions of the form

$$u = f(p) + q ,$$
$$v = f(r) + s ,$$
$$address = h(u) + v ,$$

where the integer functions $f(p)$ and $h(u)$ are precomputed and stored as integer arrays. Rather than entrust Fortran with the direct handling of array structures, I would prefer help (both from hardware and software) in the rapid utilization of mapping schemes, such as Fortran-implemented indirect addressing.

6. SUMMARY

I have tried to show the type of mathematical and computational problems encountered in quantum chemistry, and the variety, complexity, scope, and size of the resulting computer applications. Pointing out the importance of efficiency in these applications, I have discussed some aspects of the efficiency problem in the present computing environment and some possible ways for improving efficiency and convenience in the future.

ACKNOWLEDGMENT

This work was supported by the Battelle Institute Program, Grant Number B-1333-1170.

REFERENCES

1. P. A. M. Dirac, Proc. R. Soc. London A 123, 714 (1929).

2. S. F. Boys and V. E. Price, Philos. Trans. R. Soc. London A 246, 451 (1954); S. F. Boys, G. B. Cook, C. M. Reeves, and I. Shavitt, Nature 178, 1207 (1956).

3. M. V. Wilkes, D. J. Wheeler, and S. Gill, "The Preparation of Programs for an Electronic Digital Computer," Addison-Wesley, Cambridge, Mass. (1951).

4. J. C. Slater, "Quantum Theory of Matter," 2nd edition, McGraw-Hill, New York (1968).

5. I. Shavitt, The Method of Configuration Interaction, in

"Modern Theoretical Chemistry. Vol. 3. Methods of Electronic Structure Theory" (H. F. Schaefer III, editor), Plenum Press, New York (1976).

6. R. S. Mulliken and C. C. J. Roothaan, Proc. Natl. Acad. Sci. USA 45, 394 (1959).

7. S. F. Boys, Proc. R. Soc. London A 200, 542 (1950).

8. I. Shavitt, Meth. Comput. Phys. 2, 1 (1963).

9. C. F. Bender, J. Comput. Phys. 9, 547 (1972).

10. E. R. Davidson, J. Chem. Phys. 62, 400 (1975).

11. I. Shavitt, C. F. Bender, A. Pipano, and R. P. Hosteny, J. Comput. Phys. 11, 90 (1973).

12. E. R. Davidson, J. Comput. Phys. 17, 87 (1975).

13. M. Yoshimine, J. Comput. Phys. 11, 449 (1973).

14. A. C. Wahl and U. Blukis, "Atoms to Molecules," a series of film loops, McGraw-Hill, New York (1969); A. C. Wahl, Sci. Am. 222, 54 (1970).

15. Chem. & Eng. News, May 21, 1973, p. 19.

16. C. W. Bauschlicher Jr., D. H. Liskow, C. F. Bender, and H. F. Schaefer III, J. Chem. Phys. 62, 4815 (1975); D. R. Yarkony and H. F. Schaefer III, J. Chem. Phys. 63, 4317 (1975).

17. S. Chapman, B. C. Garrett, and W. H. Miller, J. Chem. Phys. 63, 2710 (1975).

18. Uses of Electronic Computers in Chemistry, National Academy of Sciences/National Research Council, Washington, D.C. (January 1967).

19. Computational Support for Theoretical Chemistry, National Academy of Sciences, Washington, D.C. (1971).

20. A Study of a National Center for Computation in Chemistry, National Academy of Sciences, Washington, D.C. (1974).

21. The Proposed National Resource for Computation in Chemistry: A User-Oriented Facility, National Academy of Sciences, Washington, D.C. (1975).

22. Chem. & Eng. News, June 24, 1974, p. 24; May 10, 1976, p. 20.

23. B. W. Arden, B. A. Galler, and R. M. Graham, Commun. ACM (Assoc. Comput. Mach.) 4, 28 (1961); B. Arden, B. Galler, and R. Graham, Michigan Algorithmic Decoder (MAD) Manual, University of Michigan Computing Center (1965).

24. D. J. Reifer and L. P. Meissner, Structured Fortran Preprocessor Survey, Report UCID-3793, Lawrence Berkeley Laboratory, University of California, Berkeley, November 1975.

25. For-Word, Fortran Development Newsletter (L. P. Meissner, editor), Vol. 1, Lawrence Berkeley Laboratory, Berkeley, California (1975-76).

26. For-Word, Fortran Development Newsletter, Vol. 2, No. 2 (April 1976).

COMPUTER ARCHITECTURE IN THE 1980s

Harold S. Stone
University of Massachusetts

ABSTRACT

Continuing advances in device technology will result in substantially higher speed devices at rapidly diminishing costs. These changes will in turn have a significant impact on computer architecture in the next decade, and on the wide-scale proliferation of computer systems in new applications.

The microprocessor of today will eventually evolve to a processor with the power of a minicomputer or perhaps a medium-scale computer, and will be ultra-compact and low cost. Non-mechanical auxiliary memories are likely to be available as well. The computational power and low cost of these computer systems will see them used in the home, office, and industry where they have not been used before.

Medium-scale systems will tend to be total systems that are service oriented rather than hardware oriented. A major service will be that of the information utility to provide data to a widely distributed pool of on-site computers. Data may include library programs, text, mail, numerical data, or other similar items whose value depend on timeliness, completeness, and cost of creation.

Large-scale computer systems may achieve two to three orders of magnitude speed improvement over the next decade. A large portion of this will come from the faster devices. Another significant portion will come from higher replication factors. For large numerical computations, the vector processor of today may evolve to a hybrid vector processor-multiprocessor to provide efficient operation on both scalar and vector types of computations. Large arrays of microprocessors may be constructed to solve special classes of problems where the low cost and high-replication factor might achieve gains unavailable in a vector processor of similar cost.

I. INTRODUCTION

As computer systems find their way into countless new applications, the impact on society is profound. The past two decades have seen truly phenomenal advances in computers, but the potential of computers has barely been realized. It is only in recent years that the average consumer has directly confronted computer systems through the proliferation of point-of-sales terminals and calculators. The advances in computer technology anticipated in the next decade will be so wide-spread that computers will directly affect the living habits and quality of life of almost every person in the United States.

What will the computers of the next decade be like? This paper focuses on the architecture of the computers to come with the intent of indicating the present trends and projecting them forward to see their potential impact. Since computer architecture is largely driven by device technology and software interfaces, Section II of this paper is devoted to an analysis of the devices that may be available in the 1980s, and to the smaller end of the computer scale. Here's where growth will be most rapid. Medium-scale computers are treated in Section III, where we project that medium-scale computers will tend to be better oriented to the specific needs of the user than their predecessors of today. Finally, for large-scale computers, Section IV indicates that rather few new ideas in high-speed computer architecture will appear in the next decade, but there is room to attain about two to three orders of magnitude increase in speed by perfecting present ideas.

II. ADVANCES IN DEVICE TECHNOLOGIES--THE COMPUTER ON A CHIP

Semiconductor and integrated circuit technologies have consistently achieved advances in density, speed, and power consumption over the history of solid state devices. Fig. 1 illustrates some of these trends [Turn, 1974]. Densities double roughly

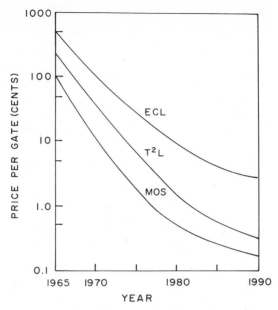

Fig. 1 (a)   Price trends

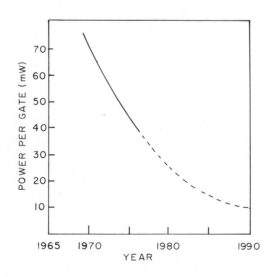

Fig. 1 (b)   Power consumption trend

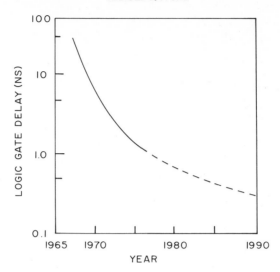

Fig. 1*(c)* *Logic speed trend*

every two years at the present rate. Assuming that this continues and a 16K bit chip is a standard in 1976, then the megabit memory chip may appear late in the 1980s. Since the cost of a single chip depends on process yields and pins per chip, but not directly on gate count, the megabit chip should cost only about double the cost of the 16K-bit chip. Unfortunately, this projection neglects limitations on the resolution of the optical systems involved in the masking for diffusion and conductor etching. To obtain densities leading to megabit chips, it may be necessary to achieve new breakthroughs in the resolution of the etching process by moving from visible light to electron beam scanning techniques or beyond.

Apart from achieving greater resolution, there are other gains to be made from new processes. In the past decade, processes based on MOS (metal-oxide semiconductor) techniques have been characterized by high density, low power consumption, but low speed. The competing technology is bipolar, with high speed, but roughly one fourth the density and additional complexity in its fabrication. TTL (transistor-transistor logic) has been the favored type of bipolar technology for implementation of reasonably fast logic, and ECL (emitter-coupled logic) is another bipolar technology that attains the fastest logic speed. Unfortunately, the power consumption of ECL is very high, and its density is low, thereby leaving the designer no clearly best choice for a logic family.

Recent changes in technology seem to have pointed bipolar and MOS processes in the same direction. MOS circuits diffused onto a sapphire substrate instead of the traditional silicon substrate attain notably higher speeds than standard MOS circuits, but this technology has not yet overcome some obstacles that have impaired its development. In the bipolar technology, a new offshoot known as I^2L (integrated-injection logic) greatly simplifies the masks for active gates, thus increasing circuit density while retaining speed. I^2L logic has a speed more nearly that of ECL rather than that of the slower T^2L logic. Given these changes, it is difficult to predict how the tradeoff between bipolar and MOS devices will continue. If either I^2L or silicon-on-sapphire technologies succeed in attaining their respective goals, then one may have high speed, high density, and low cost all in one family.

Projecting these developments into architecture has a very interesting impact on the innovation known as the *microprocessor*. A microprocessor is essentially a complete processor compact enough to be constructed on a single chip. Actually, one often finds several chips used to make up a full-fledged computer with one chip consisting of the arithmetic logic and processor registers, another chip holding control memory, and yet another chip used for random-access memory. Input/output interfaces may be on yet other chips. As density of fabrication increases, the chip boundaries will grow larger and the number of different chips will be reduced.

We have three data points on the power of microprocessors. The 4-bit microprocessor was introduced in quantity in 1971, the 8-bit in 1974 and the 16-bit will be shipped in quantity in 1976.

This is consistent with the claim that density increases by a factor of two about every two years. The chips themselves are increasing in size, too. Again projecting this forward by several years, we find that the complexity of the arithmetic unit of a microprocessor may attain that of sophisticated medium-scale machines of today by the 1980s. To be more realistic, we have to look at more than just the arithmetic unit, and this yields the estimate that a microprocessor may have the computational power of a 370/145 processor by the middle or late 1980s. Fig. 2 illustrates a speculation on where the trend may lead.

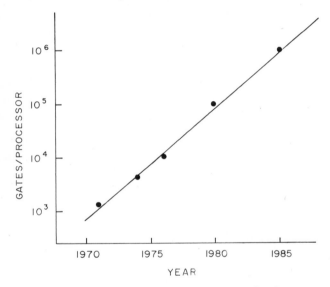

Fig. 2. Microprocessor complexity

With this in mind, the current interest in microprocessors as being distinct from larger computers is purely temporal in nature. A 4-bit machine is indeed an entirely different beast from the 16-bit mini or 32-bit medium-scale computer. Since the 4-bit computer is so limited in computational power, you must use special tricks in programming it and interfacing it. The present body of knowledge built upon larger computers does not quite fit. But the 4-bit microprocessor is already obsolete, and in the 1980s, a microprocessor will be quite similar to the

ordinary computer, perhaps what we call a minicomputer today, or
even what we call a medium-scale computer today. At that point
the 4-bit and 8-bit microprocessors will be curiosities of the
early 1970s.

Since costs do depend on pin counts, the microprocessor
designs of the next decade may differ somewhat in architecture
from more conventional computers. For example, instead of having 32 pins for the output of a 32-bit word, there may be only
eight pins, with the 32-bit word output as a sequence of four
8-bit bytes. This, of course, costs speed, but the speed of a
partly serial computer may be quite satisfactory for a microprocessor if it is used in conjunction with mechanical devices
or in close interaction with a human, since the system speed
will be determined not by the microprocessor but by the slower
input/output.

The architecture of microprocessors in the 1980s will be
largely identical to the minicomputers of today, with perhaps
some exceptions. One exception is the word size and address
size. Memory costs in the 1960s have kept this down to 16 bits
in a typical minicomputer. In the 1980s, 16-bit words may yield
to 32-bit words in the least expensive microcomputer systems if
memory costs drop sufficiently low. Another exception is the
input/output structure. In typical minicomputers, input/output
is performed by the central processor a word at a time, or is
done on a cycle-stealing basis by a direct-memory-access controller. The controller is itself a processor but is specialized to
input/output functions and is of different design than the
central processor. Since replication of identical chips is so
inexpensive, the microprocessor systems of the 1980s will undoubtedly make use of several copies of the same chip for performing the input/output functions in parallel with normal computation. Thus the central processor and each direct-memory-
access controller will be the same basic chip programmed to
specialize it to the particular function it performs.

Although microprocessors will have the power of today's minicomputers, or more, in the 1980s, there is a major obstacle that must be crossed before microprocessor based systems can lead to substantial cost reductions in conventional minicomputer systems. The obstacle is the availability of low-cost auxiliary memory. Modern device technology indicates that the cost of the control logic of a computer system can be pushed to near zero. Main memory prices can be pushed down as well, but as it goes down, memory sizes tend to increase to offset the price decrease in part. Mechanical auxiliary memory is not achieving equal gains in cost, performance, and reliability as have been obtained in the solid-state technologies. Typical $100,000 minicomputer systems delivered today have costs allocated 10% to the central processor, 20% to main memory, 50% to auxiliary memory, with the remainder allocated to other peripherals and controllers. As the hardware costs of the processor, controllers, and main memory are dropping more rapidly than auxiliary memory, the major cost in the system is auxiliary memory.

Fortunately there are several possible nonmechanical replacements for auxiliary memory in various stages of development. Magnetic bubble memories are nonvolatile magnetic shift-register memories in which storage densities comparable to MOS memories have been achieved. Since the technology is magnetic, reading and writing of data in memory inherently involves a transduction between electronic and magnetic media. Transducers are physically large compared to the size of the bubbles carrying information. Consequently, to achieve high storage density a single transducer is shared among many bits, with the resulting requirement that a bubble must be moved physically from its current resting position to a transducer in order to be read. This takes a time much longer than the access time to a cell in an integrated circuit memory, so that bubbles are not likely to be used in main memory. Random-access time may be as low as 20 microseconds, more likely somewhat higher, but still some 100 times faster than access to rotating mechanical devices.

Another attractive storage medium is also shift-register oriented, and known as *charge-coupled device* (CCD) technology. CCD memories are volatile shift-registers made up of capacitors. Charge in capacitors must be kept in circulation, unlike bubbles in magnetic bubble memories, but otherwise CCD performance characteristics closely approximate magnetic bubble memory characteristics. The first CCD memory chips for computers announced commercially appeared in 1975 and had 16k bits per chip. This puts CCD technology slightly ahead of magnetic bubbles, since bubbles did not reach the market place by 1975.

One other technology today is a candidate for replacing mechanical auxiliary memory, namely electron beam addressable memory (EBAM). This technology uses electron beam techniques to deposit charges in a small region of a surface, and to read them out at a later time. There is some irony in looking at this technology as a technology of the future since the Institute for Advanced Study computer built by von Neumann and his associates in 1948-1950 had a main memory that was functionally similar to the proposed EBAM memories. Von Neumann used Williams tubes for storage, which were basically cathode ray devices in which the beam could deposit and read-out charge stored on the face of the tube. EBAM, of course, is much smaller and denser. EBAM is several years behind the development of CCD and bubble memories, but once perfected could be a strong contender since access to memory is by random beam addressing rather than by serial access to shift registers. The shift register structures of CCDs and bubbles can be supplemented with small cache memories to improve performance, however, so there still remains much speculation as to which of the three auxiliary memory technologies will eventually survive.

Under the assumption that costs for microprocessors and memory drop to near zero by the 1980s, and that nonmechanical

auxiliary memories are available, it is perfectly conceivable
that the typical $100,000 minicomputer system mentioned earlier
can be marketed for $1,000. Input/output will undoubtedly be the
most expensive portion of the computer, and the only portion with
an appreciable failure rate and service demands. By the late
1980s the now ubiquitous hand calculator may actually be more
nearly an IBM 370/145 than an adding machine.

III. MEDIUM-SCALE COMPUTERS

Computer manufacturers have to face the 1980s with a mixture of joy and grief. The joy stems from potential unit sales
of 100 to 1000 times the present number of systems sold as computers move into every imaginable application. The grief is due
to the decreasing cost of the hardware itself so that total sales
volume of the hardware may drop precipitously even while unit
sales are growing enormously. All the while this is happening,
the end-user finds that a paltry sum buys him hardware of incredible potential, but to make it do his job he has to pour many
thousands of dollars into software and program development.

The solution to end-users' problems and to the computer
manufacturers' plight lies in treating computer systems as
hardware/software/applications systems, that is, as total systems, rather than as hardware alone. Thus pricing of computer
systems will depend more on the services they perform than on
their cost of replication. The purchaser may be quite satisfied
to pay N dollars for a system that benefits him by 2N dollars,
even though unit costs are N/100, exclusive of hardware and
software development costs. Software, for which replication
costs are insignificant compared to development costs, will be
reduced in cost to the end-user by amortizing development over
more systems.

So how will these trends affect the computer architecture
of medium-scale machines? Medium-scale computers will be
designed to use inexpensive additional logic wherever possible
to facilitate flexibility, and enhance the range of services

that can be done effectively on the machine.

Among the several trends for medium-scale computers that
are perceptable are the following:

1. A "rich" instruction set is included that permits many
    higher-level operations to be done efficiently.

2. The use of microprogramming with a writeable control
    store will be prevalent, so that new instructions can
    be implemented by the user after physical delivery of
    the machine. New instructions might be included for
    each compiler target language to increase efficiency
    of execution of object code, and these instructions
    could be easily changed to become a function of the
    particular compiler language in which each program is
    written. Emulation of one architecture by another will
    be commonplace.

3. Large memories, both real and virtual, will simplify
    problems of writing programs of large size.

4. Executive and control functions will be done by special
    purpose hardware insofar as is possible to simplify the
    operating system and control program.

5. Virtual machine architecture will be widely used to aid
    the writing and debugging of the control software that
    cannot be implemented in hardware.

There has been a great deal of interest in several innova-
tive areas of computer architecture of late, and it is interesting to speculate on how successful these ideas will be in the
medium-scale computers of the 1980s. Some of the ideas and this
author's opinions are offered here.

Push-down stack instruction repertoires. The stack machine is
a departure from von Neumann's original concept of a register
machine, and it has met with a great deal of success in the
KDF-9 computer and the Burrough's B-5000 and others in the
Burrough's line. It is widely used in instruction repertoires
to facilitate subroutine entry and exit, because the push-down

stack is the natural data structure for this. One attribute of
push-down stack architecture is high code density, and another is
ease of programming and compiler writing. One problem is that it
runs somewhat slower than machines with explicit high-speed registers, because only the top elements of a push-down stack are
directly available in high-speed registers.

As memory costs drop, the code density is not a strong
asset for push-down stack instructions. Slower speed due to the
limited number of high-speed registers available is a distinct
disadvantage. It may be difficult to build a strong case for
pure push-down stack computers in the 1980s, except perhaps
because of the simplification achieved for compiler writing. A
hybrid instruction set, consisting of stack instructions and
register instructions both, may emerge to achieve high-speed
where necessary by using the high-speed registers in the inner
loops of programs. This tends to speed-up programs where they
spend their most time, and permits stack instructions to be used
in the remainder of the programs, where speed is not essential,
and slower speed is not a serious handicap. Stacks for subroutine entry and exit have proved to be useful and will undoubtedly
be widely used by the late 1980s, regardless if the arithmetic
instructions are register, push-down, or hybrid instructions.
High-level language architecture. Numerous proposals have been
made to develop computers in which the native instruction set
is strongly oriented to execution of some high-level language.
Bashkow et. al. [1967] described a FORTRAN machine, for example,
and the Burroughs B-5000 and B-6700 are examples of ALGOL
machines. Compilation for these machines becomes quite trivial
in principle, and object code is highly compact. Given the
trends expected in the 1980s, it is not clear how high-level
language machines will be of great service. The disadvantage
of high-level language machines may be that there is little
discernible advantage for the end-user who is interested in

purchasing services and cares little about the native instruction
repertoire. Users today are still running IBM 360s in emulator
mode emulating their programs from the previous computer generation. These users care primarily about the service being done,
not about whether the instructions are IBM 360-like or IBM 1401-
like. The user of the 1980s like the user of today will care
somewhat about computation speed, but a high-level language machine does not necessarily improve computation speed over a more
conventional machine running with a highly optimized compiler.

Virtual memory and auxiliary memory. The large address space
of machines with virtual memory has been a great boon for programmers. The ease of dealing with one level of memory instead
of both main memory and auxiliary memory has led to greatly
simplified program development and reduced costs. Large address
spaces will continue to be used in the 1980s and if anything,
will grow larger. The 24-bit address of the System/360-370
machines, for example, has proved to be large enough for the
1960s and 1970s, whereas 16-bit addresses are now viewed as
insufficient, and 18-bit addresses as marginally sufficient. By
the end of the 1980s the 24-bit address may have to yield to the
31 or 32-bit address to provide an internal architecture commensurate with the capabilities of physical hardware.

A major problem in the use of virtual memories today is the
problem of memory management. It is extremely important to have
the active areas of program resident in high-speed memory to
avoid the penalties of page faults and disk accesses. This
problem is actually a characteristic of the technology available
today and may be greatly alleviated by advances in technology.
At the very least, main memories will be several times larger
than the norm today, thereby providing greater area for program
working sets. Backing up main memory we expect to have nonmechanical auxiliary memories with access times measured in tens of
microseconds. Thus the penalties of page faults when they do
occur will be orders of magnitude smaller than costs incurred

today.

Cache memory. In several models of the System/370 computer series and in the Amdahl/470 computer, among several others, there is a cache memory available that acts as a high speed buffer for main memory, in much the same way that main memory is a buffer for auxiliary memory in terms of the virtual memory system. The cache, of course, is much faster, roughly ten times faster, than main memory, but is more expensive per bit to implement. The objective is to obtain a memory whose performance is roughly that of the cache memory at a cost comparable to the cost of main memory. As long as the fast integrated circuit memory technologies are more expensive than the slower memory technologies, the cache will play an important role in medium-scale computers. Earlier we mentioned that ECL and T^2L logic families are faster than MOS, but have lower densities, and thus have higher costs. An MOS or magnetic core main memory with an ECL or T^2L cache is economically viable as long as the costs and speeds are sufficiently different. The trend, however, is to achieve low costs of the higher speed logic through innovations like I^2L logic while attaining higher speed of the low cost logic through silicon-on-sapphire technology. As these two developments become successful in erasing the differences between high-speed and low-cost logic, the economic grounds for using a cache to buffer main memory may disappear. It is much more likely that main memory will, in fact, be a very large cache for a nonmechanical auxiliary memory.

Medium-scale computers as centralized computing resources. When computation facilities were very expensive, they necessarily were treated as precious resources. In general, no single user could afford to pay for an entire computer system, and even if he could, his project may not be sufficiently large to occupy the facilities for a significant part of the duty cycle. From this grew the methodologies for sharing computer systems, first as batch processors, then as multiprogramming systems, and with terminal access as time-sharing systems. Now that the costs have dropped substantially, hardware is no longer a precious resource. Many users have purchased their own equipment for relatively small costs instead of using centralized facilities, and use the equipment with a low duty cycle in preference to sharing the equipment to reduce costs further. The economics are clear. The programmable calculator of 1976 can do many computations that a smaller user would perform on a high speed computer in 1960, and the purchase price of the calculator is on the order of the expenses of a week or so for computer time and programming services of the 1960 computer. The calculator user would never conceive of "selling time" on his device, nor is it cost-effective for him to purchase time on a shared facility to do a problem that can be done on the calculator.

Projecting this trend forward to the late 1980s, we see that a device comparable in cost and size to the electric typewriter could be as powerful as a medium-scale computer of 1976. This will have a great effect on decentralizing the computer center as we know it today. What will be the function of shared-resource medium scale computers then?

When hardware and software replication costs are low, there will still be need for central computers for computer users to access. Access will be less for computational power than for information from central data files. The data will be a resource and a commodity of trade by that time if it is not already now. The central data base accessed by a user may have service programs to which he submits his own data and receives analyses, or may have library programs that he purchases for transmission to his local site for execution. The user will almost certainly use the central data base for numerical data, catalogs, bibliographies, mail, and text, quite apart from uses he makes of programs stored centrally. Since information is created in real time, a computer user must tap that information through access to one or more centralized data bases even when he is able to satisfy his computational needs for that data through the purchase of inexpensive hardware. Thus data base management and information retrieval will be a principle function of the medium-scale computer of the 1980s.

III. LARGE-SCALE SYSTEMS

By eary 1976 a number of very high-speed computing systems had been installed and were in operation. Some of the sytems use a standard serial instruction set, and use a number of clever design techniques to achieve high-speed. For example, the CDC 7600 system uses multiple functional units that can operate simultaneously, and uses an intricate instruction scheduling mechanism to keep these units busy as much as possible, even executing the instructions out-of-order if that results in a net increase in speed.

One trend that has emerged in recent years is that of using a computer with a vector instruction set. Each vector instruction in such a machine operates on entire vectors instead of single elements. When a vector instruction is issued on a vector computer, that one instruction manipulates all of the elements of the vector operands, and achieves a great deal of parallelism of operation with a large gain in speed.

Two distinct types of computers with vector instructions have been delivered. One type is the *array computer* of the ILLIAC IV class in which each element of the vector is treated by an independent processor. Fig. 3 shows a control unit linked to 64 processors in an array by a broadcast bus. Each instruction issued results in 64 responses, each on a different element of a vector of length 64. The other type, the *pipeline computer*, as exemplified by the CDC STAR, has the computational unit partitioned into successive stages, each of which can be busy simultaneously. A vector operation is initiated by placing the first operand pair into the first stage of the computation; as they pass on to the second stage the next pair is passed into the empty first stage. Thus if there are N stages in the pipeline,

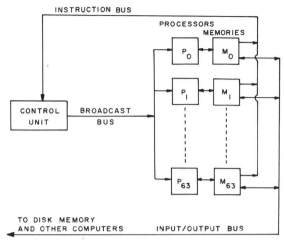

Fig. 3. An array computer (ILLIAC IV)

N different operations may be in operation simultaneously, each
in a different stage. Fig. 4 illustrates the structure of a

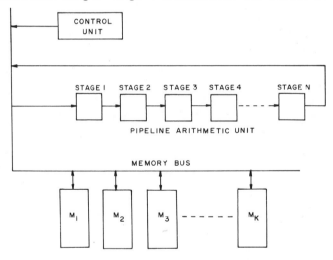

Fig. 4. A pipeline computer

typical pipeline computer. Floating-point operations can be
conveniently divided into about eight successive stages, and the
pipelines themselves can be replicated to give additional parallelism.

To give some idea of the parallelism achieveable on the

271

present machines, ILLIAC IV has 64 processors, but each processor can do two single precision operations simultaneously, so that 128 different computations can be executed at once. The CDC STAR has an effective parallelism of about 32. The parallelism achievable is impressive, but is representative of designs in progress well over five years ago. The ILLIAC IV uses an integrated circuit memory, but no large-scale integration. The CDC STAR uses neither integrated circuit memory nor large-scale integration. It is obvious that technological changes available today can be included in the next generation of these computers to gain a potential speed improvement of approximately another factor of 10 at no increase in cost. If we take into account the advances that are certain to appear in the next five years in integrated circuit technology, then this could contribute a total factor of 50 improvement in speed over machines in operation today.

Unfortunately, a factor of 50 is not enough for the very large scale problems for which these computer systems are built. Most notable of the massive calculations are fluid dynamics problems and weather analysis. In crude solutions to typical problems in these domains, one might run a computer capable of delivering 1 million operations per second for 10 hours, resulting in roughly $36 \cdot 10^9$ operations. Solutions to the Navier-Stokes equations in three dimensions can require up to 10^{18} operations without simplifying assumptions, and anywhere from 10^{12} to 10^{15} operations when acceptable approximations are available. The ILLIAC IV, CDC STAR, and CDC 7600 each run in the range of 1 to 10 million operations per second (MOPS), so that they come close to being able to solve highly idealized versions of the Navier-Stokes equations in three dimensions, if run for sufficiently long periods. A factor of 50 improvement in speed reduces a 10 hour computation to 12 minutes, and puts many crude solutions to the Navier-Stokes equation within striking distance. But even with the factor of 50, and running a computer for 10 hours, we are still a factor of 10^5 too slow to solve the full-scale equations.

The obvious answer is to increase the degree of parallelism where possible. When logic costs drop very low, the number of identical units that can be put into a design of marketable cost, can increase from 10^2 in 1976 to perhaps 10^3 or 10^4 in the late 1980s. Unfortunately, the speed increases attainable fall short of being equal to the replication factor.

Vector computers have a tremendous advantage over conventional serial computers when computations fit the vector format well. A good vectorizable serial computation is one that is iteratively structured, where each iteration is identical and independent of the other iterations. This computation can be cast into vector form by identifying each vector element with one iteration. All iterations are performed simultaneously while carrying out the vector operation.

A number of lessons have been learned from experience with vector computers like STAR and ILLIAC. A few of the principle ones are given below.

1. When algorithms can be cast in vector form there are significant advantages due to elimination of unnecessary overhead for individual elements. Vector algorithms developed for STAR were moved back to the non-vector CDC 7600, and achieved substantial speed gains on that machine over conventional serial algorithms largely because of overhead reduction and the ability to minimize conflicts while keeping numerous computational units busy simultaneously.

2. It is possible to incur substantial overhead in vector algorithms in communicating information among elements of a vector when operations on one element are influenced by the value of another element.

3. There are numerous tricks for casting serial algorithms into vector form. A programmer may have to experiment

273

with various alternatives to obtain the best alternative.
For matrices, for example, he may have to consider
sweeping by rows, columns, diagonals, reverse diagonals,
and block subarrays before finding the most efficient
method. The best vector algorithms for particular
problems may be quite unconventional and, in fact, may
not be very efficient when performed in equivalent
serial form.

4. Major bottlenecks occur when sequential scalar operations have to be done in between vector operations.
   This reduces the effective speed of a highly parallel
   machine drastically and the effect becomes more pro-
   nounced in machines as the parallelism increases.

By all appearances the vector machine is not the final
answer, although the range of problems for which vector machines
are well-suited has proved to be much larger than anticipated
because of innovations in parallel algorithms and architectural
features.

Where will additional speed increases be gained in the
1980s for the super computers of that decade? This is highly
conjectural and extremely difficult to estimate at this time.
There are several possibilities, each with its own promises and
pitfalls, no one of which appears to be the ultimate answer.
We discuss several of the approaches here.

Serial control processor plus parallel array processor. T. C.
Chen [1971] among others observed the performance deficiencies
from intermixing parallel and serial processes. Fig. 5 illustrates a typical duty cycle for an array processor in which one
processor is kept busy initializing a vector process, then all
N processors are ganged together performing the vector operation.
Chen observed that a pipeline computer duty cycle figure has
the form of staircase in Fig. 6, to show how each successive
stage initiates activity slightly later than its predecessor
stage. The shaded region in dark boundaries is exactly equal

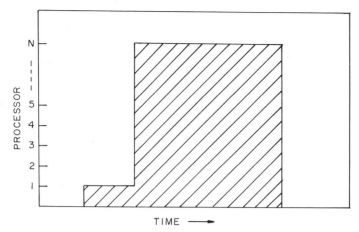

Fig. 5. Duty cycle for an array computer

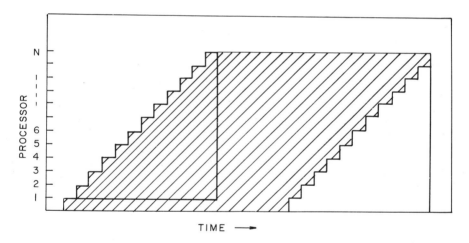

Fig. 6. Duty cycle for a pipeline computer

to the unshaded region in dark boundaries, so that the shaded area of the pipeline computer duty cycle is exactly equal to the shaded area of an array processor computation as shown in the previous figure. With this observation it is clear that there is a potential performance decrease in a pipeline computer due to a phenomenon very much like the serial overhead prior to a vector computation in an array computer.

The ILLIAC IV is designed to perform the computation shown

in Fig. 5 as shown in Fig. 7, where the serial computation is

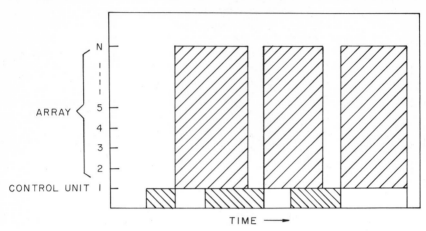

Fig. 7.   ILLIAC IV duty cycle

done in a single control unit, and is done while the previous
vector operation is in progress in the arithmetic processor
array.   This vastly reduces time lost due to interspersing
serial and parallel operations.   The equivalent processing duty
cycle for the pipeline computer is shown in Fig. 8, which simply
shows one vector operation initiated before the termination of
the prior one.   The CDC STAR pipeline computer presently does
not have the facility to execute in this manner.   Thus, the STAR

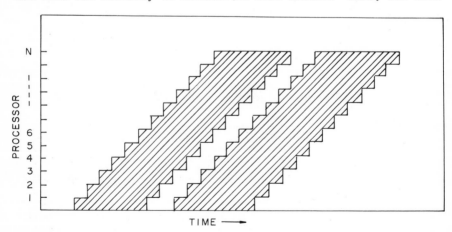

Fig. 8.   Duty cycle for pipeline equivalent of ILLIAC IV

duty cycle is more like that shown in Fig. 9.

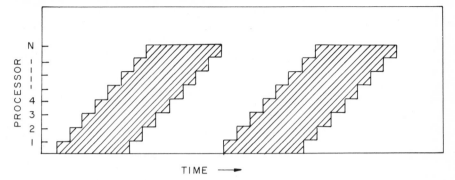

Fig. 9. Duty cycle for STAR

To achieve better total performance than is predicted by Chen's pessimistic analysis, it is clear that the architecture of the 1980s will have a mix of processors, some of which are dedicated to serial types of tasks, and some dedicated to highly parallel or iterative types of tasks. Execution overlap among processing units will have to be significant to attain the speed potential of having many arithmetic units.

Multiprocessors. To overcome the obstacle of the vector structure for algorithms that do not lend themselves to this structure, computer systems may eventually contain many identical and independent processors, each capable of executing its own program while synchronizing and communicating with other programs. Today, multiprocessors exist, often with two to four processors, and with as many as 14 for the Bolt, Beranek, and Newman Pluribus and 16 for the Carnegie-Mellon C.mmp. The problem here is one of finding how to partition among a large number of multiprocessors, and to control and synchronize the computation, so that high performance is achieved. Since the processors are not ganged together as they execute, it is extremely difficult to predict where conflicts will arise, what queueing delays will be, and where the essential bottle necks will be. Programming for multiprocessors has all of the richness of programming for a

vector computer and more, leaving this problem virtually untouched. The few investigations that have been done such as
Steele's [1975], show that as in the case for vector algorithms,
conventional serial algorithms might perform rather poorly when
partitioned naturally on a multiprocessor system, whereas a
relatively unconventional, perhaps inefficient serial algorithm,
might give the best performance on a multiprocessor.

The study of multiprocessors has reached the stage at which
hardware construction has been reduced to practice; control and
synchronizing functions are within the state-of-the-art, but
require additional study; methods for interconnecting individual
processors in large numbers are still matters of conjecture;
and programming techniques for high-speed computation are virtually unknown.

Large-scale numerical problems rarely need the full power
of individual multiprocessors because they involve thousands of
identical computations for the most part rather than a large
number of highly individualized computations. The reason that
vector computations are not completely adequate is that meshes
may be irregular, with nonuniform spacing, with portions of a
mesh satisfying a different system of equations than another
portion, or with the equations coupled by boundary conditions
of some intricacy. Moreover, the lack of complete homogeneity
may be time-varying unpredictably during the course of a computation. A multiprocessor certainly has the generality required
for inhomogeneous mesh calculations, but the penalty for using
a multiprocessor is the additional time lost due to overhead in
synchronization, conflicts, queueing, and other aspects of the
multiprocessor.

One potentially good idea that may appear in an architecture in the next decade is a processor system that displays both
vector and multiprocessor capabilities. When independent calculations are needed, the processors split apart and perform
individually. At points where the computation is highly vector

oriented, the processors combine and synchronize to broadcast
instructions to take advantage of the efficiencies of vector
mode. To some extent, this capability was designed into ILLIAC
IV, which was designed to consist of four quadrants of 64 processors each. Quadrants have been designed to gang together into
larger arrays of 128 or 256 processors, or to split apart into
individual quadrants of 64 processors, and to do so dynamically.
However, the cost of one quadrant is sufficiently high to moot
the question of purchasing additional quadrants, and only one
quadrant has ever been delivered.

Microprocessor arrays. With microprocessors so inexpensive,
there is an obvious motivation to construct vector or multiprocessor computers from arrays of microprocessors. While the individual speed of any one microprocessor may be moderate, the
ability to gather 10^3 or 10^4 processors together in a single
computer can lead to a very-high speed computer with tremendous
computing power for reasonable cost. Hardware advances have,
unfortunately, outstripped architectural and algorithmic advances to the extent that it is now possible to construct arrays
with incredible computational power, except that it is not clear
what form the arrays should take and how calculations should
proceed in them.

McGill and Steinhoff [1976] describe a microprocessor array
used for a Monte Carlo simulation of a flight system. The array
is configured to reflect the flight dynamics equations, much
like operational amplifiers and integrators are configured in
an analog simulation. Initial conditions are set by Monte Carlo
techniques, and the computer system thereafter traces the behavior of the flight system in question. The technique is remi-
niscent of digital differential analysis techniques, except that
the equations solved need not be limited to differential equations. The system described exists only on paper but is indi-
cative of one way to put many microprocessors to work on a computation that is not easily vectorized.

279

If this approach is to survive and be viable for the late
1980s then the programming of the system for a particular problem involves a configuration of the interconnections as much as
programming the individual processors. Interconnections might
be configured either by hardware or by programmable switches.
Effectiveness also depends on memory being sufficiently large
to contain the entire problem, since each microprocessor is
allocated to a particular function, without provision for swap-
ping new functions in and out of a processor's memory. Nevertheless we see a distinct possibility that users with a need for
very large-scale computation facilities could use large arrays
of microprocessors and memories especially configured for a
specific class of problems.

To summarize the current trends for high-speed machines,
a factor of 50 speed improvement is possible by the end of the
1980s from technological advances in devices, but the demands
of very large problems will stimulate evolution of the architecture itself. Vector machines look more promising than multiprocessors for large scale problems for the long term future,
but some hybrid of the two may emerge and prove to be the best
solution.

V. CONCLUSIONS

With technological advances leading the way as we move into
and through the next decade, computer architecture will evolve
to enhance the proliferation of the microprocessor, the utility
of the medium-scale computer, and the sheer computational power
of the large-scale machine. The most dramatic changes will be
in new applications brought about because of ever lowering costs,
smaller sizes, and faster switching times. There is no evidence
at this time that the rate of advance in computer technology
will slow significantly in the 1980s. We are truly undergoing
a Computer Revolution of the scale of the Industrial Revolution.

ACKNOWLEDGMENT

The author wishes to thank Dr. Thomas Whitney for suggestions and information used in this report. He is also indebted to Mr. Paul Jones for drafting the figures. This research was supported by NSF Grant DCR 74-20025.

REFERENCES

Bashkow, T. R., A. Sasson, and A. Kronfeld [1967]. "System design of a FORTRAN machine," *IEEE Trans. on Elec. Comp.*, EC-16, No. 4, pp. 485-499, August 1967.

Chen, T. C. [1971]. "Parallelism, pipelining, and computer efficiency," *Computer Design*, pp. 69-74, January 1971.

McGill, R. and J. Steinhoff [1976]. "A multimicroprocessor approach to numerical analysis: An application to gaming problems," *Proc. of Third Annual Computer Architecture Conf.*, IEEE Pub. 76 CH1043-5C, pp. 46-51, January 1976.

Steele, Guy L., Jr., [1975]. "Multiprocessing compactifying garbage collection," *Comm. ACM.*, 18, No. 9, pp. 495-508, September 1975.

Turn, Rein, [1974]. *Computers in the 1980s*, Columbia U. Press, New York 1974.

MINICOMPUTER COMPLEXES: PROGRESS AND PROSPECTS

Wm. A. Wulf
Carnegie-Mellon University
Pittsburgh, Pa.

Abstract

The economics of computers have reversed since the early 1960's;
at that time a phenomenon known as "Grosch's law" seemed to hold.
Grosch's law asserted that the power of a computer was related
to the square of its cost. More recently, however, mass production of mini and micro computers has made them more costeffective
(in $/computation) than large machines. This reversal has a num-
ber of implications, one of which is that the "right" way to
build large machines may be as an assembledge of a large number
of these smaller processors.

This implication was recognized several years ago and spawned several research projects; each of these projects took a somewhat
different approach to the problem of interconnecting many small
processors to deliver the power of a large machine. This paper
will: (1) expand on the problems and potentials of interconnected
mini (or micro) computers, (2) assess the progress to date in re-
alizing the potential of some of these systems, and (3) take another look at the future prospects for these systems.

This work was supported by the Advanced Research Projects Agency
of the Department of Defense under contract F44620-73-C-0074 and
monitored by the Air Force Office of Scientific Research.

INTRODUCTION

Recently, that is during the first half of the 1970's, there has been a substantial and growing interest in the interconnection of a number of mini- and/or micro-computers. There are a number of reasons for this interest, including:

- the economics of LSI technology

- reliability

- total system "power" and/or "throughput"

- incremental expansion

- more effective utilization of existing equipment

and others. The explicit manifestation of this interest has been the construction of a number of computer systems in research organizations which couple mini's and micro's in various ways -- although, interestingly, none of the major manufacturers has announced such a system.

In this paper I shall try to explain more fully the rationale behind this interest, to describe some of the systems which have been built, to assess the degree to which these systems have achieved their potential and the problems they have uncovered, and to make some personal observations (and guesses) about the future.

Before proceeding I would like to emphasize that the phrase "mini-computer complexes" was chosen with some care to be neutral with respect to the interconnection technology of these systems. There are many ways in which the several computers could be interconnected: at one extreme they might be very tightly coupled, say by sharing primary memory as in the classical multiprocessor. At the other extreme they might be loosely coupled, say via communication lines as in the classical network. Beyond the physical interconnection strategy, the operating systems of the several computers could be largely or wholly autonomous, or a single operating system could control the entire complex. The space of design alternatives is very rich, and relatively little of it has been explored; moreover, there is no reason to believe that any single one of the design possibilities will achieve all the potentials of complexes.

MOTIVATION FOR MINICOMPUTER COMPLEXES

In this section we shall explore some of the more important reasons behind the interest in the interconnection of a moderately large number of mini- and microcomputers.

Economics of Current Technology

In the early 1960's it was widely believed that a phenomenon known as "Grosch's law" held between the price and "power" of a computer. This "law" asserted that the power of a computer was related to the square of its cost; thus if one were willing to pay twice the price, one would obtain four times the power. It is difficult at this point to tell whether or not this "law" was the consequence of technology or a particular pricing strategy. However, it _is_ clear that it no longer holds -- and in fact that quite the opposite is true. Figure I plots the cost effectiveness (measured in memory-bandwidth/dollar), as a function of the price of the smallest configuration, for all the computers listed in Computer Review (2). Although there is a considerable amount of scatter in this graph, note its generally negative slope. It appears that the more expensive machines are not as cost-effective as the less expensive ones. In particular, the $10,000 systems, the minicomputers, appear to be at least an order of magnitude more cost-effective than the larger machines. There are a number of reasons for this tendency:

1. LSI technology tends to favor the small machine. These machines can effectively utilize, for example, the large ALU and memory chips; larger processors tend to require specialized logic to speed up the ALU functions, and faster memories than are possible with the larger, denser memory chips.

2. Economies of scale favor the small, mass-produced machine. By virtue of their larger volume, production techniques can be used for mini's and micro's which are not feasible for the larger machines.

3. Hardware and software development costs are amortized over a much larger number of units in the case of mini's and micro's. These costs are certainly not less initially for large machines, and may be larger; thus the per-unit burden for the small machines is several orders of magnitude lower.

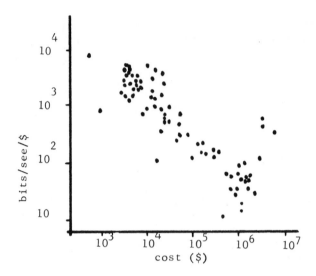

Figure I
Cost/Performance vs. Cost

In contrast with the trend data of Figure I, which deals only
with single processors, Figure II shows the results of a specific comparison of one minicomputer complex, C.mmp (8), with several implementations of a large uni-processor system, the DEC
PDP-10. This figure is reproduced from Fuller (5) and I shall
not try to explain all the rationale behind it. It shows the
relation of price/performance (measured in instructions/sec/dollar)
to both memory cost and construction technology of the processors.
(The KA10, KI10, and KL10 are progressively more modern implementations of the PDP-10; the PDP-11/40 is roughly the same technology as the KI10 and the dotted lines represent a hypothetical
implementation of the PDP-11 using current (1975) technology --
specifically the Intel 3000 bit-sliced microprocessor chips).

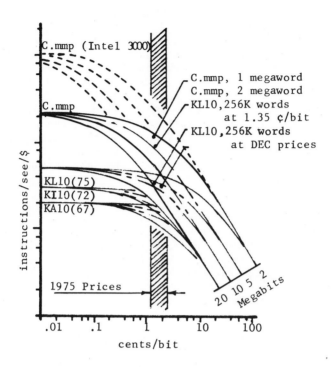

Figure II
Cost-Performance Comparison of C.mmp and PDP-10

As may be seen, as memory cost deminishes the cost of the processor dominates and the mini-computer complex becomes a factor
of 4 to 10 more cost effective than a uniprocessor.

Reliability

On purely intuitive grounds it seems that any system in which
there are a number of independent units - processors in this case,
each of which can perform a task—should be more reliable than a
system without such redundency. Thus the advocates of mini-computer complexes (including the present author) have argued that
such systems are inherently more reliable -- arguing, roughly,
that the loss of a processor should merely result in the loss of
one n[th] of the processing power of the system.

With one notable exception, the BBN Pluribus (6), this hypothesis seems to be largely untested, and even in the Pluribus case the picture is not completely clear. The problem, of course, is that the interconnection of independent units adds to the complexity of the whole: to the physical system itself, to the decomposition of the programs, to data communication, to synchronization of both data and control, and to the protection of the individual program units. To be sure, all of these problems appear in uni-processor systems as well, but the interconnection exagerates them. While the problems imposed by the additional complexity may presumably be overcome, and in fact may not be too severe relative to the increased redundency, the data is simply not available yet on a wide variety of systems.

The case of the BBN Pluribus is an interesting one in this context. I shall discuss the system at greater length below, however it is a multiprocessor utilizing Lockheed SUE's as the processing elements. It was constructed to serve as a communications node in the ARPANET and, as such, was intended to span the spectrum of low-cost, low data-rate nodes (possibly involving only a single processor), to much larger nodes handling heavy traffic. Reliability was of prime concern in this application, and substantial success has been achieved in fulfilling this goal. Unfortunately, the general applicability of these techniques is unclear for two, related reasons: First, the system involves a single, dedicated application; thus a great deal of application-specific knowledge could be incorporated in the reliability techniques. Second, the particular application is _externally_ reliable in the sense that failures of a node appear as messages which do not get through to their destination; the programs which utilize the network are prepared to recognize such situations and retransmit -- possibly via a different route. Thus a node may "fail-soft", in the extreme, by simply shutting itself off. General purpose systems do not generally have this luxury. Nevertheless, the Pluribus reliability achievements are impressive and may point the way toward more general methods.

Power and/or Throughput

The brief history of computing has been characterized by a constant pressure for both more, and more cost-effective, computing. At any given point in time technology imposes limits on both the maximum power available from a single processor and the minimum cost for obtaining a given amount of power, again from a single processor. Any attempt to circumvent these technological limits must be done by organizational techniques, e.g. by the interconnection of several processors. One may wish to obtain additional power in order to apply it to a single problem; this tends to suggest tightly coupled parallelism as in the ILLIAC IV or CDC STAR. Alternatively, one may wish simply to increase the power available to an aggregate of users -- as in a time-sharing utility; less tightly coupled systems, such as the coupled mini's discussed here, seem more reasonable in this context.

Incremental Expansion

One of the more attactive aspects of coupled mini's, at least for the computation facility manager, is the notion that the power of a configuration can be increased by "simply adding processors". Although most manufacturers now offer a family of upward compatible machines, it is still the case that increasing computing power by replacement of the existing machine is a tramatic experience.

As with all the potential benefits of interconnected processors, expandability is not without its own set of problems. A system can be designed to be expanded essentially indefinitely, but generally there is a cost in terms of the time required for one processor to communicate with another, or to access data held by another. Whether or not this is important depends on the application area envisioned for the assemblage.

Utilization of existing equipment

An oft-cited advantage of interconnecting a number of mini-computers is to enhance the utilization of a pre-existing collection of mini's; we shall examine one such system, constructed at Bell Labs, below. This rationale is quite different from those cited above, which generally presume that the system is not constrained to function with predefined, autonomous software. It is a very real advantage in many situations, but not one I will consider further.

THE DIMENSIONS OF INTERCONNECTION

Given that the notion of interconnecting a number of mini or micro computers might be a good one, a fundamental question remains: how? As one might expect there is no clear answer since: (1) although a number of systems have been built, data on them is still meager, and (2) in all probability, the answer depends upon the relative weight one places on the various benefits listed above.

In order to discuss the relative advantages and disadvantages of any particular interconnection strategy one first needs a characterization of the possible alternatives. Since this section was first written a survey and taxonomy of interconnected computers by Andersen and Jensen has appeared in Computer Surveys, (1); among other things it contains a comprehensive bibliography. Although I shall not follow their terminology and taxonomy completely, the following material has been modified in the hope that the interested reader may pursue their more complete treatment without severe clashes in either terminology or perspective.

There are at least three major parameters which distinguish between the more obvious interconnection strategies: control, topology, and bandwidth, where:

- By control we mean the mechanism used to determine the routing of information between processors and/or processors and memory. Three choices seem possible: implicit (by the structure only one choice is possible), central (a single entity, be it software or hardware, chooses among alternative routes), and decentralized (any, or all, of several entities choose the path).

- By topology we mean the physical interconnection topology, i.e., whether every processor is directly connected to every other and/or to every memory, or certain processor-to-processor(memory) transfers are only possible through intermediaries. In addition, under this term we shall distinguish between those cases in which a physical path is dedicated to transfers between a single pair (processor-processor or processor-memory) or shared.

- By bandwidth we simply mean the maximum rate at which information can be exchanged.

While these three parameters do not serve to distinguish between all the systems which have been built, it does seem that varying any one of them significantly alters the character of the system and the software which attempts to use it.

Perhaps the most striking difference between interconnection strategies is based on bandwidth: those which seek high bandwidth share memory, those that don't, don't. In the former case bandwidth is essentially unlimited since an arbitrary amount of data can be exchanged by simply exchanging a pointer (address) to the data. These systems are the classical multiprocessors; the systems which do not share memory are the classical networks. (Of course this is an oversimplification, and there are examples of intermediate points -- such as those which share secondary memory).

The Multiprocessors

Among the multiprocessors, all of which permit any of several processors to access any of several memories, control is nearly always implicit. These systems are designed to permit rapid access by any of the processors to the common memory, hence there is little time for complex routing decisions to be made. However, there are significant differences in topology; Figures IIIa-c illustrate three different approaches.

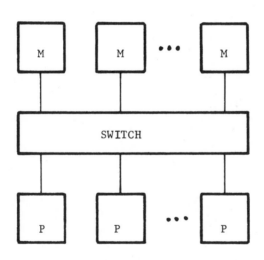

Figure IIIa
Multiprocessor with a Central Switch

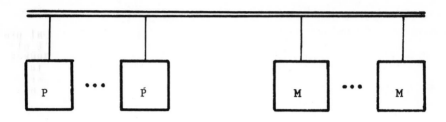

Figure **IIIb**
Multiprocessor with a Common Bus

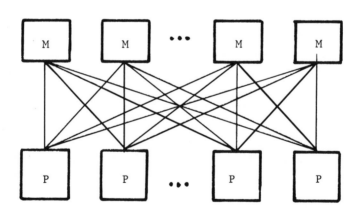

Figure **IIIc**
Multiprocessor with Decentralized Switch

Figure IIIa illustrates a multiprocessor in which there is a single centralized switch between the processors and memory. C.mmp, discussed later, is an example of such a system. Figure IIIb illustrates a multiprocessor in which all processor-memory transfers are performed on a single time-multiplexed bus. Figure IIIc illustrates a multiprocessor in which the switching function is distributed between the processors and memories. The BBN Pluribus, discussed briefly above and more fully below, is a blend of the latter two styles of interconnection topology. In all these figures "P" denotes a processor and "M" denotes a memory; later "C" will be used to denote a complete computer.

The centralized switch is probably the most rapid of the three schemes, but suffers in several respects: the central switch may be the reliability "bottleneck", expandability is limited to the predefined switch size, and, because the complexity of the switch grows as the square of the number of interconnected elements, there is a technology imposed limit on the number of processors that can be interconnected this way. The shared bus is conceptually the simplest of the three schemes, but is also limited in expansion potential, and may be slow. The distributed switch is more expensive than either of the other two for large systems, but is easily expanded and the cost is low for small configurations.

The Networks

In many ways the space of network designs is even richer than that of multiprocessor designs. Two control structures are common: those with specified routing nodes and those without. A special case of the former are those networks with a single designated routing node. The topologies may be classified as either regular or irregular. The latter permit arbitrary interconnection between nodes and thus generally do not have designated routing nodes. The regular networks conform to one of a few recognized graph structures: trees, loops, etc. Figures IVa-IVc illustrate some of the alternatives.

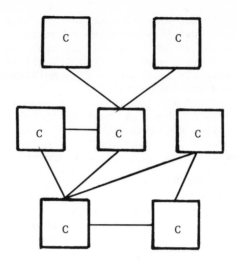

Figure IVa
Irregular Network

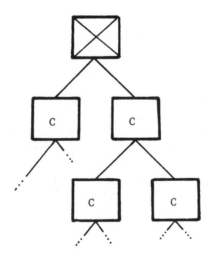

Figure IVb
Tree Network with Designated Routing Node

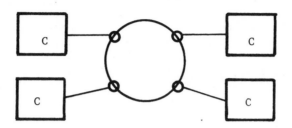

Figure IVc
Loop Network without Designated Routing Node

SOME EXAMPLE SYSTEMS

A moderate number of systems have been constructed which interconnect several minicomputers; in this section we shall describe
a few of these. The systems described were chosen to illustrate
alternatives in the design space, not to completely cover the
work which has been done.

C.mmp: A multiprocessor with a Central Switch

C.mmp (8) has been constructed by the author and his colleagues
at Carnegie-Mellon University and is a "cannonical" multiprocessor.
The architecture, illustrated in Figure V, permits the interconnection of up to 16 processors to 16 memory modules through a
central switch. The processors are various models of DEC PDP-11;
each memory module may be as large as 2 megabytes. A path through
the switch is established for each memory request and up to 16
separate paths may exist simultaneously -- thus the memory appears as a single uniform address space to each processor. Address translation is provided to map the small, 16-bit, processor-
generated addresses to the larger, 25-bit, addresses required in
the shared memory (Dmap provides this function). Interprocessor
communication is initiated through an interprocessor interrupt
mechanism, Kinterrupt, but data associated with the communication
resides in the shared memory. A common clock, Kclock, makes time-
of-day available to all processors.

Although several large research projects, notably a speech-
understanding system, motivated the construction of C.mmp, it is
envisioned as a "general purpose" machine. The operating system,
Hydra (9,11), does conventional multiprogramming of user processes on each of the processors,and user programs may run on any
(or all) of the processors; specifically, the history of the execution of a single process may involve periods of activity on any
of the processors, but the user is not, and need not be, aware of
this.

At the present time 9 processors are connected to the machine
(5 11/20's and 4 11/40's) together with 1.5 megabytes of shared
memory. Expansion to 16 processors and 2.5 megabytes is expected
by summer '76. The system is available to users about half of
each day and is being used by a number of research projects, including the speech system mentioned above (7).

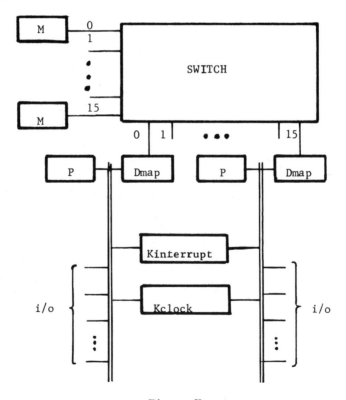

Figure V
C.mmp: A Multiprocessor with a Central Switch

Pluribus: A Mixed Strategy Multiprocessor

Pluribus (6) has been constructed at BBN (under contract to the Advanced Research Projects Agency of DOD) as a replacement for the IMP nodes of the ARPANET. A multiprocessor approach was adopted for several reasons, including the ability to provide in-expensive configurations for low traffic nodes as well as large configurations capable of handling significantly more traffic than is possible with the present IMPs. Reliability was an ex-plicit and central requirement for these machines.

The architecture of Pluribus is a mixture of the single-bus and decentralized switch schemes. The processors are Lockheed SUE's which themselves use a bus to which zero or several processors, together with several memories, may be connected. Control of the bus is centralized in Kbus. Thus, as shown in Figure VI, Pluribus utilizes several of these SUE buses, some with two processors and some local memory, others with only memory, and still others with only connections to i/o devices. The buses are connected by a decentralized switch implemented as a set of cables; the inter-faces to these cables provide address mapping. A special device, the PID (pseudo-interrupt device), maps both hardware and software generated events into a priority-ordered set and thus provides substantial hardware assistance in scheduling.

Because of the dedicated nature of the task envisioned for Pluri-bus it is reasonable to keep separate copies of the most frequent-ly executed code in the local memories attached to those busses which also have processors attached to them. The speed of the processors and memories are matched so that there is little or no interference between the processors in accessing this memory. All shared data, eg. message buffers, are kept in the shared memory; although the access time to these memories is significantly longer than to the private memories, the frequency of access is suffi-ciently low that little performance degradation is observed.

The IMP program on Pluribus is organized as a set of tasks, called strips, which are scheduled as the result of an entry made in the PID. Strips are intentionally short, and once initiated are run to completion (any processor may execute any strip).

A number of Pluribus systems have been constructed. One of these has 14 SUE processors (the maximum envisioned by the designers) and is used on a test basis at BBN. One of the systems is now in production use at the Seismic Data Analysis Center in Alexandria Virginia.

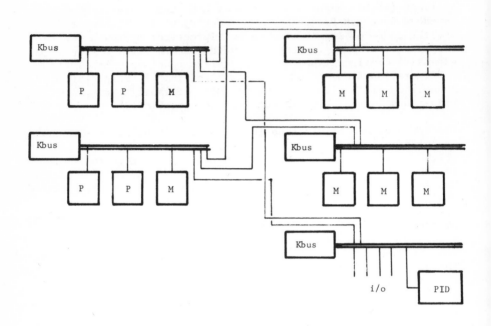

Figure VI
BBN Pluribus: A Mixed-Strategy Multiprocessor

DCS: A Loop Network with Decentralized Control

The Distributed Computing System (3), DCS, has been built by
D. Farber and his colleagues at the University of California,
Irvine. It is a loop topology network with decentralized control.
The technology of the communication lines are standard, moderately fast (2×10^6 bits/sec.), transmission lines. Processors are
connected to these lines through a "ring interface" which recognizes software-defined process names. Hence messages on the ring
are addressed to logical processes rather than physical processors, and the ring interface will recognize messages addressed
to processes which reside on a particular processor and accept
(store) only those messages. Other messages are permitted to continue to circulate around the ring (provision is also made to
recognize those messages which have gone full circle without being

298

accepted because, for example, the intended receiver has crashed).

The goals of the DCS design include both load sharing and the sharing of unique resources (e.g., a large capacity file store) on the Irvine campus. As with all networks, however, individual jobs, once initiated, execute exclusively on a single processor. Load sharing is achieved by a relatively elaborate "bidding" scheme. Prior to initiating a task, say a Fortran compilation, a "request for bid" is broadcast to all processors; those processors with both the ability and excess capacity to execute the task respond, with a bid which, presumably, is proportional to the available capacity on that machine. A "contract" is then signed with the low bidder and that portion of the user's program is executed on the winning processor.

DCS currently consists of five minicomputers (two Varian's and three SUE's) and is available 24 hours per day.

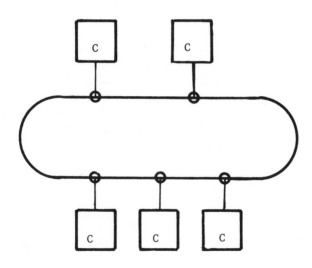

Figure VII
UC Irvine DCS: A Loop Network

Spider: A Loop Network with Centralized Control

A network somewhat similar to DCS has been built by Frazer at Bell Labs (Murray Hill) to interconnect the many minicomputers used to control experiments within the laboratory; it is an example of a network built largely to more effectively utilize existing hardware and, in this case, to provide isolated minicomputer users with access to support facilities on larger machines. The system utilizes three (1.5 megabaud) loops intersecting in a central (minicomputer) routing node.

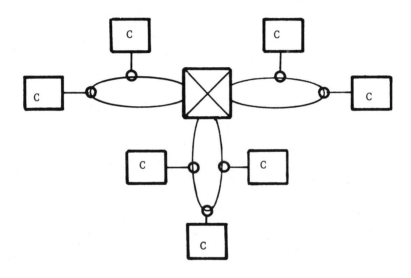

Figure VIII
Spider: A Loop Network with Central Control

STATUS AND PROSPECT

Let me begin this section by clearly labeling what follows as
largely opinion, my personal opinion. I alone am responsible for
any misrepresentations it may contain.

Let's begin by asking what we know as the result of the systems
that have been built. All of the systems mentioned explicitly
have been under way since the early 70's, hence it's reasonable
to assume that some hard data is available. Unfortunately the
assumption is not wholly justified, but we do know a few things:

> 1. Cost: The intuitive justification for cost reduction
> are supported by data such as that gathered by Fuller
> (5). His data, however, did not measure the performance
> of C.mmp under a full user load -- the test programs were
> run in a "stand-alone" mode (albeit using the Hydra oper-
> ating system). Thus one must consider the issue still
> open. This author is not aware of comparable cost/perfor-
> mance data for the other systems mentioned, although in
> dedicated applications such as the one for which Pluribus
> was designed, for example, the case for cost reduction
> seems exceptionally strong.

> 2. Reliability: Again, there is no data in the published
> literature that I am aware of. I have been told informally
> that Pluribus is extremely reliable, and given the nature
> of the application and the techniques used in its con-
> struction, I believe it must be. C.mmp, the only system
> I have first-hand familiarity with, is still quite un-
> reliable (MTBF is roughly an hour), however I don't be-
> lieve this is indicative of the ultimate reliability of
> the system since it is intentionally destabalized (e.g.,
> by adding additional processors) each time we reach a
> reasonable level of reliability. However, I do not believe
> that a comprehensive view of how to structure software so
> as to exploit the potential reliability of these systems
> has emerged (See(10) for this authors description of the
> software structure for reliability in the Hydra operating
> system. It is interesting that virtually all errors are
> detected by the software and result in an automatic reload
> of the system).

> 3. Memory Contention: An almost classic concern with
> multiprocessor systems has been memory contention -- a
> loss in performance due to the fact that some of the pro-
> cessors may have to wait for access to the memory if an-
> other processor is currently accessing it. Taking quite

different approaches C.mmp and Pluribus have demonstrated
that this need not be a problem. Pluribus avoids
the problem by simply replicating the most frequently
accessed code in memories local to a pair of processors.
C.mmp based its design on an analytic model which predicted that if the memories were sufficiently fast relative to the rate at which processors were making requests,
congestion does not occur (see 8). Although the model has
not yet been validated to 16 processors, it appears to
predict the contention for smaller configurations quite
well.

The situation, then, seems to be that none of the potential advantages of aggregrating minicomputers has been shown to be un-
realizable, but the definitive answers are not yet available. We
do have a collection of existence proofs and they span the alternatives sufficiently well that an individual with clearly defined
objectives can take advantage of the experiences of one or more
of these systems.

The next question we might ask is what, on the basis of these
systems and our knowledge of the history of computing, we can
predict about the future. I personally find the economic arguments
in favor of aggregated mini (micro) computers so compelling that
I must start from the premise that many, though certainly not all,
and especially not the "supercomputers" of any given generation,
will be built from many small processors. Beyond that, my reading
of the history of computing suggests that there is always a tendency toward the "general purpose" machine. At various points
technology has been biased in favor of various devices and computers have been built to exploit these technological anomalies.
Almost invariably these computers demanded awkward, unnatural
programming styles, and hence as soon as the technological balance
shifted, machines tended back to more familiar structures. In
particular, since software costs will certainly dominate hardware
costs in the future, I expect this tendency to continue.

Although applications will always exist which justify almost any
control/topology/bandwidth solution one can imagine, I suspect
the dominant systems will be those with a fairly regular structure -- the multiprocessors with essentially uniform access time
from any given processor to any given memory, and the networks,
such as DCS, in which the routing mechanism is minimally visible
to the user. Networks in general, however, do not allow many processors to be brought to bear on a single problem without considerable preplanning of the data communications requirements; thus
I suspect there will always be a need for nontrivial amounts of
memory and processor power at each node.

Finally, lets ask what the most important remaining problems are and whether we are likely to find the answers to them from the existing systems. As I see it:

1. Reliability remains a major intellectual problem. Specifically, hardware alone cannot solve it; software must be constructed in a manner which allows detection and correction of hardware or software errors. The problem is not unique to minicomputer complexes, of course, but it is accentuated there because of the reliability potential of these systems. The techniques used in Pluribus are clearly and directly applicable to other dedicated applications, but other techniques must be found for the general purpose systems.

2. Address space: All of the existing systems suffer from the small address space of the processors used (typically 16 bits). This, I sincerely hope, is one of those technological anomolies and will disappear in the future.

3. Languages and Operating Systems: Formulating an algorithm to execute on any of the systems discussed seems qualitatively more difficult than on an ordinary sequential computer -- at least if one tries to exploit the inherent parallelism. To date there seems to be a paucity of good ideas for language and/or operating system facilities to aid the programmer. Although I attribute this to the fact that the systems themselves have been available for routine use for a comparatively short period, it is clear that the development of these facilities is critical to their utility.

I would like to conclude by repeating that I find the economic arguments in favor of aggregated small computers so compelling that I believe firmly that most future systems will be constructed in this way. Much development remains to be done, many tough problems solved, but the existing systems clearly demonstrate the feasibility of such aggregrates.

REFERENCES

(1)   Anderson,A., and Jensen,D. "Computer Interconnection
        Structures", Computing Surveys, 7,4, Dec. 75.

(2)   Computer Reviews,GML Corporation, Lexington,Mass.
        1974.

(3)   Farber,D., and Larson,K, "The System Architecture
        of the Distributed Computer System - The Communi-
        cations System", Proc. Symposium on Computer
        Communications Networks, and Teletraffic, 1972.

(4)   Frazer,A., "Spider - An Experimental Data Communi-
        cations System", Proc. International Conference
        on Communications, 1974.

(5)   Fuller,S., "Price/Performance Comparison of C.mmp
        and the PDP-10", Proceedings of the Third Sympo-
        sium on Computer Architecture, ACM/IEEE, 1976.

(6)   Heart, et. al., "A New Minicomputer/Multiprocessor
        for the ARPA Network", Proc. AFIPS 1973 National
        Computer Conference, 1973.

(7)   Lesser,V. et.al., "Organization of the HEARSAY II
        Speech Understanding System", Proc. of the IEEE
        Symposium on Speech Recognition, 1974.

(8)   Wulf,W. and Bell, C.G., "C,mmp: A Multi-Mini Proces-
        sor", Proc. AFIPS Fall Joint Computer Conference,
        1972.

(9)   Wulf,W. et. al., "Hydra: The Kernel of a Multipro-
        cessor Operating System", Comm. of the ACM, 17,6,
        June, 1974.

(10)   Wulf,W., "Reliable Hardware/Software Architecture",
        Proc. International Conference on Reliable Soft-
        ware, 1975.

(11)   Wulf,W. et. al., "Overview of the Hydra Operating
        System", Proc. Fifth Symposium on Operating Sys-
        tems Principles, 1975.

CONTRIBUTED PAPERS

V. R. Basili and J. C. Knight - University of Maryland and
Langley Research Center
"A Programming Language Proposal for Scientific Computing"

D. A. Calahan and D. A. Orbits - University of Michigan
"A Comparison of Matrix Algorithms for Pipelined Vector
Processors"

S. Cohen - Argonne National Laboratory
"Speakeasy"

S. L. Gerhart - Duke University
"A Classification Scheme for Programming Errors"

D. C. Graham and L. P. Gaby - Kirtland Air Force Base
"SAIL"

W. Hermann - Sandia Laboratories
"Structured Programming Approach to a Problem in Continuum
Mechanics"

L. A. Kurtz, R. E . Smith, C. L. Parks, and L. R. Boney -
Langley Research Center
"A Numerical Experiment Comparing the Method of Lines with
Finite Difference Techniques for Solving Time-Dependent
Partial Differential Equations"

J. J. Lambiotte - Langley Research Center
"Computing the Fast Fourier Transform on STAR "

N. Lawrence - Texas Instruments Inc.
   "The Array Approach to Supercomputer Applications
   Programming"

K. G. Stevens - Ames Research Center
   "A Facility for Computational Fluid Dynamics"

R. T. Walsh - Sandia Laboratories)
   "An Application of PASCAL to the Design of a Large Scientific
   Software Package"

S. W. White and J. V. Timmons - Vought Corporation
   "GDP-1: A Preliminary Design Tool"

A 6
B 7
C 8
D 9
E 0
F 1
G 2
H 3
I 4
J 5